Seasons of the Coyote

A Year on Prairie Bluff

Jerry Wilson

Copyright © 2018 by Jerry Wilson.
All rights to text and photographs, including electronic, reserved.

Printed in the United States of America.

First edition 2018.

Cover and interior photgraphs by Jerry Wilson.

"About the Author" photograph by Norma Wilson.
Used with permission.

Scurfpea Publishing
P.O. Box 46
Sioux Falls, SD 57101
scurfpeapublishing.com
editor@scurfpeapublishing.com

For Norma, Walter and Laura and the many friends who have roamed the prairies and woods with us and shared nature's bounty of pleasures

CONTENTS

Preface and Acknowledgements   page xi

Winter   page 1

JANUARY
January 1: Resolutions
January 5: Facing Winter's Fury
January 8: Gift from a Great Horned Owl
January 11: The Aldo Leopold Bench
January 14: Eagles by the Dozen
January 16: A Colony of Voles
January 19: Seeking Balance
January 26: Life in a Geo-Solar Womb

FEBRUARY
February 2: Groundhog Day
February 6: Probing Coyote Poop
February 9: How to Find a Walnut Tree
February 12: Darwin Meets Lincoln on the Bluff
February 14: Memorial to Fallen Friends
February 20: January Thaw
February 23: Requiem for a Possum

MARCH
March 1: The Life and Death of Coons
March 5: Death Feeds Life in Winter
March 9: Trumpets of Spring
March 13: Cardinals Convene
March 16: Dancing with Sandhill Stars
March 17: Into the Briar Patch

Spring page 43

March 20: Breaking Hibernation
March 30: Waging Cedarcide

APRIL
April 1: House Hunting
April 5: An Anything-but-Cocky Bird
April 6: Agh! Snow Again
April 10: Hiking North Alabama Bend
April 11: Easter Groundhog Day
April 13: Choosing a Sustainable Future
April 17: Turning the Earth
April 20: A Time to Burn
April 22: Earth Day Planting
April 28: What Ducks Like

MAY
May 4: Birds Are Back
May 11: Eating from Earth
May 18: Hunting Morels
May 19: A Beautiful Invader
May 20: Bring on the Cows
May 22: Welcoming the Bees
May 25: Thinking Like Other Animals
May 27: Season of the Coyote
May 28: Magical Morning at the Pond

JUNE
June 2: Waiting for Rain
June 4: Serpents and Voyeurs
June 9: And the Rain Came
June 16: Patience and Survival
June 19: Streamlined Kitty with a Fluid Drive

Summer page 105

June 21: How Sweet It Is!
June 23: Eating What Bugs Us
June 27: Chilling Out in the Cool Tub
June 30: Calling Coyotes

JULY
July 1: Harvest Time
July 4: Independence Day: Protecting Natural Land
July 8: Making Hay
July 12: Welcoming Walnuts
July 17: The Valley of Ashes Blooms
July 21: Holiday in San Antonio
July 27: Living High Off the Hog
July 29: My Toady Friends
July 30: Rescued Robin

AUGUST
August 3: Buffalograss Lawn
August 4: A Killer on the Loose
August 6: Nature's Plan B
August 10: Canoeing the Missouri
August 14: Beyond Our Horizon
August 17: Swallow Symbiosis
August 24: Living with Irony
August 29: River Trail Flotilla

SEPTEMBER
September 3: How Not to Fell a Tree
September 7: After Apple Picking
September 14: The Monarchs Have Flown
September 15: To Bee or Not To Bee
September 16: River Appreciation Day
September 21: My Axis of Evil Burs

Autumn   page 167

September 22: The Season of Letting Go
September 23: Heron and Wood Duck Heaven
September 25: Fifteen Flitting Flickers
September 28: Prairie Rumination

OCTOBER
October 1: The Ecology of Native Prairie
October 6: Prairie Fire
October 13: Ready for Winter?
October 19: Stones, an Eagle and Red-tailed Hawks
October 21: Skull and Bones Society
October 24: Reflections in a Spider's Eye
October 26: The Season of Death
October 28: Outwitting Coons
October 30: Blue-Tongued Deer

NOVEMBER
November 2: Coyotes, Cranes and Day of the Dead
November 6: Licking Salt and Locking Horns
November 9: Canoeing Clay Creek
November 11: The Time of Fire
November 13: Drama at the Bird Feeder
November 16: Blazing and Following Trails
November 17: A Maddening Death
November 21: Airborne Raccoon
November 25: Skating a Crystal Universe

DECEMBER
December 4: Turkey Hunt
December 7: A Bridge to Somewhere
December 9: Digging Out
December 14: The First Skis of Winter
December 15: Birds Great and Small

December 16: Lighting a Christmas Tree
December 19: Joyfully Immature

Winter Again page 231

December 21: Winter Solstice and Hope

About the author   234

Preface and Acknowledgements

My wife, Norma, and I have lived one-third of a century in the geo-solar home we carved into the Missouri River bluff in South Dakota. Our children grew to adulthood on our sliver of prairie hills and woods, and though they now live in distant places with families of their own, they have taken this land with them in their hearts and minds. It is part of them, as it is of us. Some day Walter and Laura may inherit the land in the conventional sense, but that is less important than the good fortune and insights they have already received. For all of us, this scrap of natural landscape is not a mere commodity. It is an evolving *kapuka*, to borrow a Hawaiian term for a pocket of vegetation surrounded by a sea of lava. Our *kapuka* is an island of diverse flora and fauna amidst a landscape degraded from its natural state by mechanical and chemical means to a sea of corn and beans.

Several years ago, Norma and I executed the legal documents necessary to ensure that this *kapuka* and all its wild and native inhabitants are protected from development or exploitation in perpetuity by a conservation easement. We owe it to this land, and to future generations of "owners," to ensure that this microcosmic ecosystem remains intact. We named our place Prairie Bluff.

Our Earth and the fragments for which we each are responsible face many threats. Climate change, pollution, invasive species, indifference, and I fear at times my own hand ignorantly applied, all of these and more threaten the health and vigor of the land. Neither we nor our children nor our children's children will live long enough to restore the virgin health of this 150 acres, land that for more than a century before we came sustained a succession of settlers and farmers who, it must be said, did not always provide the care the land needed and deserved.

Much is already spent; the loss of soil fertility will require millennia to restore, and the diversity of native species can never be fully regained. But we have tried, to the best of our knowledge and ability, to live in harmony with this land, to learn from the land and from fellow creatures, to appreciate what the Lakota call *wama kaskan*, all living things. We have worked to preserve and restore as we have found the means. Along the way I have recorded routine and extraordinary encounters with the birds, mammals, insects, plants, weather and other aspects of life on the Missouri River bluff. I have tried to make sense of the struggles, delights and insights they have provided.

Besides the people who live in these pages, this book honors the many creatures who do not read books—the coyotes, foxes, raccoons, possums, squirrels and woodchucks, the scores of birds who reside here or visit, the native grasses and prairie flowers, the earthworms that work our soil, the bees that make our honey and pollinate our vegetables and flowers, and all else that comprises the magnificent ecosystem of which we are part.

I wish to thank those who read my evolving manuscript and made helpful suggestions, challenged my thinking and saved me from embarrassing errors—my wife and ever faithful reader Norma; my brother Paul; my biologist friend Jim Heisinger; fellow writer Fraser Harrison; and of course my editor, Steve Boint.

My eco-memoir, *Waiting for Coyote's Call*, detailed a quarter century of life on our scrap of Missouri River Bluff—explorations of the land's history and ecology, our efforts to promote sustainability, and some of what we had learned from the land and fellow inhabitants. But nature's gifts—and her lessons—continue, and across the ensuing decade, I continued to record ordinary and extraordinary encounters with the birds, mammals, plants, weather and other aspects of life on this land. Some of the stories and essays in *Seasons of the Coyote* first appeared in my blog, coyotescall.wordpress.com, and a handful were published in the Black Hills Writers Group's 2012 anthology, *Granite Island, Amber Sea*.

Like Henry David Thoreau, I have compressed events of more than a single calendar cycle into *Seasons of the Coyote: A Year on Prairie Bluff*. The organic continuity of the unfolding seasons seems a natural way to explore observations of an ecosystem, and the best way to experience and convey the perpetual miracle of regeneration—of birth, death and rebirth, restoration and renewal. These stories of life on the bluff I offer to all who love the natural world and wish to see it whole.

Winter

JANUARY

January 1: Resolutions

    I awake, thrilled by the cries of coyotes on the southern hill, two long howls, a series of maniacal yaps, now the voices mingled in a chaotic jumble. The clock says six a.m. I throw off the covers, slip on sweater and jeans and grope my way to the door. The air is calm, but near zero. My breath produces a cloud of fog. Except for a sliver of moon in the eastern sky and stars that light the snow, darkness reigns. The sun will not clear the horizon for two more hours; the first hint of dawn is an hour away.

    The coyotes are now south of the pond, nearing the spring. Their Latin name is *Canis latrans*, barking dogs. I wish I could decipher the meanings of the many voices in which they speak. Studies of coyote vocalizations suggest that the alpha pair howl most frequently, often to delineate the boundaries of their territory. The cacophony erupts again, mournful howls mingled with gargling yips. How many individual voices I cannot tell. Perhaps the adults are calling last spring's pups back to the pack, back to the den where they will shelter until night falls once more. Perhaps they have found prey—a cottontail, a family of mice, carrion. I will eat breakfast soon, and I hope that they too are well fed. Their life is difficult, but their vision is clear. I take joy in their closeness, their wildness, their resolve. I would be more like them.

    I close the door and flip on a light. I build up the fire,

make coffee and settle into my favorite chair to wait for sunlight. But already the new day and the new year have begun. Today many will respond to an ancient ritual, taking stock of the past, setting down certain pledges for the year to come. What promises should I make? I will not resolve to eat less, since decades of experience have taught me that the thin layer of fat that holidays and winter indolence bring will be burned by spring gardening and my summer hoe. I will not drink less, since moderation in all things—including moderation—has been my motto for decades. I should try to be more civil with people I am inclined to dismiss, to see whether through tolerance and dialogue I might learn more and possibly teach more than through confrontation or disregard. Yet I will not promise to be less argumentative, since I regard skepticism and questioning as the fundamental duty of human citizenship—and an essential path to learning.

So what does that leave? If I am to be a better man at year's end, where should I begin? What goals and tasks should I set for myself as a new year unfolds?

I resolve to spend more time gazing out the window at the changing seasons, the moments of the day, the slants of light, the fellow creatures that come to visit. Perhaps I can gain a deeper understanding of the dozen species of birds that daily dine on the sunflower seeds I provide. If I watch faithfully, a bird I have never seen may appear.

I resolve to grow a better garden this year, to profit from the mistakes of last season, to invest more time in comprehending the needs of soil and plants and the life cycles of both the insects that pollinate our crops and those that feed upon them. Perhaps I can discover which life ways I should encourage, which I must combat, and with which I may coexist or share.

Though long experience has taught me that New Year's resolutions are lofty goals from which I will undoubtedly fall short, I will hope to cultivate the life of the mind, to read more attentively, to think in contrary ways that might reveal a hint of truth. I will faithfully carry my notebook and pen, recording the small moments with nature and life that might hold some kernel of truth, something I might someday translate into understanding.

I resolve to face mortality, not just the eventual end of life as I know it, but the mortal life that is my daily blessing, with good humor and fun. Am I about to give up breathing, in-spiration? Hopefully not anytime soon, but all living things are moving inevitably toward that precipice from the moment they are born, and as any actuary would tell you, I have expended a majority of my allotted years. So I must couple work with play, and while facing head-on the grim and ugly realities of our time, laugh at every joke provided by fate or friend.

I remember the words of William Wordsworth from his poem "Intimations of Immortality," written more than 200 years ago:

> What though the radiance which was once so bright
> Be now for ever taken from my sight,
> Though nothing can bring back the hour
> Of splendour in the grass, of glory in the flower

But I might revise Wordsworth's title, for I am alive today and would live every day as if it were my last. It is more complete mortality that I seek.

January 5: Facing Winter's Fury

We are past the winter solstice, but little practical benefit has ensued. The upper two-thirds of my thermometer remain useless, and if the days have lengthened by a minute or two since December 21, I haven't noticed. There is no January Thaw on the horizon; it seems that winter has come to stay. The ten inches of snow that covered the bluff in late December has melted on some sunny southern slopes, but elsewhere has hardened to ice and crust. I enjoyed skiing half a dozen times in December, alone and with family and friends, but when I tried it on New Year's Day I careened uncontrollably down an icy slope until I hit a pile of cedar brush. Enough of that until fresh snow falls.

A world encased in ice is tough on my four-legged and feathered neighbors. The colder the day, the more frantic the activity at our bird feeders. We have scores of house finches, dozens of gold and the occasional purple. There are juncos, various sparrows, blue jays, cardinals, red-bellied, hairy and downy woodpeckers, nuthatches and one flicker that flicks past on some errand but rarely stops. And all of the above remain vigilant, for the moment they drop their guard, the merlin that lurks in the cottonwoods may fall from the sky and snatch the slowest bird.

After weeks of cold, the deer have grown tame. When I toss handfuls of corn on the frozen snow, they materialize as if from nowhere, but really from where they have bedded out of the wind in the tall prairie grass. Yet, on a recent evening their abrupt scattering caught my eye; A sleek coyote was trotting down the creek bank below the house. Though he likely harbored little hope of dining on venison, the deer weren't taking any chances.

Meanwhile, the January sun reaches deep into our solar home, and without burning fossil fuel or even solar energy stored in the cells of oak, ash, hackberry or elm, we live in comfort, warmed and sustained by the ultimate source of renewable energy and power. Yet, for ultimate comfort, when the sun goes down I'll throw a couple of logs in the stove.

January 8: Gift from a Great Horned Owl

Under an ash tree by the spring, a large gray object amongst fallen leaves catches my eye. At first glance it appears to be the scat of some large predator. The thing is cylindrical, about three inches long and nearly an inch in diameter. If it were the excrement of some prowler of the bluff, it had to be one of the larger denizens of our prairies and woods. The object appears to consist mostly of hair and bones, presumably the remains of some unfortunate creature or creatures that provided somebody's dinner. The contents are similar to what one commonly finds in the dung of a coyote, but it doesn't take long to rule that out. The diameter is simply too large.

I pull off my gloves and break the pellet into halves. I put one half in my coat pocket to take to the house for future examination and pick the other half apart. Yes, it clearly consists of hair and bones, mostly hair. The hair is gray, the color of a cottontail rabbit or of any number of rodents—mice or voles. But I quickly rule rabbits out. As I pull the mass apart I see that every bone is small. There are tiny femurs, half an inch long and thinner than pencil lead. I find scraps of what appear to be a pelvis, paper thin. There is a pair of miniature incisors, shiny white ribs like narrow blades of grass, a crushed skull that my little finger cannot fit inside. It is possible that some of the bones are those of a bird, though the absence of feathers makes that seem unlikely. I can draw no conclusions about a particular species that the predator has eaten, but it is apparently one, or perhaps several, of the smallest mammals with which we share our home.

Perhaps someone with specialized training could rearticulate enough of the unlucky creature to give it a name, though many scraps are broken or crushed beyond recognition. But the further I poke, the clearer the conclusion becomes. This is not the excrement of a mammal. It has been dropped under the ash tree by a bird. But instead of excreted, this pellet has been regurgitated from the gizzard of a great horned owl, a creature whose diet is even more varied than that of the omnivorous coyote.

The *Bubo virginianus* is our largest and most common owl. Its wingspan can exceed four feet. Not that they are plentiful in this region of tilled fields and monoculture, but along the bluff they find adequate habitat for nesting and roosting, and usually abundant prey. The food intake of the great horned is said to be the most diverse of all American predators. They are capable of killing mammals as large as themselves, including skunks, rabbits and prairie dogs, but they also eat any bird they can take down, frogs and other aquatic species, rodents, even insects and carrion when times are hard. Their talons are incredibly powerful, strong enough to crush the vertebrae of many mammals and birds.

As their name suggests, great horned owls are readily recognized by their large feathery ears, which by the way, are very efficient in detecting the movements of their prey. Their eyes are large, the pupils wide, the retinas equipped for excellent night vision. Though the great horned's eyes are fixed in their sockets, the owl can swivel its head for a 360-degree view. Add to this that the soft feathers of their wings make them stealthy fliers, and they are not likely to go hungry as long as other birds and mammals share their terrain.

But what really sets owls apart from fellow creatures of the bluff is the manner in which they digest their food and eliminate their waste. Like other birds, owls swallow small prey whole, or rip it apart into manageable pieces. But unlike most birds, owls lack a crop, a sack in which food is stored for later digestion. Instead the owl has two stomachs. The first, the proventriculus, produces enzymes, acids and mucus that break food down. The second stomach, the gizzard, or ventriculus, separates what is soluble from what is not—fur, bones, feathers and teeth. What is soluble passes into the intestines for further digestion, while insoluble materials are compressed into a pellet by the gizzard and travel back to the first stomach. When it is time to eat again, the owl regurgitates the pellet so that new food can be admitted. The pellet that I hold in my hand has made this journey to the interior of the owl and back again. The still intact half will lie in the sunroom with scores of other artifacts from my natural world, a talisman of life feeding life.

January 11: The Aldo Leopold Bench

Today is Aldo Leopold's birthday. He was born in Burlington, Iowa, in 1887. Google "Aldo Leopold bench," and you'll find a dozen sites—from *Organic Gardening* magazine to woodworking sites to the US Environmental Protection Agency—that will tell you how to build an authentic bench. Some sites use this portal to usher you into the house that Leopold built—the literal shack he and his family rehabilitated for a weekend cabin on their farm in "Sand County," Wisconsin, but also the house of ideas inhabited by generations of conservationists who have been inspired by Leopold's actions and words.

"To spy a Leopold bench in someone's yard is to know something about the family who there resides," says the EPA, "even if you haven't read Leopold's opening lines [of *A Sand County Almanac*], 'There are some who can live without wild things, and some who cannot. These essays are the delights and dilemmas of one who cannot,' you will appreciate this easy-to-build bench…. Its form, resting alone under a tree or in congregation around a fire pit, reminds us of Leopold's thoughtfulness."

It is true. As one who discovered *A Sand County Almanac* half a life ago and whose thoughts, writing and life have been inspired by Leopold, I take particular pleasure in resting from my labors, whether with pen or hoe, on a Leopold bench. But today it is far too cold to sprawl under a leafless tree, even on such a bench. Today is a better day to plug in the table saw in the relative warmth of the garage and build one as a promise for the return of summer days.

Any feature of Leopold's plan can be altered to fit large

or small bodies, and the materials can range from stock lumberyard boards to hand-hewn slabs or exotic woods. For example, I will use two-by-eights for the seat instead of two-by-sixes, and I will widen the bench to fit Norma and me together—should one of us choose to welcome the other to share reverie or joy.

I built two of the benches a few years ago: one for the patio, the other for the fire pit on the hill behind the house. Lumber for another has waited in the garage until the time came to trade laptop for saw. I could not argue that Aldo's benches rival my recliner for comfort, though the simple design strikes the correct angle of back to legs. But perhaps ultimate comfort was not Leopold's intent. I think simplicity was. Anyway, best not to get too comfortable, Leopold might say. There is more work to be done. Just rest a few moments, contemplate the work you have done or are about to do, enjoy the fire or the flowers or the robins ripping worms from the grass, or simply lose yourself in mindless pursuit of mind. But a life well lived is more than contemplation; there is work to be done.

On the Prairie Bluff it never ends. Yesterday Norma and I cleared scores of small cedars that had grown under an ancient ash deep in the woods. We cut the ash's fallen limbs for firewood, thus creating a proper clearing where on another day we might picnic or lounge with a book to read or a notebook to record observations or thoughts. This morning I shoveled away the snow that fell last night. This afternoon—after I finish the bench—I must write letters to legislators urging action on environmental bills. No, there is no end to work, especially if one is officially retired and has no good excuse, like going to work, for not doing the work that needs to be done.

But I digress. Time to turn off the computer, get out of the recliner, take measurements of Leopold bench number two and cut the boards for number three. When spring comes I will lug it through the woods to the creek. Then I will have earned the right to relax on the bench, listen to the voice of the spring, contemplate the shape of the water that tumbles over the stones, watch the slow progress of a fallen leaf toward the precipice from which it will be swept away.

January 14: Eagles by the Dozen
More snow today. The sky is bleak and wind howls through the barren ash trees west of the house, but we are protected by cedars, pines and deciduous bushes and trees, and by our earth-sheltered home. A big chunk of hackberry blazes in the stove.

Yesterday we drove with friends Clarence and Sandy to the Missouri River to look for eagles. Below Gavin's Point Dam near Yankton, we counted twenty bald eagles, *Haliaeetus leucocephalus*, perched in cottonwoods on the south bank. Three or four were fully-grown but not yet "mature"; those over two years old are distinguished by white tails and heads. Nine of the magnificent birds occupied two adjacent cottonwoods, nine eagles in a space of fifty yards. They eyed the flocks of floating and diving ducks, canvasbacks, mergansers and golden eyes.

Occasionally an eagle would leave its limb and swoop across the current, dipping to strike a duck or a fish, particularly a fish that might be stunned by its recent trip through the turbulence of the hydro generators. But in this cold the eagles cannot afford to wet their wings, so they are careful to only skim the surface. Ducks that see them coming have time to dive or dart to avoid the deadly talons; most forays yield no success.

From a high hill above the dam, where for half a century turbines have churned electricity from the river's power, we counted twenty-one turbines churning wind power near Crofton, Nebraska. It is one of two wind farms nearby, facilitated by the Nebraska Unicameral's near unanimous passage of C-BED legislation, a law that encourages community-based energy development. I wondered when or if the South Dakota Legislature will summon the wisdom to follow the lead of Nebraska, Minnesota, Iowa and other neighboring states in promoting development of our vast but largely untapped renewable energy resources—wind and sun.

Sometimes we dread or curse or hide from nature's powers, forgetting that we can also work with those forces to enhance our lives, to reverse the trends of over-consumption and reliance on non-renewable and polluting fuels that threaten the future of the only Earth we have. That we can change our thinking and our ways is obvious. The bald eagle's dramatic resurgence from near extinction proves that Americans are capable of recognizing our errors or our ignorance, of changing our ways, of letting our own better nature take the lead.

January 16: A Colony of Voles

I sit by the fire writing, my mind immersed in another realm, when a movement catches the corner of my eye, a tiny flash of dark against the snow. I glance up but see only birds at the feeder. Probably a junco, I think, and return to my task. Then I see it again. The shadow that flits across the snowdrift below the feeder can't be a bird. It disappears, not into the air, but into the snow. I face the window to watch, but see only juncos and finches, the discarded hulls of sunflower seeds, and here and there a whole seed kicked out by a careless or inefficient bird. Back to my work.

Moments later the thing emerges again, a momentary glimpse and gone. I get up from my chair and stand at the window to watch. Another moment passes and it reappears, a round brownish-gray shape in the mouth of a finger-sized hole near the base of the feeder post. The shape darts out, grabs a seed and is gone.

A mouse? No, the tail is too short, the body stubby and round as a bullet. It has to be a vole. But which vole, meadow or prairie? Both are common in our native prairie in summer, and when the snow melts in spring we find their narrow trails through jungles of grass. Like their cousins the pocket mouse and the meadow jumping mouse, they dine on seeds, but voles complement their diet with salad. The drift below the feeder would provide the perfect combination—sunflower seeds and bluegrass that remains green beneath the snow. The two species of voles are similar in size, shape and color, and both are major elements in the food chain of carnivorous mammals and birds.

Based on the barrel-shaped body and the short tail, our visitor is probably the prairie vole, *Microtus ochrogaster*. If so, it is a generally monogamous mammal that typically breeds only in spring and fall and may produce two to four litters in a year. If, on the other hand, it is the meadow vole, *Microtus pennsylvanicus*, it is even more important to coyotes, owls and hawks. Meadow voles reproduce "like rabbits" but faster. A female meadow vole reaches sexual maturity within a month, the gestation period is three weeks, and individuals can live up to a year. Thus a female meadow vole can produce dozens of offspring in her brief lifespan.

I step outside for a closer look at the heap of snow I had scooped off the patio. Closer examination reveals that the mound has not one, but many doors. Clearly this vole—or voles—has created a subsurface city, a system of tunnels in a meter-wide radius around the pole, the unending source of food. Soon I confirm that the vole has company. How many I can't tell, but two appear simultaneously on opposite sides of their hill. I imagined what lies below, numerous paths that perhaps converge in a great room, a room likely littered with discarded sunflower hulls that serve as insulating carpet and a comfy bed nestled in the bluegrass lawn.

When the snow begins to melt, whether in a January thaw or sometime next spring, perhaps I will see a family of voles emerge for the last time and seek another home. Or perhaps they will disappear into the night, and when the last snow melts I will find nothing more than the remains of a winter's banquet—that is if the little rodents are cautious enough not to show themselves while Luna the cat is sunning herself on patio stones.

January 19: Seeking Balance

In the balance I seek between physical and mental activities and between work and play—between hoeing and hiking, trimming and skiing, planting and harvesting, research and reading, writing and quiet contemplation, the physical often holds the stronger grip. I must mentally chain myself to the chair to get my indoor work done. The balance is less difficult to achieve, however, when winds roar outside and snow swirls around the bird feeders as they have done this middle week of winter's siege. For the past few days I have contented myself with hours by the wood fire, probing the wisdom of Edward O. Wilson.

Wilson—no, unfortunately no cousin or uncle of mine—was among the inspirations behind my eco-memoir *Waiting for Coyote's Call*, as well as this present book. It was Wilson's book *The Diversity of Life* that provided one of my favorite quotes, one which keeps my spirits high in trying times: "There can be no purpose more enspiriting than to begin the age of restoration, reweaving the wondrous diversity of life that still surrounds us."

Now I am savoring Wilson's more recent book, *The Creation*. In a chapter entitled "The Pauperization of Earth," Wilson observes that the great cataclysm that sent the dinosaurs to oblivion sixty-five million years ago—the crash of a giant meteorite off the Yucatan peninsula of Mexico, was actually the fifth disturbance of this magnitude in the previous 400 million years of Earth's history, each of which, the fossil record demonstrates, obliterated most of the living species of their time. Now, Wilson laments, "a sixth spasm has begun, this one a result of human activity. Although not ushered in by cosmic violence, it is potentially as hellish as the earlier cataclysms." He cites the conclusions of a team of climate experts, that human-induced climate change "if left unabated, could be the primary cause of extinction of a quarter of the plants and animals on the land by midcentury."

Wilson names five causes for the decline of Earth's biodiversity, which he summarizes with the acronym HIPPO. The order of the letters, he says, corresponds to their rank in destructiveness: Habitat loss, Invasive species, Pollution, human overPopulation and Overharvesting of nature's bounty. In short, we humans seem to have lost our sense of balance, or perhaps even the wisdom that balance is required for the health of both living creatures and the Earth.

Our personal quests for balance, I am convinced, must proceed on dual fronts: the public and the personal. We can neither wish away climate change and other environmental threats nor stave off their ravages by simple contemplation or by individual choices, important though those might be. Collective political action will be required. But I am equally convinced that collective action proceeds from minds and bodies prepared by lives lived in harmony and balance. Like happiness, balance is less an achievable goal than a quest, but balance we must seek. Now I leave my keyboard and venture out to feed the birds.

January 26: Life in a Geo-Solar Womb

In spite of global warming, we've endured a colder than average January—which makes us especially appreciate the earth-sheltered womb we inhabit. On sunny days, of which one can't have too many in January, we need no heat beyond the sun. But even on the coldest and dreariest of days and nights, little supplemental energy is required to keep us warm. That is because the main floor of our home is nestled into a wind-and-cold-impervious south-facing hill.

We designed our house in 1981 with these basic principles

in mind: In keeping with the "organic" architectural philosophy introduced a century ago by Frank Lloyd Wright, we wanted our house to blend with the landscape, to complement the land to the extent possible. In function, it had to meet the needs of human animals, pathetically comfortable only in a narrow range of temperature hovering around seventy degrees Fahrenheit. But this comfort had to be achieved with minimal consumption of non-renewable fossil fuel. Thus, the general design was clear. We would do as coyotes do—face the sun and burrow in. On the northern plains, that means a geo-solar house.

In the coldest winter our climate can deal, frost creeps no more than three feet down; another foot below the frost line the soil temperature remains near fifty degrees. Our north and west external walls are steel-reinforced concrete, backed by insulation and then earth, so little energy is required to keep the interior warm. Our lower floor is an "open basement," the south wall mostly insulated glass facing the sun, the floor poured concrete covered with heat-absorbing tile.

As determined by the winter and summer angles of the sun at our latitude, 42° 54', our windows are sized for maximum exposure in winter, as well as the necessary overhang to block unwanted summer sun. At winter solstice, December 21, the sun warms the floor a full sixteen feet from the south wall. By late January it still reaches well over half way into the great room.

When the sun doesn't shine we build a fire, releasing energy the sun has patiently stored over decades in wood. Over thirty-five years in this home, our typical consumption of wood is at most two cords per winter, two big pickup loads. The annual cost of staying warm is two days of labor, cutting and splitting wood, and a few dollars to maintain a saw. The added bonus is conveyed by the adage that wood heats thrice: when you cut it, when you split it, and when you burn it in your stove.

FEBRUARY

February 2: Groundhog Day

Today dawned cloudy, so if Mr. Groundhog emerged, he didn't see his shadow. The groundhog, *Marmota monax*, also known as the woodchuck, is a short-legged, heavy-bodied brown furry rodent of eastern and northern North

America. Few people ever see a groundhog, February second or any other day. Groundhogs are sluggish and reclusive, and on the Northern Plains, pass much of the winter asleep. They emerge occasionally to urinate and defecate, or perhaps to bask for a while on a sunny day, but mostly they remain torpid in their burrows for the coldest months.

In three decades on the bluff, I have seen a woodchuck engaged in his pursuit of happiness only four times. A deceased groundhog I found one spring after the snow had melted. Had he emerged from his burrow too soon—fooled by a cloudy day—only to perish in a February storm? More likely his body had lain under snow since fall, when luckier friends entered hibernation. Two of those whose lives I observed dwelt at different times in a den below a pile of limbs and ancient junk behind the barn, one I spied camouflaged amidst the summer foliage of a mulberry tree beside our garden, and the fourth we found lounging on her front porch on Easter Sunday. (More about that later.)

Whether other woodchucks lie in deep sleep somewhere below the frozen soil of our woods, I do not know. If one should poke his head from his burrow today and gaze through leafless trees to the clouded sky, and if he should be so foolish as to believe the lore of Groundhog Day and venture forth in search of spring, he would surely be disappointed, for regardless of today's sky we will likely endure six more weeks of winter, and probably more, before spring truly comes to the Plains.

Yet Groundhog Day is significant to my calendar of hope. In the half of my life I have invested in the Northern Plains, I have learned to suppress all thoughts of spring through the long and dreary months of December and January. But at last, February has come. We have miraculously survived beyond the mid-point of another winter, both spirit and flesh intact, and it now seems less foolish to entertain dreams of spring.

Thankfully, February is our shortest month. In four weeks, by the first of March, I will awake one morning to the far-off but familiar honking of geese. I will spring from bed and dash to the door to strain my eyes south for the faint shifting V of an angle of geese, rushing north toward summer nesting grounds, pushing the boundary of winter toward Canada and beyond. But whatever the calendar says, we'll know that storms may still be gathering in the Rockies. Yet despite lingering doubts, in another month I will tell myself that spring is nigh!

February 6: Probing Coyote Poop

I find them on every trail I hike—the unmistakable three-or-four-inch-long scats that coyotes leave behind. In size and shape they closely resemble those of their domesticated cousin, a good-sized dog. But unlike the slimy, stinking excrement that dog food produces, the coyote's waste is—well, almost free of waste. Because the coyote's digestive system is remarkably efficient, even when "fresh," the coyote's droppings are rarely offensive; the excrement commonly consists mostly of hair and shards of bone.

In spite of a couple of neighbors' best efforts to eradicate them, and even despite annual efforts by certain legislators in the state capitol to find new ways to exterminate South Dakota's state animal, coyotes still thrive on our bluff—partly because they find both shelter and abundant food in our rehabilitated native prairie and untamed woods. They might dig their dens where I will never find them, but on their nightly errands they resemble me and many fellow residents, as creatures of habit. They follow the same trails followed by rabbits, raccoons, deer, mice, voles and me. What makes for convenient passage through a thicket of grass for a small mammal is also convenient for the coyote, and that is where the encounters he seeks are most likely to occur. And thus, he may relieve himself on trails I am likely to share. In my meanderings, I often pause to stoop and study the reassuring reminders that my favorite mammal still thrives in our neighborhood.

I have been enamored of coyotes since the age of six, the night my brother and I saw the glowing eyes of a pack who watched us from the edge of a clearing where we huddled in fear by a dwindling campfire, convinced that we would not see another sunrise. But the coyotes did not eat us for dinner, and by morning I had reached an appreciative accommodation to wildness that has remained with me to this day. If any animal holds the place in my mind that the Maya would call my *waigel*, my spirit animal, it is the coyote.

Though my laboratory is far from sanitized and my tools the most primitive, I often drop to my knees, grab a convenient twig or sliver of stone and dissect the droppings to see what my neighbor has had to eat. Whose bones are these? Is that the hair of a rabbit, a mouse or a fallen deer? What fruit produced those seeds and what insect's leg have I found in the coyote's scat?

Except for humans, and for the occasional cougar that might wonder through, the coyote is the top predator on our bluff. He has competition, of course; various hawks, owls, foxes and other mammals eat many of the same things that coyotes eat. But despite his lofty position near the top of the local food chain, the coyote is also remarkably omnivorous. He will eat almost anything he can catch, pick or find. And so it falls to me, as overseer of the bluff, to monitor his diet, to see what he has dined upon.

In spring, coyotes eat birds' eggs if they can find reachable nests, and also birds if they are lucky enough to catch one. I have found scraps of shell from small eggs swallowed whole, splinters of shell from turkey eggs, and sometimes feathers, though whether they are from a bird freshly-killed or from carrion encountered by chance I cannot say. In summer the coyote's dung may contain various fruits—wild plums, mulberries, and fruits from our orchard—and the exoskeletons of June bugs, grasshoppers, cicadas and other insects. But after years of informal investigation, I was still not prepared for the mystery that presented itself this winter.

The best time to learn who is about is the morning after a light snow, when tracks are still distinct and easy to follow. One can learn in which brush pile the cottontail makes her home, whether the possum has company in his trek to the compost pile, how many mice and voles have not yet fallen prey to one of the many birds and mammals that love to eat them, and whether turkeys, pheasants or other prairie birds have wandered by.

On such a morning in December, I was surprised to find coyote tracks less than twenty paces from our front door. I checked to see that Luna the cat was still cuddled in her nest in the garage, then set out to follow the trail. I hadn't gone far when I found the coyote's calling card. It contained the usual components—hair and bones—but there was something else, small flakes of something smooth and shiny with shades of amber and red. The scat was likely just a few hours old, but already frozen so stiff I couldn't pry it apart with a twig. Since I routinely use my pocketknife to peel apples or cut fruit, I was reluctant to use the tool for the present inquiry. Thus I proceeded down the trail, but carried the question with me. What had the coyote eaten that would have a shiny colorful skin?

Certainly not an insect at this time of year. Perhaps a wild plum that had fallen and had been preserved by a layer of leaves? But I hadn't pursued either the trail or the inquiry far before another set of tracks distracted me, and I began chasing rabbits, or specifically following the unmistakable trail of a cottontail hopping through snow—front tracks wide apart, rear feet close together—until I found the brush pile where he sheltered.

But the question of what unusual thing the coyote had eaten would not go away; it required further investigation. From that day on I stopped to dig through every coyote scat I found. I discovered that all contained tiny slivers of the strange, reddish skin. It must be a fruit of some kind, I surmised, but what at this time of year? And then at last I found a larger scrap intact, a piece of peel half an inch across.

Eureka! It could be only one thing. Our apple tree had produced an abundant crop, and the neighbors at the bottom of our hill have an orchard of a dozen apple trees. Each tree produced fruit by the bushel in August, far more than anybody could gather or use. I went to see. Sure enough, protruding from the snow under the neighbor's trees were freeze-dried apples by the hundreds. People and deer and other creatures had eaten all they could of this amazing crop, and we had picked our own apples from July until frost. Still, apples remained.

And so, this winter the omnivorous coyote's diet is ever more balanced. Besides his various meats—rabbits, mice, voles, the remains of deer, he has all the freeze-dried apples he might want. I rejoice in coyote poop!

February 9: How to Find a Walnut Tree

How to find a walnut tree? Simple. Just live near it for three decades, but stick to familiar trails. Don't venture off the worn path or crawl through the brush. Then one day, lost in thought, simply amble off the path for no particular reason. Keep your eyes on the ground, where perhaps you subconsciously expect to find some answer to whatever question is on your mind, but be sure to reserve some small corner of your consciousness to survey the here and now. That way, when you happen to pass a tree trunk with fragments of rough-ridged black shell littering the ground, the variation from earth and fallen leaf and broken twig may catch your eye. You'll stop in your tracks, puzzle for a moment before you realize what you're seeing, evidence of a tree that does not fit in these woods. Or at least you didn't know before now that it does!

How many times I had passed near the walnut tree without actually seeing it, I couldn't say. I had often traversed a path through the thicket in which it stood, but mostly in summer when trees and underbrush held their leaves and produced a nearly impenetrable barrier, or in winter when the ground was covered with snow. I had cut dozens of small redcedar trees in this piece of woods, but with that task, my focus was confined to the ground, looking for upstart cedars that had sprung to life from seed left by mature females I had long since eliminated from the copse. I had even invested hours of a night nearby, waiting at the mouth of a coyote den for my wily friend to emerge. And near that walnut tree, I once spent an entire fine fall day felling and cutting up a huge American elm that had given up the ghost and was ready to be dismantled into hundreds of chunks of firewood.

    But I digress. On this particular February day I had set all tasks aside—except the vital task of enjoying daily exercise and fresh, cold winter air. I had sauntered as usual across prairie hills with no particular destination or aim in mind. Suddenly, without warning, my feet turned themselves from prairie grasses to woods. Perhaps it was the biting northwest wind that communicated the altered course to my feet, but choose it they did.

    There was no trail here that led into the woods. But winter is the time for avoiding trails, ducking under low branches, climbing over fallen trunks and limbs and backing into briars and brush that one would avoid in a short-sleeved shirt, but which are navigable when armored in a heavy coat, hat and gloves. So in I plunged. Seeking the passage of least resistance, my eyes half registered the debris on the forest floor, the scat of birds and mammals, twigs and seeds, decaying leaves of every size and shape. Until the tiny object that didn't fit caught my eye.

    I stooped and picked it up, one wall of a tiny black vessel, harder than most any wood, a roughly ridged exterior, but smooth inside. The only part that was anything but black was the edge, recently grooved by a squirrel's teeth. My eyes skirted a small circumference around the base of the tree. They were everywhere. Most were camouflaged by late winter leaves, but in every barren spot lay the discarded containers of a squirrel's snack.

My eyes fastened on the bark of the trunk and followed it up to the limbs. No intact leaves remained to confirm the identification, neither on the branches, nor at my feet. But the bark was not that of an ash, not a mulberry, not a hackberry, not a box elder, not an oak or elm.

Black walnut trees are considered a native tree here—just barely—but they are not common in Clay County. We are on the fringe of the tree's vast range, a range that covers most of the eastern half of the United States. Here the tree's native habitat is confined mostly to wooded ravines and waterways, and even there it is rare. We had planted black walnuts in three places on our bluff, but this was the first naturally-occurring walnut I had found.

So, thank you to the squirrel or the blue jay or whoever long ago brought a black walnut to this place on the western edge of a small natural grove on Prairie Bluff. My world is now wider, more enriched. And to the squirrels that dined on this tree's largess, I have one request. Eat all the nuts you want next fall, and tell all your squirrel descendants where to find this tree. But now and then spare just one nut from your dinner. Carry it to another place in this or some other wood. Bury it for a future snack, and then forget where it lies. Perhaps you can extend the range of the black walnut, maybe a hundred yards in your next generation and perhaps a quarter mile in your grandson's time.

Feb 12: Darwin Meets Lincoln on the Bluff

On February 12, we celebrate the birthdays of two towering nineteenth century figures, Abraham Lincoln and Charles Darwin. Born on the same day in 1809, the two never met. Neither man saw the Missouri River bluffs, though President Lincoln helped shape the early Euro-American history of South Dakota, and upon Charles Darwin's investigation and insight is built modern man's understanding of how the Great

Plains ecosystem evolved and how natural processes continue to reshape, and in some instances restore, the modern ecosystem of which we are part.

Dakota Territory was established by Congress in February of 1861, the bill signed by President James Buchanan a few days later. In 1862 President Lincoln signed the Homestead Act, which accelerated white settlement. Yankton was designated the capital of Dakota Territory, and Lincoln appointed his personal physician, Dr. William Jayne of Springfield, Illinois, as the first territorial governor. But by then, Inglebrigt Severson had already arrived, one of the first white settlers to arrive on our piece of the bluff, probably in 1860, a year after the Yankton Sioux were removed from the land by the Treaty of 1858. It was Inglebrigt and his wife Serena who in 1869 built the two-story log house that still stands on our land, a structure in which three generations of their family would pass the next hundred years, and a structure that required most of my spare time for two summers to stabilize and preserve.

On November 24, 1859, as Inglebrigt made plans to cross the Missouri River from Nebraska Territory and take this piece of the bluff, Charles Darwin published *On the Origin of Species by Means of Natural Selection*. Darwin's observations had grown from his study of the insulated ecosystem of the Galapagos Islands off the coast of Ecuador. His observation that the beaks of isolated finch communities varied in size and shape, depending on their diet, was a prime exhibit in his emerging theory of evolution.

Finches are the most numerous birds at our feeders—house finches most prominent, followed by goldfinches and an occasional purple. I have not measured their beaks, but they all seem to relish sunflower seeds. The sunflower seeds are an exotic variety, of course. Not much across the Plains retains native virginity. Most of the plants, birds and mammals—including humans—that inhabited the bluff 150 years ago are extinct or removed, or exist only in small communities on scraps of prairie that have escaped cultivation, overgrazing or human development. Yet the legacy of two great men, born two centuries ago lives on, still contributing to our understanding of this place on Earth, to the processes of degradation and restoration, and to our obligations to the land, the ecosystem and the peoples of which we are a part.

February 14: Memorial to Fallen Friends

Valentine's Day. What kind of man would take his sweetheart to the woods on Valentine's Day, especially a cold Valentine's Day? I would. And she would go. Partly because if there's no snow on the ground, winter is the time to look for bones, especially for fallen antlers.

So off to the deepest woods we go. In summer, thrashing through thickets of leafed out and sometimes-thorny underbrush is not my idea of fun. A summer explorer stirs swarms of mosquitoes and gnats and provides transportation for everything from ticks to the barbed seeds of invasive weeds. Equally important, the reward for summer incursions is slim; whatever lies beneath the understory, the feathers of roosting turkeys, pellets regurgitated by well-fed owls, the bones of fallen mammals and antlers shed by winter deer, all are hidden for the season.

A February day with little snow is perhaps the best time to look for antlers. The mating season is long over, so bucks no longer need their crowns for impressing potential mates or for backing down rivals. Winter is also the hungry season, the season for browsing branches and dried fruits and scrounging for whatever can be found, making an impressive pair of antlers an impediment. Why carry around the extra weight and limit your movements to spaces that only a broad rack can pass through if the need for your insignia has passed? Time to throw out the old to make room for the new. In a couple of months, the nubs of next year's even more substantial antlers will emerge as velvety knobs.

If the hunter of discarded crests waits much later in the winter, the most imposing antler may be damaged by gnawing rodents who find it a good source of calcium to build their own bones. Sure every mouse has to eat, but let them chew on other bones and inferior antlers, I say. The perfect eight-point crest comes home with me—if I can find it.

I try to keep eyes and mind open to other encounters, but it is the search for antlers that dominates our attention; what we find instead is a surprise. It is past mid winter, the time when hunger stalks many a native inhabitant of the bluff. The coyote is no exception; getting a single coyote through winter requires the death of many a mouse, vole, rabbit or bird, along with whatever carrion, fruit or rubbish a coyote can stomach. But on this particular day, while trudging up a steep and brushy hillside, we spot scattered coyote fur. We begin to search for bones. Nothing to be found. The hair is spread over a long stretch of hillside—a common pattern of dispersal where coyotes eat other animals, dismembering the victim and quarrelling over favored parts. On a hillside, the moveable feast of course spreads down.

We search that course, then circle back up the hill. Eventually I find what remains of the unfortunate coyote besides his fur—the intact skull, complete with hair, teeth and glazed eyes. So what would consume an entire coyote, I wonder. Would other coyotes dine on one of their own? Turkey vultures and raccoons and others might do their parts as well. But where were the skeletal remains, the bones of legs and spine? Might this coyote have fed a mountain lion, something capable of crunching every bone into food, and if so, why not the head?

The ground on this shaded hillside is still frozen hard, and what snow remains is icy crust, so of course no tracks or other clues remain. The manner of death and what other life the coyote fed will remain unknown. But I pick up the skull and carry it home. Atop the stone retaining wall beside our house, I had stacked sections of a hollow log—not just any log, but one inside of which mushrooms had grown. Inside each I had installed an antler—my version of found art. From the central log I withdraw the antler and replace it with the coyote's skull. Some might find this morbid or even perverse, displaying a coyote's head. But excluding my human neighbors who carry guns, my spirit animal is commonly the top predator on the bluff. So the coyote deserves a central place in this shrine to fallen friends. Sometimes even I am momentarily startled when I find myself meeting the coyote eye to eye. And why this fascination with the remains of other creatures? I couldn't say for sure. It is not worship as at a sacred shrine, but perhaps an affirmation of admiration and respect, as well as a comforting reassurance that life remains diverse and wild on Prairie Bluff.

February 20: January Thaw

We waited thirty-one days for the usual January Thaw to come, but the weatherman had other ideas. Finally on a sunny afternoon in early February the temperature reached the mid forties, and melting snow began to move. At first tiny rivulets trickled a drop at a time down icy drifts. By late afternoon, thousands of droplets had coalesced and water was trickling down hillsides and crevices to lower ground. Here on the north forty, the destination of flowing water is the pond below our house.

For three months the pond has been encased in ice, but by the time winter's skin had grown thick enough to support humans in early December, the surface was also covered by snow, rendering the pond unskatable. With the tentative thaw, that began to change as the first melted snow reached the valleys. Another week of above freezing afternoons passed, and most of the snow from surrounding hillsides flowed as icy water to the pond and covered the snow and ice. Because the air trapped in ice makes it lighter than water, eventually the old ice cracked across the middle, broke loose from its earthly moorings around the edges and rose. Then on Valentine's Day, Arctic air returned.

The thermometer the next morning read ten degrees; surely the time for skating had come. I dug the skates from the closet and Norma and I headed for the pond. The surface was a glossy sheen from bank to bank, except for early winter's iceberg protruding in the middle. A broad ring around the cottonwood and willow edges seemed the perfect skating run. I stepped out onto ice. A high-pitched crackle splintered across the surface and I quickly retreated to the safety of earth. The time for skating had not yet come, so on that day we headed for the woods instead.

Now it is President's Day, and two more days in the twenties with nights near zero have thickened the ice to at least a couple of inches, so we'll gather friends and try again. But we will stay near the edge; life's pleasures are never without risk, but why take foolish chances by skating on thin ice?

February 23: Requiem for a Possum

I saw it as we drove out the driveway, a dark lump on Frog Creek Road. Gray fur, a mammal of some kind: cat, rabbit, raccoon?

No, there was no mistaking the long, tapered hairless tail. It was a possum, *Didelphis virginiana*, our only marsupial, the order of mammals whose embryos complete their maturation riding in their mother's nipple-lined pouch. I got out of the car and crossed the road. The possum—this one was a male—was freshly killed, sometime in the night. His eyes still stared, but vacantly. His hair ruffled gently in the wind.

Almost as he looked yesterday when he scurried into the hollow log beside our lawn when I approached to fill the bird feeders, the log I had brought up from the woods years ago, dragged to the pickup and hauled home atop a load of firewood. It was a long-dead elm trunk sprawling beside a ravine, its limbs fallen away. It was too far gone even then to consider for the stove, but there was something about the way the tree had grown that I chuckled over each time I passed it on the trail. Apparently, in its younger days the tree had sprouted two rival trunks, but those trunks had long since rotted away, leaving what appeared to be two vacant eye sockets, perfectly positioned above a long, hollow snout. I rarely relocate decaying logs, but there I was with a pickup full of wood headed for home, and this oddity of nature might as well ride along.

For the first couple of years, it lay alone at the edge of the yard. The second year I arranged a pair of deer antlers above the eyebrows to create a hybrid prairie creature that I thought might amuse friends, a deeragon, my version of the jackalope, the man-made hybrid of jackrabbit and antelope that one finds in western gift shops. I'm not sure anybody else appreciated my stroke of artistic genius as much as I did, but then I'm easily amused.

A year ago, as often happens in spring, I decided another flowerbed wouldn't hurt. I got out the shovel and spaded a ten by twenty-foot patch at the edge of lawn, partially sheltered by a spreading juniper bush. The back edge I planted to native perennial forbs—blue flax, purple coneflower, stiff sunflower and blanket flower. The front I reserved for colorful annuals—petunias, marigolds and moss roses. When I finished, it occurred to me that the back side, under the juniper, needed a proper edge, a border to set off the riot of color from the untrimmed grasses beyond. And so the deeragon moved once again.

At the time, I didn't think of it as a refuge or a home. Presumably it had been occupied at least occasionally in the woods, but not here at the edge of a mowed lawn and a flowerbed under a juniper bush in plain sight of our front windows. What I had not considered is that humans are not the only ones who enjoy breakfast in bed, or at least bedroom and kitchen in close proximity. Above the log and a few feet away was a bird feeder.

Anyone who puts out black oil sunflower seeds knows

that most every winter bird is pleased. More than a dozen species come to dine—everything from house and gold finches to four kinds of woodpeckers to nuthatches, blue jays, cedar waxwings, cardinals and more. The presence of so many potential avian diners attracts rough-legged hawks, merlins, kestrels and other birds of prey. Wild turkeys and pheasants sometimes wander by to eat what other birds have scratched off their plate. What they miss may be munched by squirrels or licked up by deer. One winter when snow was deep, the drift below one feeder held an elaborate system of tunnels where voles lived and dined. And always raccoons and possums had done their part to prevent the waste of a single seed.

In the past I had even photographed a confrontation between a hungry possum and a pair of young deer, a contest in which the possum prevailed. But this winter's resident possum was different. The first time I saw him munching seeds, I simply watched in amusement and wonder. He licked up a tongue's breadth of whatever lay on the grass, chomped open mouthed like a hog, a little saliva dripping from the lower lip, then swallowed and scooped up some more.

I opened the front door and spoke. "Hello, possum," I said. "I hope you're enjoying your dinner." No reply. His beady eyes registered my presence for as long as it took to chew a mouthful, then he went on with his dinner, seemingly oblivious to my interruption. I of course was delighted to have the visitor, though it did occur to me that he might find his way through the cat door into the garage and assume a share of the food we put out for the cat.

I took a few steps in his direction. Again he glanced up,

but gave no sign of being perturbed. I came closer, now not more than half a dozen paces away. Still no reaction or alarm. Of course he did have a mouthful of finely chiseled teeth, so I suppose he had little reason to fear. I took a few more steps, halving the distance between us. At last he looked up with what seemed like irritation, not just a pause in licking up seeds.

"What are you doing here, eating all my birdseed?" I demanded. I made a sudden lunge, and at last he responded, lazily to be sure. No sign of true alarm, no dash to the freedom of the woods. Instead he ambled slowly to the head of deeragon and sauntered in. I knelt at the end of the snout and engaged Mr. Possum in a staring contest. He didn't blink. He was clearly prepared to wait me out. And so it went. Until today.

I lifted the bloodied possum by his wiry muscular tail and carried him away from the road toward the woods. I laid him gently on last fall's leaves beside an arching box elder tree. Here he would go back to the spirit world of possums, if such a world exists, or decay into the earth, or more likely be devoured by the first hungry coyote that wandered down the path.

Now the hollow log is empty, a hollowness echoed in my soul. My days are somehow less complete. We still share the bluff with myriad other creatures, and I'm sure that somewhere other possums roam. Perhaps another will make the log his refuge or home. But this fellow creature, crushed by a speeding car in this curvy strip of road where the speed limit is thirty-five, is no more.

MARCH

March 1: The Life and Death of Coons

As often happens, some of the nastiest weather of winter

comes when we've earned the right to expect better. In the past few days we've had freezing rain and then snow, and below zero nights have kept it all around. It's too icy to work outside, and there's not enough snow to ski. It's too cold for much of anything besides sitting by the fire and swapping yarns with friends. Like the one about the raccoon that might have done me in.

The *Procyon lotor* is among our most prolific animals, and our contact with them is frequent. On our treacherous drive home from town late last night, we counted a dozen raccoons in as many miles. Ten were alive and engaged in a frigid search for food. Two lay freshly killed in the middle of the road. It is an unusual night drive if we don't see a few pairs of glowing eyes, at least one or two of them coons ambling across the road, especially near a neighbor's feedlot. But the profusion of raccoons last night brought to mind the one that might have killed my housemate Errol and me in the winter of 1971.

We were living in a small two-bedroom house on a backstreet in Del City, Oklahoma. The place was heated by a gas-fueled floor furnace, a common and practical type of heater in that place and time. There's no faster warm up—not even a wood stove. Turn up the thermostat and stand directly over the rising heat. It's especially effective when your pant legs are wet.

One winter evening we heard a vague rustling sound under the house. We figured a neighboring cat, or perhaps a rat or other wild creature had taken refuge in the crawl space below the floor. Come Saturday, we'd have a look. The next evening, the scrambling and scratching continued. Directing more attention to the phenomenon, we concluded that the sound was confined to a small area in the middle of the house near the floor furnace. On the third evening all was quiet under the house, so we assumed that whatever had taken up residence had moved on. So, Saturday came and we saw no need to investigate.

About the middle of the next week, we began to notice the odor of decaying flesh. Maybe the creature—whatever it was—had not escaped after all. By the next Saturday the stench could not be ignored. We opened the foundation vent and crawled inside the reeking two-foot space between floor joists and musty earth. We shined a flashlight all around the perimeter of the little house, but saw nothing. Then we recalled that the rustling had seemed to come from the center of the house, next to the furnace. We saw that the furnace was vented out the side about a foot off the ground. The pipe ran horizontally into a round eight-inch clay chimney pipe that was supported by a pair of bricks. Crawling toward the furnace, our noses told us that whatever was decaying under the house was in the chimney!

How to get it out? Everything was tightly sealed. We crawled back out, borrowed a ladder from a neighbor, and climbed onto the roof. We shined the flashlight down the chimney, and sure enough, something furry lay at the bottom—fifteen feet below.

Being an occasional fisherman, Errol remembered his rod and reel. He attached his biggest treble hook to the line and lowered it down the chimney pipe. After a bit of "fishing," he snagged the unlucky creature and began to reel it up. Unfortunately there was a joint in the pipe about four feet down, a joint with a slight offset. When the decaying body reached this impediment, it stuck. Errol tugged at the biggest catch of his life. The body almost cleared the seam before the hook pulled free of the decaying hide, and the carcass whooshed back to the bottom, sending a wave of putrid air up the pipe into his face.

And then it began to rain. So here we were, standing on the peak of our roof in the rain, repeatedly reeling a heavy body to within four feet of the top only to see it break loose and slip once more to the inner recesses of our home. I glanced nervously up and down the street, hoping none of the neighbors were watching what would no doubt have been the strangest fishing expedition they had ever seen.

After half an hour and a dozen tries, Errol finally landed his catch, a large raccoon. But not just any raccoon. Around its neck was a collar! The ill-fated creature had been somebody's pet. What to do with the body? We thought of trying to locate the grieving owner, but decided that was not likely and that whatever child had loved the coon might be better off assuming the animal had gone off to the woods to join its wild cousins. We sealed the body into a plastic bag, took it for a ride in the country, and emptied the bag in a clump of grass where the remains might return to earth.

So one less pet raccoon in Del City, Oklahoma. But as we drove down the country road it occurred to us that the coon might have taken us with him to the other world. The body, stuffed inside an eight-inch pipe, would have filled at least a foot of space—about exactly the space below where our furnace exhaust entered the chimney pipe. If that hole had been blocked, all the fumes from the gas furnace would have been forced into the closed crawl space below the house, a potential source of asphyxiation for us. Back in town, we stopped at the hardware store for a chimney cap.

March 5: Death Feeds Life in Winter

OK, I'm thinking, maybe it's time to get off the subject of death. But winter is death's favorite season, and it isn't over yet. Snow still covers the ground, and the thermometer hasn't risen since Thursday. Yet we know, at least intellectually, that the days are numbered for the season of loss. The most recent blast of ice and snow likely won't be the last, but March has come, we have gained three hours of sunlight, and any day now angles of geese will fill the sky, pushing winter back to its proper place at the North Pole. Blink your eyes and spring will come!

And yet, winter has taken its perennial toll. Trees have been stark and brittle for months. Soil that in two months will produce the first lettuce leaves is still hard as brick. Even the lovely amber and pink of native grasses has faded, heads stripped by wind, stems shattered and drab. And last week, on the hillside east of the house I found the remains of a frozen deer.

What took her life, I could not ascertain. I saw no arrow or bullet hole, which I have sometimes found in other carcasses. She looked healthy enough to be alive when I found her sheltered south of a cedar tree a hundred feet from the house, a protected slope of native grass where deer often sleep. I expected her to spring from her bed and disappear, but she did not. When I came close, the glaze across her eye proved that this was her final rest. Like sisters of a dozen generations, she had come home to die.

A hundred feet from the house is too close for decaying flesh. I picked up a frozen leg and began to pull. I tugged her to the next cedar before concluding that she was too heavy to drag up hill. I went for the tractor, picked her up with the snow scoop and hauled her to another hillside 200 yards away.

The first night, coyotes came. I heard the happy commotion from our bed. By morning her belly was opened and choice parts were gone. Then came the day shift, a murder of crows, two dozen or more, their raucous caws shrieking their glee. A week has passed, and now, should I wish, I could move what remains of her carcass with ease. The dining table where she lies is a carpet of hair, but little is left of the body but hide and bones.

When the weather warms and what remains begins to rot, vultures will dine, and then insects and worms. When winter comes again, mice who live in the nearby brush pile will gnaw the scattered bones. And someday, what nothing above ground eats will enrich the soil.

March 9: Trumpets of Spring

Spring is here! Well, not really, but the geese that announce it have come. I have learned to expect the migration of waterfowl to begin about March 1. But this year, freezing rain fell on February 26 and snow on February 27. The temperature the first morning of March was well below zero. Instead of pushing north, geese congregated on open stretches of the Missouri River and waited for nature's call.

Monday began a warming trend, and on Tuesday melted snow again streamed down the valleys toward the ponds, but still I saw no geese. Most of that day I spent indoors in county commission meetings, so perhaps birds were passing overhead and I was unaware. By Wednesday, most of the snow had vanished from the bluff. Norma and I rambled across prairies and woods, and still we saw or heard no geese. A nagging nervousness set in; why were the harbingers of spring several days late?

I recalled that when light snow fell on our bluff the previous week, parts of northern South Dakota got nearly a foot. Probably the cornfields and wetlands where migrating geese feed and rest were still blanketed in white. That could suggest to those who listen to weather reports why migration might be premature, but presumably the geese also knew that their reception farther north would be ungracious. After thousands of generations of migration, they must sense instinctively what we must rely on modern media to learn.

In any case, nervousness has turned to joy. Today thousands of Canada geese fill the sky. The recent wet snow reminds us that March is our snowiest month; I know that for weeks the earth may remain frozen, that tilling the garden is a month or more away. We may not see pasque flowers for weeks, and there will be more fires in the wood stove. Yet the first sign of spring has come—thousands upon thousands of geese rushing and honking northward across the sky, pushing winter beyond the bluff, clearing the path for yet more geese and ducks and sandhill cranes, and two months hence, even brown thrashers.

When I hear the thrashers sing, I will set out tomato and pepper plants and relegate the winter's cold and ice to memory. But for now, it is enough to strain eyes and ears toward the Missouri, waiting for the next angle of geese to clear the bluff.

March 13: Cardinals Convene

On this date, the cardinals of the Roman Catholic Church elected one of their own as the new pope. Jorge Mario Bergoglio, the first pope from the Western Hemisphere, took the name of St. Francis. Pope Francis' thirteenth century namesake was a humble man, friend of the downtrodden and the poor. But he is also the patron saint of animals and ecology; he has often been depicted in paintings and statuary with a bird on his shoulder or hovering near.

Today was the first day on the bluff that truly felt like spring. The sun was bright and strong, the temperature in the sixties, the wind a gentle southern breeze. I walked the upland prairie with the mission of trimming trees, but really looking for signs of life. Angles of geese still honked their way north by the thousands, a long line of Vs stretching south to infinity, a certain sign that the earth was thawing and that the deep awakening had begun.

I mindlessly sauntered and trimmed my way down the path toward the pond. The ice was still thick, but rimmed by open water, not yet open enough for ducks, but enough that the iceberg was loosed from its moorings, the muddy bank reclaiming its freedom from winter's long grip. Then another kind of cardinal sang, the *Cardinalis cardinalis*, a brilliant red male perched in the top twigs of a still-barren oak. I paused to take in the crisp notes, sung to attract any female who might hear.

Across the pond a second male cardinal replied, perhaps a greeting for the first or perhaps a proclamation that the other side of the pond was his. Then came a third from a distant grove of ash, and the conclave had begun. This was no secret meeting behind closed doors, no new pope was selected, and I cannot say what business was discussed or decisions made.

Of course my cardinals have not heard the news that the other conclave of cardinals had selected Francis as pope, nor that as the faithful watched the Vatican chimney for a smoke signal, a seagull alighted, foreshadowing the choice of a cardinal who would take the name of the saint of birds. The cardinals at our pond have no idea that their cloaks of brilliant red are imitated in Rome. But whatever their message or news of spring, never has an assembly of cardinals sung more sweetly, nor a council, caucus or congress proclaimed a vision more true.

March 16: Dancing with Sandhill Stars

Among the most majestic birds we see on the bluff are sandhill cranes, *Grus canadenis*. Actually we rarely see them *on* the bluff, but soaring far above. Last spring we watched a flock of 300 gobbling fallen corn in a nearby field, but since they rarely stop to visit us, this past weekend Norma and I and friends Chuck and Grete drove to the Platte River in Nebraska to visit them.

On Saturday afternoon we idled down the Platte River Road from Doniphan, south of Grand Island, to Ft. Kearny State Park, a mostly gravel road that roughly follows the river's south bank. Cranes roamed last year's cornfields by the tens of thousands, feeding on waste corn in the stubble of the Cornhusker state. Sundown found us amongst scores of birdwatchers huddled on the old railroad bridge north of the park, awaiting the birds' arrival at the islands where they spend the night safe from predators amidst the braided channels. No cranes came to roost at our feet, but thousands saluted us as they cruised the river in search of a nighttime refuge.

Sunday morning we were up at daybreak for another visit. Just after sunrise we arrived at the bridge south of Alda.

We opened the car doors to the roar of thousands of cranes greeting the rising sun. We hiked upriver through the lovely Nature Conservancy prairie, where we crouched behind grasses and trees to watch the magnificent birds strut in the shallow water of sandbars. They stand a meter high, great flocks of gray readily visible for long distances across pastures, fields or the islands that dot the Platte. But through binoculars one sees that the gray is accented by wings of subtle brown, a white face and a cap of brilliant red. They feed and dance, leaping on fluttering wings and settling back to earth, an exuberance that humans rarely match. Then warmed by the sun, they rise on eighty-inch wings to soar across the prairie for another breakfast of corn.

Arriving from the Gulf of Mexico in March, the birds remain near the Platte for up to a month, resting and putting on weight for the long flight that remains to their summer nesting grounds in the marshes and tundra of northern Canada and Siberia. Around April Fools Day, the last wave of the season will rise above the Platte and set their sights on the Arctic Circle, still thousands of miles away. If we are lucky, we will see them again in the sky above our bluff.

Only twice have I seen them feeding near our home, last spring in a field on the bluff and once in a cornfield by the Missouri. A few times they have passed overhead, so low we could see the tawny plumage of their breasts and the feathery bustles of their rumps. But usually we only hear their chortle—like the far-away tinkling of a crystal chandelier—and then if we scan the skies and look long and carefully enough, we may see them, half a mile high, circling and sailing north on favorable winds, transcontinental airliners on a nearly non-stop flight.

March 17: Into the Briar Patch

When I was a child, my mother read and reread stories from our household's two books written for kids. Among my favorites was Brer Rabbit and the Tar Baby, which I learned much later was among the tales collected by Joel Chandler Harris in 1870s Georgia, African stories passed down by Southern slaves and possibly trickster tales told by their Creek and Cherokee neighbors. It is legitimate to ask whether Brer Rabbit and perhaps other tales are tinged by racial stereotypes, but as a child I found the story charming and hilarious. The animal characters are so vividly drawn that I could visualize the action and comprehend the conflict and irony that animates the battle of wits.

The story may be summarized as follows: Brer (brother) Rabbit's frequent tricks are endured by most of his fellow creatures, but are an intolerable irritant to the wily Brer Fox, who devises an ingenious plan to outwit his rival. Mixing tar and turpentine, he fashions a life-like doll, a "tar baby," and sets it in the Rabbit's habitual path. Brer Fox lies in hiding as Brer Rabbit saunters up and greets the tar baby, who of course does not reply. Accusing the newcomer of being stuck up, Brer Rabbit punches him in the nose. His paw sticks. "If you don't turn me loose, I'll hit you again," says Brer Rabbit. And so it goes until all of Brer Rabbit's feet and his head are embedded in tar. Brer Fox emerges from hiding, laughing at his nemesis with glee. "What should I do with you," he asks. "Should I hang you, drown you, or roast you and eat you for lunch?"

"Do anything you like with me," Brer Rabbit replies. "Hang me, drown me, or roast me for lunch, but pleeeeze don't throw me in the briar patch." So that, of course, is exactly what Brer Fox does. And within moments Brer Rabbit is sitting on a log on a far away hilltop, chuckling devilishly and picking tar from his fur. He has saved himself, but perhaps as important, he has outfoxed Brer Fox.

Norma and I weren't sure what tricksters were nightly rooting for worms or insects in our flowerbeds and front lawn, but we endured the irritant as long as we could. We do delight in sharing our yard with a wide range of fellow creatures, from mice and voles to squirrels, skunks, possums, raccoons, rabbits, coyotes and deer, and we are loathe to interfere with the habits and choices of co-inhabitants. But there are limits to our patience. The daily task of replacing divots in the lawn grew tiresome, and when it came to uprooting nascent flowers from their beds, that was too much. Time for a battle of wits. We borrowed a live trap from our friends, Clarence and Sandy, baited it with a chunk of Luna the cat's favorite tuna, and waited for action.

The sun rose next morning on a battlefield. The trap lay on its side several feet from where it had been set. A big patch of lawn was torn to shreds. Inside was a fat Brer Raccoon. Like Brer Rabbit, I greeted the coon with good morning, loaded him trap and all into the pickup bed and headed for the woods. I stopped at the prairie edge and carried the caged animal down the hill and into the heart of the forest. I opened the door facing a big hackberry tree in a region where fellow coons are known to hang out. He bounded from the cage and charged at full speed toward the big cottonwood by the spring, soon out of sight in a tangle of vines—his briar patch.

The next morning dawned with the raccoon's neighbor, a possum, clawing away at the steel wires of his cage. I repeated the journey to the heart of the woods with the possum, and again I opened the hatch. Brer Possum stared long at the open portal, sniffing the trap for another trap. He inched toward the opening, then lunged as fast as his short legs could carry him to a fallen tree. He examined the trunk for a suitable hollow, but finding nothing of sufficient size, he was off again, tracing the trajectory of Brer Raccoon.

I did not threaten either of my fellow inhabitants with drowning or lynching, and I had no desire to roast and eat a possum or a coon. Neither exhorted me to throw him into the briar patch, but I suspect that was satisfactory to both. After all, they had gone—as we sometimes say of dead people—to a better place. At least I hoped they thought so, and for the sake of spring flowers, I hoped they would live happily ever after in those distant woods.

Three days passed without a catch, so I tripped the trap and put it away. The next morning we found more holes in the lawn. Out came the trap again and more Luna tuna bait.

Next dawn brought an amazing sight. The trap door was closed, the tuna untouched. But next to the trigger laid a pile of raccoon excrement! How could this be? If the coon was trapped, why didn't he eat the food, and how did he escape? Or was this his protest demonstration, the equivalent of a last laugh in Brer Fox's face? Apparently Brer Coon backed into the trap, dumped his load, then ambled out and pulled the trigger. The mystery will never be solved, but the battle of wits goes on.

Spring

March 20: Breaking Hibernation
    I hereby declare an end to Cabin Fever. Even the calendar tells me that spring equinox has arrived, but better evidence is found through a stroll outdoors. In the past week I've marveled at nine tokens of spring, and I added one of my own:

1. Nest-seeking turkey hens strolled clucking past the garden gate.
2. The last sliver of ice vanished from the pond.
3. The first pair of blue-winged teal replaced the ice, floating the open water, peeping notes of love.
4. An early pair of bluebirds briefly inspected the birdhouse by the clothesline. As Thoreau said, when the bluebird comes, "he carries the sky on his back."
5. A meadowlark pierced the morning air with his seven-note song.
6. Goldfinches have shed drab winter feathers for the brilliant yellow of spring.
7. Last night brought the first lightning and a thunderstorm.
8. The bluegrass scraps in the lawn are turning green.
9. The maple tree is covered with flowers and filled with honeybee hum.
10. On St. Patrick's Day, I planted three varieties of chili peppers in soil and peat, a down payment on the garden of my dreams.

But spring is not all admiration and joy. The season of life is also a season of physical work. Not that I'm complaining. I welcome hours outdoors and the physical tuning that only the regular exercise of muscles can bring. In the garden there will be tilling, planting, weeding and harvesting. Native prairie restoration involves removing cedar saplings, thistles and other invasive species; sowing and spreading native seeds; selective mowing and burning; walking the hills with a sprayer on my back, judiciously applying chemicals to noxious weeds that can't be controlled another way; and maintaining fences to confine the neighbors' cows when they graze here each spring.

So let the joy and work of spring and summer begin! Today Norma and I turned the soil of the flowerbeds, rooting out the sedum and starflowers that spring early from roots and bulbs to grab more than their share of territory. We chopped in humus and manure to prepare the beds for summer's flowers. Then I hiked the hills with pruners, dropping to my knees to snip off a hundred cedars that sprang in bare soil from the thousand seeds left behind by mature females I removed last year.

After a long season of relative hibernation, an afternoon crouching and crawling on knees and working the earth with my hands will guarantee a stiff back tomorrow, but the tenderness of hands will become the first layer of toughness that by May will grow to calluses across my palms. Like the plants and some of the animals that share our bluff, we have emerged from our season of dormancy, ready to embrace with exuberance the season of life.

March 30: Waging Cedarcide

What could be more contradictory for a tree-loving conservationist than to spend a fine spring morning killing trees? Yet, that was exactly my primary occupation again today. When Norma and I bought land on the Missouri River Bluff in 1981, a dozen small cedars dotted our hills. Of the thousand trees and bushes we planted, the first were more cedars northwest of our home site. But these days I cut down cedar trees by the hundreds.

The eastern redcedar embodies a number of contradictions. First, they are not a true cedar, but a species of juniper, the *Juniperus virginiana*. The eastern redcedar is the most widely distributed tree-sized conifer in the eastern United States. Its native range extends from west of the Missouri River to the east coast. It is valued as food by various birds and as shelter by both man and beast, including me. But the cedar is a serious adversary of prairie.

Though the cedar is native in southeast South Dakota, in all the centuries that man and cedars coexisted, the trees were confined to protected ravines. But suddenly in the 1980s, they exploded across the grasslands of the region. I remember well the first signs of proliferation. Peering across our west valley one winter morning in 1985, I saw three dark dots protruding from the hillside snow. I clipped on skis and glided over. Three eastern redcedars poked their tips through white. I was delighted to learn that another native species was reasserting itself on the bluff.

As these and other cedars grew toward maturity, I saw that some bore bluish berries that cedar waxwings love. I eventually figured out—but too late—that the blue seeds mean female, and that each berry is a potential tree. By then cedars were widespread along the bluff and were taking over untilled pastures across the region! Why now? The first answer is suppression of fire. Sometimes ignited by Native peoples to enhance prairie and bring bison, and probably more often by lightning, fire swept the prairie until the late 19th century, when it was brought under control by cultivation, grazing, roads and fire fighters.

Let a tongue of fire touch a branch in a dry season and a cedar bursts into crackling flame. But most fires have been controlled for a century, so why the plague of cedars now?

Fewer livestock graze the land than in past decades, and reestablished wildlife habitat, on our land and elsewhere, provides more cover and food for birds, including cedar berry-loving cardinals and cedar waxwings. More berries bring more birds, and more trees get planted. But there is another factor, second only to suppression of fire. The tall grasses that once dominated the prairie have been plowed under, replaced for a century by crops. Much of the bluff was replanted to grass in recent decades, but to imported cool-season grasses, bluegrass and smooth brome. In summer heat and drought, these grasses are dormant and sparse, allowing competitors to emerge.

    The immediate choice was clear; remove large female cedars and cut cedar seedlings every year, or let them take control. But since my years to wield loppers and saw are finite, restoration of native prairie was urgent; tall grasses like big bluestem, switchgrass and Indiangrass grow thick and tall, crowding and shading cedars and other invaders out. Thus each spring, before the seeds mature to viability in summer, I must walk the hills on cedar patrol, conducting cedarcide on the next plot scheduled for rehabilitation and removing saplings sprung from remaining seeds on already converted lands. In our ravines and woods, cedars and all the birds and mammals that love them thrive. But the meadows belong to prairie, to the forbs and grasses that evolution and we have planted, and to the birds and mammals that make their homes and earn their livings there.

APRIL

April 1: House Hunting

    It is the first day of April, the day of fools—or in my case, another good day to fool around for a while. At dawn the sky is clear and the sun rises bold and strong. I pour a cup of coffee and launch back in my recliner to watch the feeding birds.

They seem especially hungry this morning, flocking in great numbers and gobbling sunflower seeds. Luna leaps to my lap, demanding her morning rub. All is well with the world, but it's about to get better.

A flash of blue catches my eye, not the steely blue of the abundant jays, but the blue of the other bird that bears the color's name, a true bluebird blue. The early pair that appeared briefly on the first day of spring moved on, so I hope this one stays. On my calendar of birds, April first is bluebird season, and the eastern bluebird, *Sialia sialis*, is here on schedule. This one is a male. He appears to be alone, a bachelor who has yet to find a mate or perhaps a husband sent ahead to survey potential nesting places.

He is not here for sunflower seeds. He has other things in mind. He pauses briefly in an elm, then flies directly to the post upon which is mounted the nearest bluebird house. For several moments he surveys the yard from the post top. Is the open space adequate to satisfy safety concerns? Perhaps he is calculating the prospects for insect production amidst the trees, native grasses and brush piles in his purview. It is too early, of course, to anticipate the insects that might visit wildflowers or the flowers that might grow in beds. Not even a blade of future promise has broken the recently mellowed earth.

Time to take a closer look. He flutters beside the house as if surveying the construction. Is the house well built and firmly attached to the post, able to survive the storms of spring? Will the roof keep out the rain? He checks out every side, then hovers a moment before the door. He lights and pokes his head in the hole for a better look. Yes, the human neighbor–me–has cleaned the house since last season. But is it clean enough to satisfy a very particular mate? At last he disappears inside. I hold my breath, hoping he will like what he finds. But moments later he emerges and flies back to the elm.

Like people, bluebirds would be unwise to make snap judgments, so I understand that he must take his time. We have two other bluebird houses he may wish to consider, one by the garden, which is farther from the house and perhaps closer to a wealth of food, and one by the driveway. I hope that he'll choose the closest house, where I can watch him and his mate—a mate he perhaps has yet to attract—without leaving my easy chair. And even better, I hope he has friends who will choose the houses he rejects.

It is too early for nesting, of course. That may yet be a month away. And who knows, he may be a mere speculator in our yard, stopping off to dream and rest on his way to a destination farther north. If that's the case, I'll be watching for other flashes of blue—and for the paler blue of the female, upon which my future hopes and those of the visitor depend.

April 5: An Anything-but-Cocky Bird

After more than three decades of hunting, it's an uncommon day when I find a new fellow inhabitant of our bluff. By "hunting," I don't mean that I carry a gun. Sometimes I carry a compact camera and binoculars on my belt, though those are occasions when exploring the life of the prairies and woods, or at least a "nature walk," is my particular aim. More often I am at work, preoccupied by some seasonal or perennial task.

Such was the case this afternoon when I flushed a bird that I could not immediately identify. To be more accurate, it was our old Ford tractor that flushed the uncommon visitor. I had been mowing a firebreak in preparation for burning a four-acre hilltop prairie and was en route to a one-acre bottom south of the spring. As the tractor passed the lowest point, just above where the home spring seeps from the ravine, a flash of brown to my left caught my eye, perhaps a rotting branch flipped up by a tire? My eye followed the movement, and there in the grass crouched a plump brown bird.

I stopped the tractor for a better look. A variegated pallet of browns, roughly the size and shape of a bobwhite quail. Certainly not a quail, but what? My mind ran through the catalog of possibilities, eliminating them one by one, until only two remained. It had to be either a snipe or an American woodcock.

I had encountered each bird only once, the woodcock by the shore of Marindahl Lake, several miles up Turkey Ridge in Yankton County, the snipe by the Missouri River. Yes, as an Oklahoma cub scout I was dumped in the woods with a paper bag and told to wait while older boys rounded up snipes and sent them my way—then a common ritual of initiation—but no snipes came. At the time the snipe remained to me a mythical creature. I'm quite sure that the tricksters who dispatched me on that mission had never seen a snipe, much less captured one; they were likely as uneducated about birds as I was at the time. That is, they probably had no idea that such a creature as a snipe, whether bird or mammal nobody seemed to know, actually existed. And I didn't learn until much later that the bird officially shared my name, the Wilson's snipe.

So decades passed before I finally encountered and identified the snipe. It was while tromping through a rare backwater slough of the Missouri River that I almost literally stumbled across the brownish bird with a white belly and a very long beak. I got a close-enough look to confirm the sighting in my bird books when I got home. It was a fulfilling day. A mere forty years after "snipe hunting," squatting in the dark by a blackjack tree with an opened paper bag, the bird had finally appeared.

Back to the present bird. The tractor engine idled and rattled, and the bird remained crouched some four or five steps away. Odd behavior, I thought. I pondered whether turning off the engine might prompt it to fly, as sometimes happens, but decided that I could stay as long as he, so I turned the key. Except for a distant blue jay's screech, silence reigned. The ground bird's huge dark eyes stared back at me, and I had leisure to embrace details of the uncommon visitor.

The wings and back were a marvel of intricate design—layer upon layer of feathers in chevrons of dark gray, white and tan. The neck was white, the face and belly soft amber. The bird was chunky and squat, with hardly any tail. The crown of his head was marked by four crosswise bands of dark brown, interspersed with white. And then there was the beak. The bird's body was perhaps eight inches long, but the beak was close to three—long, straight, tapered to a sharp point at the end.

To this point, the bird had crouched unmoving in the dry winter grass. Indeed, if I had been on foot I might well have passed within four paces and entirely missed the sight, so well camouflaged he was. But now he rose on his short legs and began a rhythmic sway. His legs and head remained stationary, but his heavy body lunged forward and back, forward and back, a strange rocking dance. Was he ill, was this mating behavior, or was this display meant only for me?

After ten minutes had passed I decided that he was in no hurry to fly, and since he had tolerated my presence at such close range, perhaps I could creep even closer. Very slowly I climbed down from the tractor seat. Now I was on the ground, a level playing field. We faced each other eye to eye, not ten feet apart. On hands and knees, I began to crawl, and he continued to rock like an old grandmother with a baby on her lap. Oh for my camera! But I would simply have to record this encounter in my mind. I crept forward an inch at a time.

Only when he was the length of my body away did he begin to move, but at a rate comparable to mine, taking small steps now and then, just enough to maintain this strangely intimate comfort zone between us. And thus we regarded each other for another ten minutes, until I began to wonder whether I could rush to the house for the camera and find him there when I returned. I decided to take the chance. Slowly I backed away, stood and walked, then jogged up the hill toward the house. I grabbed a bird book, thumbed through until I found him—not the snipe, but his sandpiper cousin, the American woodcock, *Scolopax minor*.

I called Norma, found binoculars and camera, and we rushed back toward the spring, slowing to a creep when his turf came into view. Yes, he was still there, crouched at the base of a wild plum bush. We explored his features through binos from afar, then moved in for photographs. The light was wrong, and he was now partially concealed by brush, so the ideal photo opportunity had passed. Still we communed another long while before at last he rose as high as his short legs would permit, fanned his red-tipped tail, and flew on beating wings toward the pond.

None of our field guides promise that we will see the woodcock again. Eastern South Dakota is the western edge of his usual domain. But his choice haunt is moist woodlands, swamps and thickets, which would describe our wooded springs, so perhaps we will meet again. And who knows, perhaps his range is expanding our way. But even if that is the case, we will need to maintain a sharp eye. When the grass is brown, he is so well camouflaged that an unobservant hiker could stumble over his body before he flushed. Add the fact that the woodcock is mostly nocturnal, and the encounter made this a remarkable day.

April 6: Agh! Snow Again

"Hey, did you hear the forecast?" asked my friend Istvan over his beer at Carey's bar in Vermillion. "Ten inches of snow tomorrow!" Istvan's glee was met by grumbles and boos.

"It's spring," I said. I'd hoped to till the garden this weekend. The soil was finally almost dry, but with another layer of wet snow, who knew when that might happen? Sadly, the weatherman was right. Today a beautiful moisture-laden snow is falling fast.

Istvan was undeterred by our grumbling. He's an immigrant from Hungary, a professor at the University of South Dakota, and a fanatical devotee of cross-country skiing.

I've known him to shuffle about on an inch or two, to drive through a blizzard to find good snow, and to miss dinner because he had to do the loop just one more time. I enjoy skiing myself, and when the first good snow came last December I skied the woods and hills of our bluff almost daily until the sun burned holes in the trails. For everything there is a season, but this is not the season for snow! It is the season to watch lilac buds swell and open, robins snatch earthworms and bees gather pollen from maple trees—and for me to till the garden and plant potatoes and onions. But what can you do? No force of will could hold back the powerful moisture-laden low-pressure zone that flooded in from the Gulf of Mexico or the stream of Arctic air from the northwest. When they collide, get ready for snow. But who am I to complain? Southeast South Dakota missed the storms that kept winter-weary residents a hundred miles north shoveling snow for the last two weekends, and now those poor folks were facing a third ruined weekend in a row. Ruined unless you're Istvan, or a kid with a new sled, or you suffer from some perverse fixation on winter or an abnormal denial of cabin fever. Of course neither does Istvan have a 500-foot driveway to plow!

At least it's not really cold. That's why this snow is so wet—the temperature is hovering at the thawing mark. And by the time I had the driveway cleared and the sidewalk and patio shoveled, it was dripping from the eaves. Even if I'd wanted to join Istvan for a spring slog, by then I was pooped, and besides, instead of gliding, my skis would stick to the snow.

Yet, there are reasons for delight. I have my exercise for the day, logs are blazing in the stove, I have a good book to read, and when the snow melts under a warming spring sun the world will explode in green! And who knows—if it doesn't snow again this week, maybe next week I can till the garden.

April 10: Hiking North Alabama Bend

It's a sunny Sunday afternoon, the kind of day that fools a South Dakotan into thinking that spring is truly here. Norma and I meet Clarence and Sandy at Clay County Park for a hike down the Missouri River to explore the riparian zone from the park to the Frost Wilderness north of the Vermillion-Newcastle Bridge.

The first stretch is partly familiar. We have walked this stretch before. I say "partly familiar" because immediately below the park the trail we knew a decade ago has caved into the river. The present primitive trail has necessarily receded. It still hugs the caving sandy bank at the water's edge, but most of the cottonwoods that once lined the shore are gone. The two that fell this year lie in the river, still rooted to the shore, still alive and sprouting leaves, producing swirling whirlpools where the swift current meets the trunks.

After half a mile we enter a wider strip of woods, a rare patch spared from conversion to farmland after the river was dammed sixty-five years ago and farming the floodplain became possible and safe. Here the landowner had leased the riparian strip to the state for walk-in hunting. Given that access, people with all-terrain vehicles took license to gouge a wider trail through the woods, eroding the trail deep through shifting sand. At least the trail is easy to follow. In half a mile the path drops from the bluff to a narrow plain of accretion land, land the river has given this landowner as compensation for a bank it took from another owner across the river or somewhere upstream. It's a process as old as the river, though the Missouri's tendency to give and take away has been moderated by the dams, which generally regulate flow. Now that the radical rises of spring are controlled and the fast-moving water has cut the channel deep, the floodplain is starved of the nutrients it needs to thrive. The sediment-starved river, channelized from below our fifty-nine-mile almost-natural stretch to its convergence with the Mississippi at St. Louis, runs ever faster and cuts the bed deeper each year, encouraging high sandy banks to cave.

    The accretion land is boggy in places, a snarl of young willows, eastern redcedars, grasses and reeds, and invaders like Russian Olives, cockleburs and purple loose strife. It is the home of numerous mammals and birds, whose tracks and scat we find. We stop to examine a giant two-segmented beetle that crosses our path. Migrating ducks bob on the water and geese honk overhead. Early-arriving songbirds are looking to nest.

    Well below Clay County Park, we hit North Alabama Bend. When the water is low one can still view the wreckage of the steamboat North Alabama three miles up the river, mostly buried in the sand next to the snag that brought it down in 1870. But cartographers memorialized the wreck at this bend west of Vermillion where, since the river's course was changed by the great flood of 1881, the river has headed south for a few miles. In a 2009 process in which I as a Clay County commissioner had a hand, the US Army Corps of Engineers purchased the 565 acres of mostly floodplain from speculators who hoped to sell 468 housing lots along the river. Now, instead of suffering inappropriate development, North Alabama Bend is protected in perpetuity and in the public domain.

    The federal river frontage runs well over a mile, part heavily forested, part small dunes and scattered cottonwood trees. We pick our way through the pathless wood until we encounter a crude four-wheel-drive trail carved by the would-be developers. We follow it through cedar and ash, then cottonwood and willow forest to a higher bank that still supports native prairie, peppered with invasive exotic weeds and mature cottonwoods. The Corps bought this land as part of its environmental mitigation effort. In the future, the Corps may dredge part of the old river channel for a backwater, similar to the one they dug in a former channel another mile downstream. That backwater supports spawning for many species of fish.

Beyond the public land lies a small private tract, then "Gunderson Park," a quarter-mile strip protected by a conservation easement with Northern Prairies Land Trust, and then two miles of the Frost Wilderness, a game production area managed by South Dakota Game, Fish and Parks. The wilderness qualities of this stretch are now seriously degraded by well fields for the Lewis and Clark Water System, but otherwise that area too remains wild and in the public domain.

Six miles below Clay County Park one arrives at last at the Vermillion-Newcastle Bridge, six miles of river so far free of major development. It is the longest relatively-wild riparian stretch remaining on the South Dakota side of the longest reach of flowing and unchannelized Missouri below Montana. A wonderful hike through the crown jewel of Clay County. May it remain forever wild.

April 11: Easter Groundhog Day

On the second of February we chuckled, as I imagine woodchucks might. Yes, there was a bitterness to our laugh, because anybody who lives on the Northern Plains knows that whether the groundhog sees his shadow is irrelevant; we will endure at least six more weeks of winter and probably more. Now more than two months have passed, and even though a light snow fell last night and the ring-necked ducks on the pond had to break a new skin of ice this morning, this afternoon the kiss of spring has returned. Time to celebrate Easter with a walk in the big woods.

On my Jerry-rigged bridge, Norma and I cross Boulder Creek to the peninsula that juts into the pond between two spring-fed creeks and their ravines. We scare up two pairs of wood ducks on Boulder Creek, then a pair of mallards in the shallow water of the east neck as we proceed up the ravine toward the big cottonwood. There we will cross the stream on an even flimsier bridge, a plank dropped across the stream. This is among our most primitive trails, circling a region we infrequently explore. As we clamber north up the east ravine, the peninsula grows steep—so steep that the crumbled chalk rock bank sustains no growth and erosion is continuous. Disintegrating Niobrara chalk litters the slope, and the trail grows more treacherous. To avoid tramping through the sticky mud below a soggy seep, I long ago dragged a fallen elm trunk to span the trickle, thus providing a stable, if precarious, passage across eroding slope and mud.

Beyond the seep, a small delta juts into a bend in the creek, an easy vantage point from which to observe downstream toward the pond and upstream to the big cottonwood and almost to the spring. Scanning the opposite cliff from that point, I glimpse movement halfway up the bank where a large American elm long ago died, lost its footing on the hillside and crashed across the creek, forming a natural bridge. Piles of scat tell us that the bridge accommodates raccoons and probably possums and other woodland mammals that wish to cross without wetting their feet, or perhaps to dine with a view. When the tree fell—decades ago in the wave of Dutch elm death that ended that species' dominance in our woods—its roots ripped a hole in the bank that has never healed. The root ball and the earth it brought with it when it fell formed a flattish deck in front of the cave, which apparently had later been enlarged by a shelter-seeking mammal. It is on this terrace that something moves. I edge stealthily closer, seeking a position with an unobstructed view. Fifty feet across the ravine, lounging on his (or more likely her) front patio, is a fat and wooly woodchuck—*Marmota monax*, aka groundhog—munching lazily on a twig. Groundhog Day has truly come at last, and now we know who enlarged the den. *Monax* is a Native American name for "digger."

Norma steals to my side, to a position that offers an open view. For the next ten minutes or more we watch as the woodchuck chucks wood and enjoys the sun of spring. Now and then she stands on her hind legs, and with her front claws scratches mightily at her belly, perhaps dislodging fleas or some other parasite that annoys her, then nibbles away at the place, either eating the offending party or at least nipping it out with her teeth. And yes, she does cast a shadow against the wall of her cave.

Why do I guess it is Mrs. Groundhog that we watch? Partly because of her girth. She appears to be pregnant with a belly full of "ground piglets." After all, once our only fully-hibernating mammal awakes from winter sleep, the woodchuck's heart rate returns to normal from the wintertime rate of four beats per minute, the body temperature warms from just above freezing, and it is time to mate. She opened the door, and perhaps sometime after calendar Groundhog Day, a male neighbor from down the creek came to visit. When he was gone, she had a month or so to rebuild her weight before four or five babies would come—tiny, blind and naked offspring nestled in a grassy bed far inside the earth.

On this day, the first blades of green grass are springing from the soil. In a couple of weeks, mother woodchuck will find abundant food for herself and then for her young—grasses, forbs and the insects they attract. But for now she seems satisfied to lounge in the sun, nibbling small bits of bark, not oblivious to our voyeurism, but unperturbed.

At last my legs begin to cramp from the long-held pose and I slowly straighten. She glances my way, but does not retreat. I relax and improve my point of view. Still no evidence of alarm. At last I begin to whistle at Mrs. Groundhog, who is really quite a handsome creature, lovely brownish fur, delicate ears and nose, bright sparkly eyes. I vary the whistle, then raise the volume, but still no response beyond a casual glance. She refuses to permit disturbance of a lovely Easter afternoon. She has risen from the dead, as it were, and has no plans to relinquish the new-found joy of life. I begin to talk to her, to call out her name and toss compliments her way. I wave my arms. She will not be provoked. After all, her doorway is two feet behind her, and judging by the amount of earth composing her deck, her burrow is profoundly deep. She doesn't know about guns or other human devices that might do her harm, and a deep gulf separates her from us and any threat we might pose.

Half an hour passes. The woodchuck's lazy delight has outlasted our attention span, and we have other missions to accomplish. But I will return, next time with binoculars and camera that will enable me to better appreciate her finer features and to preserve her image for the day when winter returns, when she crawls back into the earth for a season's sleep, when I will again need assurance that spring will come, whether on February 2 or on Easter Sunday, and that she and perhaps a new generation of groundhogs will emerge, fulfilling poet Percy Shelley's promise that if winter comes, spring can not be far behind.

April 13: Choosing a Sustainable Future

In this week a few years ago, the South Dakota Board of Minerals and Environment held a public hearing at the Elk Point school gym concerning the then-proposed Hyperion refinery's Air Quality Permit. It was the last opportunity for the public to comment on the planned refinery's air emissions—which by Hyperion's own figures would have annually spewed more than ten million pounds of carbon monoxide, fine particulate matter, sulfur dioxide, nitrogen oxides, volatile organic compounds, sulfuric acid and hydrogen sulfide into the air over southeast South Dakota. In spite of opposition testimony that lasted until midnight, the state board accepted the company's claim that they would "prevent significant deterioration" of our air quality. One can only wonder what level of deterioration the agency charged with protecting South Dakota's environment would consider significant.

The refinery was to have been built on several thousand acres of prime farmland ten miles east of Vermillion. It would have processed 400,000 barrels of tar sands crude each day, bottom-of-the-barrel crude mined in Alberta, Canada, an energy-intensive process that eventually could destroy a boreal forest the size of North Carolina and leave behind gigantic pools of polluted wastewater. Among the dozens of toxins such a refinery would emit, only six were even addressed in the air permit. According to the US Environmental Protection Agency, these various pollutants and toxins can aggravate heart conditions, trigger strokes, and produce or worsen asthma, bronchitis and other lung diseases. Cancer-causing benzene was not regulated by the permit, nor was carbon dioxide, though by Hyperion's own figures their operation would have more than doubled South Dakota's output of this global-warming gas. In spite of these facts, the state's Department of Environment and Natural Resources issued the permit without requiring an Environmental Impact Statement. The name chosen for the proposed plant of course drips with irony; Hyperion was the Greek Titan who fathered the sun.

Following the public hearing, the Contested Case Hearing went forward because of intervention by three citizens' groups in Clay and Union counties. Among the immediate issues were Hyperion's failure to disclose information vital to an informed decision concerning the permit, such as the specific source and makeup of the tar sands crude they proposed to import, the locations of the numerous pipelines for importation and exportation of crude and refined products, and the specific technologies they would employ to monitor and control emissions of dangerous pollutants.

Global politics, the scientific community and common sense tell us that we must phase out our dependence on fossil fuels and move rapidly toward sustainable technologies of the future. Yet southeast South Dakota was asked to sacrifice clean water and air—and 3,300 acres of rich farmland—to an outmoded and unsustainable technology of the past, even though South Dakota has tremendous untapped potential for wind power and great promise for solar power that could supplement the hydro power upon which we have relied for sixty years.

The Sierra Club and two *ad hoc* community groups organized to oppose the refinery. After years of community meetings, scores of letters and editorials, hand-painted "Stop Hyperion" signs on farm fences, and numerous legal challenges, the death knell for the refinery was a global recession and increased energy efficiency, which together reduced demand for oil. With no formal announcement, the proposed refinery quietly faded away.

A *National Geographic* article about the planned refinery ends with this statement: "The question of how to strike a balance between the needs of today and the needs of tomorrow has been put off to the free market, and the free market's answer has been to forget about tomorrow." That leaves ordinary citizens responsible for choosing a sustainable future; it means that tomorrow is in our hands. And in this case our hands won the day. After years of hype, Hyperion is dead.

April 17: Turning the Earth

Our spinning Earth has turned toward the sun, and now it is time to turn the earth. For six decades, this has been for me an annual ritual, task and cause for celebration. Though it is not tied directly to any calendar, not even to the revolutions of moon or Earth, it is a day more profound than a solstice or equinox. The frost has gone and the soil is mellow, birds are singing and the sun is promising another year of garden sweets.

Over the years, I have turned the earth in many ways. In my earliest gardening years in Oklahoma, my father performed the task with a Ford tractor and a disk. Our soil was sandy, so it was possible to work it ten inches deep without actually turning it over, loosening the soil for easy rooting with minimal disturbance to vital communities of microorganisms. In later years, when my garden was a corner of a lawn behind a series of houses in various Oklahoma towns and then in Vermillion, South Dakota, the task was performed with a shovel, commonly known as spading the garden. The technique is ancient, but still performed by subsistence farmers around the world, though millions of the poorest farmers still lack a sharp steel shovel like the one I used.

When we arrived on Prairie Bluff in the spring of 1982, I was engaged fulltime in building our home, but still found time to turn the earth in the bottomland below our building site using a newly-acquired 1939 Allis-Chalmers A tractor and a one-bottom plow. For the first time in my life I had virtually unlimited space. I could have plowed an acre or five acres if I had chosen. But I compromised with reality and plowed only about twice the area I could conceivably give proper care in a summer when building a home would occupy twelve or more hours each day, seven days a week. The soil was bound by decades-old smooth brome sod, so turning the soil was more akin to slicing slabs of sod to build a pioneer hovel than to gardening. Even after following the plow with a worn-out single disk, the soil was tight, still bound by clumps of roots. Nevertheless, we planted a garden of more than 10,000 square feet.

Though the soil was poorly prepared, most of the seeds we dispersed sprouted, took root and grew. Sometimes, as daylight faded after a long day of sawing and hammering in the sun I would take up my hoe and work as many rows as I could before darkness fell. Despite the fact that the garden grew more weeds and grass than the things we planted, the ridiculous-sized plot produced far more vegetables that summer than we could consume.

In the thirty-five years that have passed since that first summer, I have descended the same hill from the house to the bottom each spring to turn the soil. As deer returned to enjoy the growing natural diversity of our land, I built a seven-foot fence that deprived them of the opportunity to share the fruits of our labor, and gradually we reduced the garden to a more reasonable size. Over the years, the elm and hackberry trees that were saplings south of the original plot grew into arching trees that shaded the garden from mid-day sun, and after a couple of decades of harvesting vegetables without augmenting natural fertility, the original plot grew tired and harvests gradually decreased. A decade ago, we moved one space closer to the house for a new garden plot and planted the original to native forbs—wild flowers that bloom to this day.

For a quarter century now I have turned the soil each April with a Ford tractor, the same model my father used when I was a teenager, a 1959. Actually, I have not "turned the soil" every spring. Some years ago I began experimenting with only disking the garden in alternate years, since this less disturbs organic life. But our valley soil is tight, deep with fine top soil that migrated here from surrounding hillsides during the eight or nine decades in which our land was farmed, from settlement days in the 1860s until the federal government's Soil Bank conservation program took the hills out of production agriculture and returned them to grass in the 1950s. I found that when I did not actually turn the soil, by mid-summer of dry years the earth was packed so hard that the growth of tubers and roots was impaired.

So today I mounted the plow once more. This year, once the soil is worked I will spread a pickup load of horse manure bequeathed upon us and our garden by our friends Jerry and Carrie down the road, then lightly disk it into the top inches of soil. Given anticipated summer rains, we have good reason to hope for bountiful crops.

Whatever the calendar says, the garden test for spring is when the soil is thawed and mellow, when the plow or the shovel turns it soft and loose, ready for another season's seeds. So today I turn the earth and hereby proclaim the onset of another season of garden life. Since this date last year our Earth has traveled 584 million miles in its orbit around the sun, racing through space at 67,000 miles per hour, the elliptical orbit of our tilting planet around the sun spinning us through the seasons, spring to summer to autumn to winter and back to spring. But perhaps the astronomers and physicists have missed the point. Could it be that it is the farmers and gardeners around the globe, performing the most important, ancient and universal annual ritual known to man, that really turn the Earth?

April 20: A Time to Burn

This week I am mowing firebreaks around scraps of prairie scheduled for next week's burn. I will wait for ideal burning conditions—dry weather with a light and predictable breeze—then gather the necessary equipment: propane torch, fire-suppressing swatters, gloves, my backpack sprayer and extra jugs of water. Most important, I will assemble a handful of friends to help. Some enjoy the hard work and challenge, others the spectacle and excitement of fire. All are pleased to participate in maintaining native prairie.

Why the burn? Fire is a vital component of healthy prairie life. If unburned or ungrazed, big blue stem, switchgrass and Indiangrass, the six-foot grasses of a mixed tallgrass prairie, build a thick layer of thatch that inhibits new growth. Burning releases nutrients stored in accumulated thatch and produces a burst of energetic growth.

But besides these millennia-old benefits of fire, there are other reasons to burn. In most "restored," or replanted native prairie, including ours, smooth brome and bluegrass, the imported cool-season grasses that today dominate eastern South Dakota grasslands, remain. In April, warm season native species have not yet broken dormancy, but brome and bluegrass are green and bursting with energy. While fire warms the earth and awakens native grasses, it suppresses brome, countering its annual jumpstart on the natives. Fire also scorches redcedar saplings and emerging thistles and other noxious weeds.

Before Euro-American settlement, lightning-ignited fire swept the plains on no particular schedule, invigorating native species and keeping plant and animal populations in balance. For the past century wildfire has been controlled, one factor in the proliferation of non-native species that were brought intentionally or by accident to the plains. So controlled burning remains a key feature of modern native prairie management. Research continues concerning the optimum frequency for fire, but the emerging consensus is that segments of restored prairie can profit by burning every five or six years.

Rather than burn large meadows in one season, it is better to burn a smaller plot each year. Some species besides native grasses are fire positive, enhanced by fire. Other species, including many mammals and birds and some annual native flowering forbs that depend on reseeding for perpetuation, may be negatively impacted. Thus we never burn more than half a dozen acres in a given year, ensuring that refuge remains for species that fire could weaken or eliminate. It is also essential to burn early in the season, before ground-nesting birds have laid their eggs.

Burning is never easy, always a challenge. Besides choosing the right day and time of day, proper techniques are required. With a green firebreak encircling the area to be burned and an energetic crew, it is possible to burn safely if you follow one rule: be sure the "controlled burn" remains controlled. That means beginning on the downwind edge, allowing fire to burn slowly against the wind until a wide strip is black and fire on the outer fringe is completely extinguished. Then move fire slowly around the perimeter, both left and right into the wind, crewmembers following with swatters and water. Only when the downwind perimeter is blackened and the outer rim is cool is it safe to light the head fire and watch the wind-driven flames roar madly across the prairie, consuming accumulated fuel.

Once the fire dies, we walk the perimeter again, ensuring that smoldering spots are doused. Only then is it safe to take the crew to the house for food and drinks, a reward for participation in a critical aspect of managing native prairie.

April 22: Earth Day Planting

Earth Day has now been celebrated for almost half a century. Sometimes on that day I look back over the years and feel mostly frustration that we seem to have made so little progress toward achieving a sustainable world. Instead, in important ways we seem to be plunging blindly toward the abyss—toward a variety of "tipping points" from which return seems depressingly unlikely.

Other times, I look back across the years and contemplate the progress we have made. Earth Day was founded by U.S. Sen. Gaylord Nelson of Wisconsin as an environmental teach-in on April 22, 1970. Earth Day was by no means the beginning of the environmental movement in America; the truth is that there was never a time when thinking and caring people did not see threats to the planet or to their home turf and act to ward them off. And perhaps a majority of humans have always been aware of the planet's needs and applied themselves as they could on their farms and in their backyards and neighborhoods toward nurturing the piece of Earth entrusted to them.

One key component of environmental protection in the United States, the Clean Air Act, was passed in 1963, seven years before the first Earth Day. The Clean Water Act was enacted shortly after the first Earth Day, becoming law in 1972. Many people today think of recycling and reusing as modern phenomena, but before the "trash era" in which we live began, reusing and recycling resources was for most people around the world an unquestioned way of life. So Earth Day was neither the founding of a movement, nor a sudden recognition of conservation and sustainability values. It was perhaps more an expression of alarm at how rapidly modern man was destroying wilderness, paving the planet, carting not only garbage but materials made from limited resources to landfills, burning non-renewable fuels and polluting our water and the Earth. And yes, even in 1970 the alarm had already been sounded about the threat of global warming and climate change.

And yet, Earth Day is important. It is a "teachable moment" for those willing to think and learn. It is a time for action—whether that be picking up trash, protesting destructive developments, planting trees, or just taking the kids for a walk in the woods.

This Earth Day my tasks have been many. I watered the emerging plants in the vegetable garden. I made spicy vegetable soup for Norma and myself for lunch. Tonight we will join friends to hear an Earth Day message from Francis Moore Lappé, author of *Diet for a Small Planet, EcoMind: Changing the Way We Think to Create the World We Want*, and many other books. But my central task for the day was to plant a small patch of native prairie.

Over the past quarter century we have replanted or worked to rehabilitate some sixty acres of prairie, a postage stamp compared to the vast prairie that has been lost, including well over a million acres plowed under in the five years after corn prices spiked. So on a landscape scale, today's planting was miniscule, a piece of eroded hillside the size of the manicured lawn of many a suburban home. So why is today's planting important?

An October entry in this book describes the prairie fire that was ignited by a petroleum pipeline clearing crew a few years ago. That fire burned some fifteen acres of hillside prairie and woods—at exactly the worst time of the year. We were suffering severe drought, winter was coming and nothing would be growing for many months. The hillside, stripped of topsoil by decades of inappropriate farming, was laid bare to forces of erosion.

Furthermore, some fifty hardwood trees and hundreds of eastern redcedars were dead. I wasn't particularly sad to lose the cedars, but I mourned the ash, hackberry, mulberry and elm. However, we had a big job on our hands, cutting down, moving and piling hundreds of dead trees. I hired a neighbor with a tractor-mounted shear that could cut twelve-inch trunks. I followed with my old Ford tractor and loader, pushing the cedars into half a dozen giant piles. The largest pile, mounded at the bottom of the most erodible hill, contained several hundred trees, mostly cedars of all sizes. Once the wood had sufficiently dried and the pile was surrounded by a layer of snow, I lighted a match.

It was a spectacular fire. When the last embers died several hours later, what remained was a valley of ash. And now spring has come, the time for planting prairie forbs and grasses. So this morning, Earth Day morning, I headed to the valley with a bag of mixed prairie seeds—four native grasses and twenty-nine flowering broadleaf plants. I raked the remaining branches and twigs and the blackened rocks into the valley's vortex, the steep narrow ditch that with a single cloudburst might become a small ravine. I covered sticks and stones with ash and dirt, then walked the patch in ten-foot strips and cast my seed to the wind. Then I raked the seed in—a rather imprecise planting, to be sure, but with the goal of covering the seeds with half an inch of soil. I finished the job, wiped the sweat from my brow, picked up my tools and started back toward the house. I glanced toward the cumulous clouds floating in a blue Earth Day sky, found a cushy seat in unburned grass where I could admire the just-opened pink blossoms of the groundplum milk vetch, *Astragalus crassicarpus*, and asked for rain.

April 28: What Ducks Like

What do ducks like? Water, of course, shelter and food. But each species has its own requirements and preferences, some dining on invertebrates, others mostly on vegetation, and some scooping up and filtering food from the mud at the bottom of a pond. Thus their preferences vary from wooded lakes to grassy wetlands, from shallow to deeper, and various sorts of vegetation and cover where they might nest.

In thirty-five years on the bluff we have watched the pond below our house pass through many a cycle from drought to flood, wetland to lake, parched to lush and back again. Except for a few seasons when the pond was dry, each spring and fall has brought various species of ducks, some resting on their migrations north and south, others staying to nest and raise a family of ducklings. But of all those seasons, last spring was a banner year.

April brought six species of colorful ducks to the pond: wood ducks, mallards, northern shovelers, blue-winged teals, ring-necked ducks and redheads. Wood ducks like to perch on overhanging limbs. They visit each fall and spring, and in most springs at least one pair stays to hatch eggs in the house specifically designed for their use. Mallards, northern shovelers and blue-winged teal are "dabbling ducks," surface feeders that turn tail up to feed on submerged plants, seeds and snails. Redheads and ring-necks are pochards, diving ducks that go deep for food and may reemerge some distance from where they disappeared.

So why, after all these years, was this a bonanza year for ducks on our pond? Three answers suggest themselves. First, record corn prices turned many a wetland and grassland in the migratory waterfowl flyway to tilled fields. Shallow wetlands were drained and nesting vegetation plowed under, so pressure has grown on remaining wetlands and ponds. Second, our pond offers both deep and shallow water for feeding, plenty of remaining trees for wood ducks to perch in, and sixty surrounding acres of undisturbed woods and prairie grass for nesting and cover. But the third factor has to do with the removal of a ring of cottonwoods that formerly surrounded the pond, making it more inviting to dabbling ducks and pochards that had increasingly felt hemmed in by too many trees. Here is how that change came about.

Twenty-five years ago, melting snow and a wet spring raised and maintained the water level on the pond. Then just about this time of year, the cottonwoods we had planted across the dam above the spillway level flowered. Thousands of seeds sailed away on wind-borne cotton wings to try their luck at propagation along the creek, or on far flung hills where success was only a dream. Other thousands fluttered down to form a flotilla of cotton that covered the surface of the pond. A lucky few landed at the water's edge and somehow got planted just right, perhaps by the hoof of a drinking deer or the foot of a padding raccoon, perhaps by a wind-driven wave that covered them with a thin layer of soil.

We were already realizing that the line of cottonwoods we had planted was year by year blocking more of our summer valley view. Yet I was delighted to witness the reproduction. I saw the ring of new seedlings, the offspring of cottonwoods we'd planted across the face of the dam our first year, as improved habitat. I don't believe it occurred to me that there would one day be negative impacts, even beyond the problem we now faced. It did not occur to me that every new tree would thrust its roots deep into saturated soil around the pond and drink all the water it desired. The thick mat of grasses we had reestablished on surrounding hillsides retained most of the rain that fell and the melting snow, and increasingly, much of the water that made its way to the pond would now be taken up and transpired through the leaves of cottonwood and willow trees. More lessons in the law of unintended consequences.

In most springs, the level of the pond fluctuates enough that some of the cottonwood seeds lucky enough to germinate wither as the water recedes. In other years, a heavy rain sends water gushing in, inundating and drowning emerging seedlings. Many fall victim to the same hooves that might have planted them, and some are plucked out by feeding ducks. The attrition rate is very high, but here and there one manages to survive. But in that particular spring more than two decades ago, hundreds of cottonwood saplings survived and began to grow. Of those, nearly a hundred made it through the first summer and winter and leafed again in spring.

A quarter century later, in the year of the great Missouri River flood of 2011, the intermittent creek that feeds this man-made pond flowed almost around the calendar. It began with a seep when the soil thawed, ran with melting snow and heavy rains, and continued to discharge ground water throughout the summer, fall and into winter until the deep freeze came. Thus the pond remained full through spring and summer, and the trunks of cottonwoods stood for months in several feet of water. Then the flood year turned to drought, a drought that would last from July 2011 until it finally broke two years later.

I knew the survival chances of long-submerged cottonwoods were slim. Their long-time companions, the willows that came to life the same spring as they and that had long grown in their shadows, would likely survive, since willows can tolerate long inundation. But like most other trees, cottonwood roots need to breathe. If the roots are covered with water for long periods of time, they drown. Thus I was not surprised in the spring of 2012 when the ring of cottonwoods produced no leaves.

So what to do with a hundred dead trees surrounding a quarter-acre pond? I cringed at the all-too-real expectation that one by one they would fall, brought down by rot, winds or ice, to pile together and turn a placid pool into a graveyard of tangled trunks. I eyed the falling water level as the drought intensified in the hot summer months. In August, three succumbed to wind and crashed into the pond. By September only a puddle remained, and by November the pond had turned to cracking crust. With winter approaching, I had to act.

I dragged out the chain saw and went to work. If only cottonwood was good fuel for the stove, we would have been rich beyond imagination in firewood. But that is not the case. Cottonwood produces as much ash as heat. I offered the trunks to a local sawmill, but the operator was already well-stocked with even larger drowned trees. What I faced was a massive cleanup job. A few trees leaned away from the pond, so that whenever natural forces brought them down they would only litter the banks, something that wood ducks might enjoy. About seventy-five stood straight, or more likely inclined toward the basin; there was little question which way they would fall.

Over two long days I cut the trees down, dropping them one or two at a time and pushing them with my tractor and loader into a pile in the barren basin. Some trees were from a third generation, their trunks a mere six to twelve inches in diameter. But most had grown in ideal conditions for a quarter century and had reached two feet thick. After I dropped those I had to cut them in half in order to move them, a twenty-foot trunk and a forty-foot section of limbs and branches. When I finished, the pile had grown to a hundred feet long, twenty feet wide and six feet high.

With the cooling fall air and the easing of transpiration, the seeps that fed the pond began to trickle once again. The window of opportunity was closing. On a Friday morning I gathered fire-fighting equipment just in case things didn't go as planned, and set the pile on fire. For two days it burned, the first hours a massive blaze that reached above the surrounding banks and warmed the fall air a hundred feet away. By evening the inferno was reduced to massive flaming trunks. That night I sat by the fire and watched the flames die to glowing coals.

By Saturday morning, well over half the fuel had been consumed. I passed that day pushing what remained together with the tractor, consolidating half-burned trunks so they would continue to feed off each other. On the second night the wind kicked up, though deep in the basin its effect was minimized. By now most of the wood was gone, just glowing embers in a pile reduced to the size of my tractor and surrounded by at least fifty feet of dry earth on every side. Satisfied that the risk of escape was near zero, I went to bed. On the third morning, all that remained were a few glowing embers and one stubborn stump that refused to burn, perhaps because when I cut the trees down it retained a bit of life.

So now the pond is far more open. Sixteen mature cottonwoods remain on the dam face above the spillway level, and about fifty willows and cottonwoods in the ring closer to the pond. Ducks can now readily sail in from any direction, and more importantly, escape without obstruction should a coyote, fox or other predator threaten. I have come to see that when natural selection takes one organism away, it is always replaced by something else, often something better. After several days of intervention and hard work that contributed to this particular outcome, I only hope that my intervention has been consistent with that process. I will never know what micro-ecosystem might have evolved had I let the dead trees fall and decay in the pond, but I do know that I have enjoyed watching this spring's congress of ducks.

MAY

May 4: Birds are Back!
Take a number for your turn at the birdbath! Cardinals, blue jays and robins wait in the juniper bush. Usually it's one at a time, but some birds can't wait their turn. Most bathe modestly, semi-immersed in water, fluttering wings and pecking at feathers, whether merely preening or removing offending hitchhikers I can't say for sure. But things really get lively when the just-arrived brown thrasher appears. He's all in, earning his name—thrashing like mad, water spraying from every side, perhaps washing off the residues of his travels. Once he retreats to the juniper to dry his feathers, the water level is down a good half inch.

For lovers of birds, May is a special time. Full-time residents remain, transformed from survival mode to the rites of spring—mating, nesting and marking territory with song. Permanent residents still adorning greening grass and trees or soaring overhead include cardinals, nuthatches, blue jays, crows, downy, hairy, red-bellied and red-headed woodpeckers, various sparrows, chickadees, cedar waxwings, turkeys, ring-necked pheasants, red-tailed hawks, turkey vultures, eagles and more. A few regulars have reinvented themselves for spring; the goldfinch, for example, has traded subtle winter hues for dazzling yellow.

But if this United Nations of birds isn't enough to cheer the heart—and it is—spring has brought new nations to our door—birds that winter in Mexico, Central America and our southern states. Yesterday, a goldfinch and a robin were followed at the bath by a newly-arrived pair of eastern bluebirds and a spotted towhee. I grabbed the camera, though as usual, too late. But I may have another chance; two pairs of bluebirds have moved into houses in our yard and the towhees are scouting nesting sites nearby.

Among other returning migrants—what South Dakotans who spend the colder months in Texas or Arizona might call "snowbirds," are our smallest visitor, the ruby-throated hummingbird, the red-winged blackbird, blue-winged teal, wood duck, belted kingfisher, great blue heron, flicker, meadow lark, dickcissel, killdeer, eastern kingbird, house wren, mourning dove, and my favorite if I have one, the brown thrasher, whose return always coincides with turning the calendar to May. Blue-winged teals share the ponds with wood ducks—perhaps the continent's most dramatically colored waterfowl. Kingfishers and herons hunt for fish and frogs, the latter of which proclaim the joy of spring with more vigor than any other creature on the bluff. Blackbirds nest in cattails below the pond, their shrill cry audible for a quarter mile. Flickers join year-around cousins in hammering for insects, while meadowlarks, dickcissels, killdeers, eastern kingbirds, house wrens, mourning doves and brown thrashers fill the meadows and woods. But one thing every bird has in common: this is the season to mate, build a nest, lay eggs and feed a brood of young. No other season is so filled with activity and song.

A few regular summer residents I have yet to see or hear.

I have thrilled to the repertoire of the brown thrasher, but have not heard the catcalls of his less conspicuous cousin, the catbird. The tree swallows that last summer occupied one of the bluebird houses have not yet returned. The loggerhead shrike may not show up until he can find fat grasshoppers to impale on barbed wire and thorns. The banquet of birds will not reach full adornment until yellow-billed cuckoos, rose-breasted grosbeaks and Baltimore and orchard orioles arrive. And summer will not be complete until night is filled with the screech owl's warbling wail and the whip-poor-will's plaintive call.

As I delight in sightings and songs, search for nesting places of familiar birds and new arrivals, and await the homecoming of still-anticipated friends, I also watch for the unexpected—stop-over birds who prefer northern climes to our bountiful bluff, like the yellow-rumped warbler who sang from the rim of the birdbath this morning, resting at the halfway point in his journey from a southern state to his summer home in Canada or Alaska. Like all of us, birds and humans, in the larger sense he is just passing through.

May 11: Eating from Earth

So how is *your* garden growing? It's a common question these days amongst friends who gather at Carey's bar or meet at the grocery store. Naturally we hope that the answer will lead to an opportunity to brag about the progress of our own gardens, though modestly of course. But growing one's own vegetables is a venture shared by most who seek ways to live sustainably on our good Earth.

Norma and I have our seeds and plants in the ground, rain fell on Friday, and today the sun is bright. Okra, pumpkins, cantaloupes, cucumbers, beans, corn, zucchini and crookneck squash have yet to make their appearance, but green stripes mark rows of potatoes, onions, lettuce and spinach. Closer examination reveals the tiny shoots of carrots, beets, peas and Swiss chard. Sixty bedding plants, including eggplants, six varieties of tomatoes and five kinds of peppers are thriving. Now comes the hard part: waiting for the first taste of greens.

As all gardeners know, growing vegetables involves process, tradition, hard work, patience and fun. If we are lucky, we have gained certain knowledge and skills from a parent. In my case, I gardened with my mother from the age of five. Through her ninety-third year, she visited her garden every day, and at ninety-five still had a couple of tomato plants in the flowerbed. For those who did not grow up with a master gardener, a vast array of books, neighbors and the Internet offer advice. But the best teacher is nature herself, though her lessons take time, and are sometimes less than gentle. Some of us have learned the hard way, for example, not to set out tender tomato and pepper plants too soon, for the last frost of the season may still be lurking in Canada, its icy fingers reaching our way.

If we are attentive to nature's lessons, we learn from our soil what grows best one place or another and what supplements or special care the plot might need. A sign of healthy soil, recognized by every organic farmer or gardener, is a wealth of earthworms. In my garden, every spade full of earth turns up two or three, hard at work breaking down decaying plant material and loosening the soil. That is particularly important in our garden, where the texture is dark but tight.

Gardening does more than produce the most healthful food on earth. The work is good for body, mind and soul. But there are other fringe benefits to enjoy. The morning air is filled with the songs and calls of mating birds—the whistles of cedar waxwings, the crow of the pheasant rooster, the cooing of turtle doves, the "pechur, pechur, whit, whit, whit, whit," of the cardinal—and in the pond the exuberant croaking of chorus frogs. The bluebirds that nest by the garden gate flit from their house when I enter, but soon return to the task of incubating eggs.

The first phases of my work are over, tilling and planting; soon the weeding, cultivating and mulching will begin. Most of the garden's bounty will not mature until July and August, but if we are lucky, we'll be eating freshly-picked salads by Memorial Day. When the bluebirds' work of harvesting insects for gaping mouths begins, most of our work will be finished, and the most tangible rewards of gardening will be yet to enjoy.

May 18: Hunting Morels

After two weeks of roaming the woods, we've finally hit pay dirt. The morels are out! Last evening I came upon the largest concentration of mushrooms I've ever seen—four dozen large, prime morels, freshly sprung from the earth beside a pile of decaying brush. Four dozen in a space the size of my living room. This morning Norma made morel omelets. They were delicious, the mushrooms augmented with diced onions and peppers and folded into fresh, brown, free-range eggs from our neighbors down the hill.

For the uninitiated—deprived city folks and recent transplants who have yet to discover this delectable natural delicacy—our favorite local mushroom is the *esculenta*, a member of a family of edible mushrooms of the genus *Morchella*. When freshly sprung from the earth they are tan in color, ranging from small in a dry season to four inches long in a wet spring. They are sometimes called sponge mushrooms for their sponge-like cap. Some mushrooms are poisonous, so eating unidentified fungi is not wise. But morels are easily recognized. Their surface texture resembles a human brain, though of course the mushroom is not divided into two lobes.

Over the years, Norma and I have experimented with various methods of preparation—sautéing in butter, grilling with vegetables, adding to stir-fry, and most recently, mushroom soup. In lean years, we generally eat the entire meager crop fresh, but when they are more abundant, morels can be preserved by drying or freezing. Dried morels regain most of their original size, texture and flavor when properly cooked, and frozen morels are nearly indistinguishable from fresh in mushroom soup.

Part of the attraction of mushroom hunting is the unpredictable nature of their appearing. When and where can they be found? The best time to look is a warm day in May following a rain. The best place is less predictable. In the many years I have hunted our woods, I have never found them twice in exactly the same spot. There are, however, certain places to look closely, including near decaying elm trees on the east slopes of hills. But elusiveness is part of their charm, which also makes it easier to be vague when other hunters pry you for information.

But I'm not like those hunters who selfishly guard their favorite hunting grounds. I will gladly reveal where I found this year's bounty. It was immediately west of a downed elm near the middle of the wildest and least accessible forest on our bluff.

May 19: A Beautiful Invader

The problem with hunting morels is that I find things I don't want to find. Things like budding thistles and the spreading leaves of burdock, non-native invaders that propagate themselves by riding the wind or the fur of passing animals or the pants legs of humans. But this year I came to terms with a much bigger problem, one I can no longer ignore. Throughout the big woods, in every semi-shaded clearing where morels might appear, I also find buckthorn, *Rhamnus cathartica*.

I've known about buckthorn for a few years, ever since ecologist friend Carter Johnson, on a spring stroll through the woods observed casually, "I see you have some buckthorn on the slope above the creek." He pointed out the shiny dark leaves of a shrub that stood as tall as a man, quite a beautiful plant, really. I guess Carter assumed I knew all about buckthorn, and thus didn't insult my intelligence, such as it was, by a sermon on the evils of this particular invader. I wrote the name in my notebook, intending to look up the plant when time allowed.

There are reasons to admire the shrub. It grows in dense thickets, its glossy leaves reflecting the sun. No doubt the shiny black fruits I had admired the previous August would feed a variety of birds. It was later that summer that I found time for formal investigation. I learned from the Minnesota Department of Agriculture that common buckthorn had been brought to that state in the mid-1800s as an ornamental hedge. It didn't take long for people to realize how invasive the bush was in natural areas, but nurseries continued to sell it until the 1930s. In those many decades, it had spread virtually everywhere that people or birds happened to transport its seeds.

I have no idea when buckthorn arrived in our woods. It may have been decades ago or it could have been during our tenure here. I'm sure I saw its glossy leaves glinting in filtered sunlight before Carter identified it for me, but it was part of the undifferentiated jungle of undergrowth that has always thrived in clearings visible from the maintained trails. In winter when I tend to thrash my way through brush, leaves are brown or shed, so attempts to identify the unknown are difficult if not futile. But now that my eye is trained, I see buckthorn in many a partially-shaded clearing, a virtual cancer on the native forbs and shrubs that grow below the trees.

"Why is buckthorn a problem?" the agriculture department rhetorically asks. The list of answers is long: it out-competes native plants for nutrients, light and moisture. It degrades wildlife habitat. It shades the forest floor, disrupting the natural succession of native trees. Its seeds remain viable in the soil for years. And the list goes on, but the last item is perhaps the most disturbing; like many an imported invader, it has no natural enemies—no insects or diseases to check its growth. Nor am I likely to slow its spread with low-tech means. I have long controlled musk thistles and burdock with my hoe, but for buckthorn the hoe is a useless tool.

Having established identification and listed the threats posed by this lovely woody invader, the experts move on to methods of control. If one has a single plant or a small patch of buckthorn in some corner of the lawn, he can dig up the roots, or cut the plants at the surface and apply herbicide to the stump to kill the roots. But if buckthorn already dominates entire clearings in the woods, chemical warfare is the only recommended option. Glyphosate will allegedly kill buckthorn, but it kills everything else it touches. Triclopyr is the recommended chemical. It kills only all the broadleaf plants it contacts—not just buckthorn, but native forbs and the saplings of native trees. At least it spares the grasses, so application will not denude an entire area and leave it open to reinvasion, not only by buckthorn, but by other undesirable vegetation as well.

Presumably there was a time—either before or after we took possession of these woods—when it might have been possible to eradicate buckthorn with hand tools and minimal application of herbicide. That time is unfortunately past. Perhaps a forest fire would control this and other underbrush, but a "controlled burn" of the forest is out of the question. And for me, so too is the widespread and relatively unrestricted use of herbicides.

So what to do? I will purchase a jug of Triclopyr, drag out the backpack sprayer once again and walk the trails, hoping to beat the invader back a few feet from the edges. Perhaps the grass that grows feebly in semi-shade will occupy more of this space, but I fear that my plan will yield only temporary results. I fear that to keep trails open, periodic spraying combined with mechanical removal may be required. Not a happy thought, but another chapter in the book of unintended consequences, the unforeseen results of man's attempts to manipulate the natural world, in this case the importation of foreign plants without knowledge of their properties or whether they might escape control.

It is too late to undo this invasion, just as it is too late to avoid leafy spurge or Canada thistles or many another non-native plant. It is the ultimate dilemma of one whose goal is to restore native plant communities. Yes, many of the natives are extinct, but at least as disturbing is the fact that so many non-native aggressors are firmly entrenched in otherwise natural environments. Rooting them out entirely seems nearly impossible, at best an odious task. But I must try.

May 20: Bring on the Cows

To some conservationists, cows may be anathema. Yes, there are reasons to move beyond cows. We know that the space, energy and food devoted to producing calories from beef make cows among the least efficient uses of natural resources. We know that over-consumption of meat, especially red meat, is bad for our health. And we have seen vast stretches of the American west—including millions of acres of public lands and most of the lands on the Missouri River bluff—overgrazed to the point that most native grasses and other beneficial species, both flora and fauna, have been replaced by weeds. So why would I want cows grazing the native prairies we have carefully nurtured back toward health?

The answer is that just as cows can be destructive to native prairie and natural habitat, they can also be a conservation tool. Years ago, I would have rejected that idea. I grew up with cows, and my father wisely employed rotational grazing, moving cattle from pasture to pasture before a particular plot was overgrazed. But even when we arrived on the bluff more than three decades ago, the results of overgrazing were obvious; my inclination with our land was to take whatever restorative measures we could and then manage by benign neglect. However, experience and experimentation have reinforced what my father and other responsible cattlemen have long known. Grazing is a natural part of prairie ecology and can be an important conservation tool.

The prairies of the Great Plains evolved, after all, with grazing herbivores, principally bison, the ideal prairie management animal. Not only do they graze selectively, their hooves also plant the seeds that their shaggy beards collect and distribute as they graze. But bison are not practical for us. Our fences would never contain them, and they require a much larger range where they can drift from area to area throughout the year. So cows are the fallback grazers for us. They lack beards, but like bison, they graze as a herd, their hooves bury seeds and they leave fertilizing manure in their wake.

The key, as with every helpful tool, is proper use. When Norma and I more than doubled the property for which we are responsible by purchasing adjoining bluff land at auction in 1998, much of the newly-acquired land had been overgrazed and abused for decades. One twenty-five-acre parcel, in particular, appeared to support nothing but cedars, thistles, leafy spurge, brome and brush. I was reluctant to take it on; I saw only work. But Norma saw beyond the present condition to what the land had been and what it might be again, so the work began.

In the beginning, I invested many hours walking the hills with my backpack sprayer, spot-spraying the worst infestations of noxious weeds. Within a couple of years, the thistles were reduced to the point that we could control them with a hoe, and by then, I was also collecting flea beetles, *Aphthona nigriscutis*, and relocating them to the worst infestations of leafy spurge. In half a dozen years, prairie remnants began to reemerge. This particular bluff pasture had been grazed by the same neighbor's cows for several years before our purchase, so we agreed to continue that relationship—but with certain restrictions. The cows had to be out by the first of July.

In wet years this arrangement worked fairly well; the cow-calf pairs grazed the hillsides while the cool season grasses—brome and blue grass—thrived, and the native species had time to recover and produce abundant foliage, seed and habitat by summer's end. But in dry years, recovery was far from satisfactory. So in 2013 we moved up the cow-out date to the last day of spring, June 20. I now believe that we have found the proper formula for cattle grazing as a helpful prairie management strategy.

To suggest that this is some new discovery would be absurd. Good grassland managers have known this for centuries, and their teacher was nature herself. Long before white settlers brought cattle to the Northern Plains, bison grazed these same hills in a sustainable way that benefitted all species that had evolved together across the region. Prairie burns, whether ignited by lightning strikes or by Native American land managers, brought an exuberance of prairie growth in the ensuing spring. That, of course, attracted great herds of bison, which attracted native hunters, but which also left behind abundant manure to fertilize the area's recovery the following spring. Bison tended to crop a particular area short before they moved on, but next summer would find them in other valleys and on other hills, leaving the previous year's grazed area to recover.

Many good range managers have also inherited this wisdom from fathers and grandfathers, a formula for maintaining prairie health: take half and leave half. Those who by necessity, ignorance or greed took more year after year soon found their land degraded, dominated by invasive and exotic grasses, woody plants and weeds, its productive capacity reduced to a fraction of its natural prairie potential. Today, wise managers whose livelihood requires pasturing their lands for the entire growing season perpetuate grassland health by rotational grazing, moving cattle or other livestock frequently from one parcel to another.

That is not our situation. We simply sell forage on our land for about a month for a fraction of the going annual pastureland rate. To ensure preservation of this practice into the future, our grazing strategy is prescribed in the perpetual conservation easement that governs land use after we are gone. So grazing has become a standard tool in our conservation kit. We have still conducted occasional controlled burns—though burning, especially in dry seasons, is risky work. Flea beetles continue to do their part, pursuing their symbiotic relationship with leafy spurge and slowly bringing many infested areas under control. In a recent year we invited a neighbor to mow unfenced areas for hay, and I also occasionally mow small prairie plots that can be neither pastured nor burned, though this requires burning a few gallons of fossil fuel. But we have come to rely on controlled grazing as an essential tool, and most of our prairie is now included in the grazing plan.

There are other benefits, as well. The rent checks pay the property tax, and browsing cows help deer control some emerging woody plants and weeds. Unlike burning or mowing, the impact of grazing on nesting prairie birds is minimal. But most important: if timing is right, cattle thrive on invasive but nutritious non-native early season grasses, preventing those grasses from achieving maturity and producing seed, thus leaving the land relatively free of competition as summer heats up and the native species reach full stride.

I have not forgotten my father's mantra from a well-managed farm in Oklahoma: Only if you take care of the land will the land take care of you. But I also learned from neighbors who carelessly took more from their land than it was able to give and thus broke the cycle of sustainability in disastrous ways. And I have learned from non-human managers, the birds, mammals and insects with which we share the bluff, that working within natural processes helps maintain and even enhances the health of our biosphere. For any person who possesses land, that is what a land ethic requires. So today we open the gates to our neighbors' cows for the last month of spring. On the first day of summer they will be gone, leaving the prairie to the management of native inhabitants for the rest of the year.

May 22: Welcoming the Bees

He (or she) who would rise before the summer sun must set the clock early, five a.m. But by the time I was dressed, had a cup of coffee, and drove a mile north to Grace's house, she had the hives prepared for transport. Grace, her professor husband, Harry, and their three children were about to depart for a semester at sea, a journey in which Harry would teach between stops along the Atlantic coast to Nova Scotia, across to Ireland, down the European and African coasts to South

Africa, across the Atlantic to Argentina, then back north through the Caribbean and home. Grace didn't invite us to go along, but she asked us to babysit her bees.

Norma and I were bringing scant and largely unsuccessful experience with honeybees, *Apis mellifera* to the venture, as I will explain. Yet Grace trusted us to care for her bees, or perhaps she didn't see any better options, or more likely delivering her bees to us was a typical act of generosity and trust for which she is known. In any case, I backed the pickup up to the hives at first light and we muscled two hives onto the tailgate, threw in a jumble of equipment and headed back to the bluff.

By the time we had unloaded the hives onto a shipping pallet, the much-jostled bees were buzzing madly, eager to be out. Grace pulled off the tape that blocked their door and out they poured. Likely some had seen this terrain before, since they routinely fly far more than the mile from the Freeman house to ours in search of pollen and nectar. We hoped they would readily adapt to the new circumstances, since for honeybees home is less a geographic spot and more a hive and queen.

We positioned the hives on a slightly southeast-sloping hillside halfway between our vegetable garden and the pond, blossoms and water each less than 200 feet away. The hives were already heavy with honey, likely made from the nectar of the creamy white flowers of linden trees, Grace conjectured. Other early flowers were blooming, so we had reason to hope the bees would quickly resume their work. Before Grace left for the six-month trip we would work with her to learn the processes of harvesting and extracting honey.

This was not our first effort as beekeepers. Among our first projects when we arrived on the bluff in 1982 was to establish a hive. An elderly friend, who also did his best in a largely futile effort to teach me to play guitar, set up a hive of bees near our house. The first year, with Willard's guidance, we did gather enough honey for the winter. But the second

summer, Willard died, and almost immediately so did our bees. At least they disappeared, and I was too busy at the time gardening, planting trees and finishing the interior of our house to try to figure out why. And there was no chore girl, as in John Greenleaf Whittier's 1858 poem "Telling the Bees," to drape the hives in black and sing to the bees: "Stay at home, pretty bees, fly not hence! Mistress Mary is dead and gone!" Perhaps, as New England tradition would have it, the bees vanished because nobody came to tell them of their benefactor's demise. More likely the reason might have been determined by a more scientific approach.

In later years two friends kept bees on our land, first Frank, and later Grace. Both saw disappointments balanced by success. When Grace moved her hive home I wasn't overly concerned, since they weren't going too far to continue their work here, and since we still had wild bees. But that was before the alarming phenomenon known as colony collapse disorder swept across the land. It was a mystery that several years later is not entirely resolved, let alone satisfactorily addressed.

Unanswered questions provide good reasons to go on living. I don't expect to solve every mystery of the bluff, not if I live a hundred years, and neither did the great naturalist Aldo Leopold. "It is fortunate, perhaps," Leopold observed in *A Sand County Almanac*, "that no matter how intently one studies the hundred little dramas of the woods and meadows, one can never learn all the salient facts about any one of them…. Every farm is a textbook on animal ecology. Woodsmanship is the translation of the book." But while the disappearance of honeybees is likely not a phenomenon of nature, it is a drama that I and many others would like to see solved. I fear that the causes may lie beyond the boundaries of our meadows and woods.

Bees have long inhabited the bluff. For years wild pollinating honey makers inhabited a leaning burr oak beside our creek. Suddenly several years ago, they vanished. I pondered the disappearance for several weeks before the calm summer afternoon when, strolling past the pond downstream, I heard the unmistakable hum of bees. I looked up to see scores of the golden insects entering and exiting a narrow slit in another oak, an unhealed wound where a limb long ago fell away. Our wild colony had apparently found a new hive. Perhaps it was no coincidence that within weeks after the bees abandoned the earlier tree, it crashed across the trail.

For four years we watched the bees come and go in their new home, a strong, stately oak well-watered by the pond, the time of year and the daily temperature dictating the intensity of bee activity. Then, as suddenly as they came, the bees again disappeared. Why? Where did they go? Did the colony follow the queen to another hollow tree, or did something more sinister happen? Was the cause natural or human? For the next three years we saw no bees except those at work in our prairies. But to my delight, bees resumed residence in the same cavity this spring! Whether they are descended from the earlier inhabitants, followed a rebel queen from another hive, or are perhaps of undomesticated origin I cannot say.

Our little mystery is of course a microcosm of a years-long national, and even international, mystery of vanishing bees. As honeybees disappear across the country, billions of dollars worth of flowers, fruits, nuts and vegetables are at risk. Just as we don't miss the water until the well runs dry, most people won't concern themselves about this loss until the foods they love don't grow because there were no bees to pollinate them. For years commercial beekeepers have lost up to one third of honeybee colonies each year, but according to a joint study by the U.S. Department of Agriculture, Apiary Inspectors of America and Bee Informed Partnership, in 2014 about forty-two percent of the nation's honeybee colonies died. South Dakota fared slightly better than the national average, but corn-intensive Iowa and Illinois lost more than sixty percent of their bees.

    Researchers have asserted and investigated various hypotheses to explain the disappearance. The proliferation of parasitic mites might be a factor, or perhaps a virus that targets bees' immune systems. Commercially-managed bees suffer stress from being trucked across the nation from one monoculture to another to do their work, from fruit orchards and commercial vegetable gardens in the south to almond groves in California and back. Some investigators point to the widely-used herbicide glyphosate, the active ingredient in Monsanto's Roundup which, by killing every plant except the desired plant—corn or beans—replaces biodiversity with monoculture. It is chemicals like glyphosate that make monoculture without manual labor possible, and that model pervades modern agriculture, hundreds of acres of a single crop. A single plant that flowers briefly and is done replaces the summer-long supply of a variety of flowers from which bees and other pollinators gather pollen and nectar.

    Other scientists point to the genetically modified organisms themselves. GMOs and chemical control not only deprive bees of diverse food sources; seeds are now even infused with nicotine-derived neonicotinoids before planting. The systemic neuro-active insecticide is taken up by the plant and transported to all tissues—roots, leaves, flowers, pollen and nectar. Neonicotinoids protect the chosen plant from insect pests, but evidence suggests that they also may weaken bees and impair their navigational powers, rendering them unable to find their way back to the hive.

Researchers in Europe, and particularly in France where a third of the bee colonies were disappearing each year, thoroughly examined the hypothesis that systemic pesticides are at least partly to blame for the loss. When results were in, France succeeded in banning the use of such agents. A year after the ban was imposed, populations of bees seemed to be rebuilding. Achieving such a ban in the United States is unlikely. Here the Department of Agriculture and the Environmental Protection Agency often rely on researchers employed by the very chemical companies that produce new compounds to test their own products and declare them safe. In America, chemicals are considered innocent until proven guilty. It is up to the victims to do the research and to then overwhelm political opposition to doing the right thing.

Perhaps colony collapse disorder springs from a combination of factors, including some not yet recognized. But one thing is certain; both the domestic bees we once housed and the wild hives that for years made their living and their homes on our bluff had the abundant food sources and water that bees need to thrive—a spring-fed stream and acres of restored native prairie with dozens of flowering forbs as well as local fields of alfalfa and clover. If our wild bees died instead of simply relocating, we don't know why.

The first summer after the colony disappeared, I held to hope. Bees continued to visit the birdbath in the front yard, so maybe the colony had simply moved again. When they left the water they flew northeast, so perhaps they had found a new hollow in one of the century old cottonwoods in a nearby grove, a new home from which they could continue their vital work. We may never learn all of Leopold's "salient facts" pertaining to our local mystery or the national crisis of bee disappearance, but I continue to hope that we can learn why these miraculous creatures are disappearing across America…and that we will exert the will to save them, and thus also save the flowers, fruits, vegetables, nuts and other plants we love and need.

Many garden plants require pollination, so in the summers before Grace's bees arrived I determined to try my hand at artificial insemination. In recent years I had found very few pollinators in the garden, lots of blossoms on zucchini, yellow squash, cantaloupe and pumpkin, but little evidence of setting fruit. Lacking the finesse of the honeybee, I went to the medicine cabinet for cotton swabs. I didn't fly, I didn't buzz, and the fibers of my swab were crude compared to the tiny hairs on the bee's body that collect and transport pollen. But delicately as I could, which did not approximate the grace of bees, I went from blossom to blossom, gently stroking the male stamens and anthers of each blossom and dusting the pollen around, hoping that grains might light on the female pistils of the blossoms, that the timing might be right for fertilization, and that given the abundance of flowers, the alchemy might work on at least a few. For each vegetable—zucchini, yellow squash, cucumber, pumpkin and cantaloupe—I used a new swab, reducing the chance of cross pollination, that my work would produce hybridized fruits we could not use.

Was my bee substitute work effective? Perhaps to some degree; each species produced a few fruits, though certainly not abundance. But only a honeybee or other specialized pollinator can truly do this delicate work. It was clear to me that we should get bees again and do our best to keep them alive. We do love honey, but beyond that, and beyond the inherent value of bees as a species, their function of pollinating crops is invaluable. And now the bees were back.

May 25: Thinking Like Other Animals

Anthropomorphism: The attribution of human form, characteristics or behavior to other creatures. In spring I find myself thinking this way. I watch orioles and robins working tirelessly to build their nests, and I remember our own frantic twelve-hour days and seven-day weeks building our home with a toddler at our heels and another baby on her way. When turkey toms fan their tails and strut before seemingly unimpressed hens, I remember my friends and me slicking our hair and polishing our cars. The fearlessness of the mother skunk that dines in our compost pile reminds me of human mothers who would do whatever it takes to protect their young.

What mental processes guide the army of ants that labor as a team to haul the carcass of the grasshopper from the patio? What dreams lull or disturb the cat that sleeps on my lap? Why do bluebirds try out every house in the yard before choosing a favorite, and what mental checklist accompanies that decision? I observe the actions of fellow animals and, perhaps erroneously, find them remarkably like my own.

It is commonly believed that the evolution of opposable thumbs made humans superior to other mammals, and in recent millennia we have learned to make and wield tools to accomplish hitherto unimaginable goals, but could the human with the most refined use of fingers—the most adept brain surgeon or the concert pianist—build a passable oriole nest? I doubt any human could do with his hands what a small bird does with her beak. Some dismissive humans say that the accomplishments of fellow fauna are guided by "mere instinct." Yet lacking lips, some birds learn passable human speech, while no human has ever mastered the brown thrasher's songs.

Beyond admiring their actions, I speculate about the thoughts of other animals. What is the nature and scope of their rational powers? One thing seems clear. The concept of "dumb animals" is not valid. But are their thought processes on a plane with ours, or perhaps in some ways we fail to comprehend, even superior? If only we knew the languages in which to ask our neighbors, "what do you think?"

Unexamined condescension to fellow creatures allows humans to feel superior and also to exploit other animals in merciless ways. When I see thousand of pigs confined for their entire short lives in stinking concentration camps, for example, I remember Joey, my 4-H pig. I came home from school one fine fall day to find Joey racing madly about his pen, gathering leaves and twigs and hauling everything he could grasp in his mouth to a far corner of his shed, where he arranged them in a cushy bed. We humans had no idea that before morning the first storm of winter would come howling in, but Joey knew. He not only knew; he produced and executed a rational survival plan. That's more than I can say for some fellow women and men.

May 27: Season of the Coyote

It is evening in the woods, the moment of revelation between the last crimson rays of sun and the definition of stars. We pick our way down the trail past the pond and rise toward the meadow above. Darkness closes as we climb, but emerging from woods we are compensated by the still-glowing western sky. This weekend, Memorial Day, our daughter Laura will marry Sam, and Sam's mother Megan, father Rob and sister Francis have come to Prairie Bluff en route to the celebration.

In this change of shifts from day to night, all is silent but the occasional buzz of a mosquito and the swish of shoes through greening grass. We arrive at the summit and pause to drink the cool night air. From the oak grove a whip-poor-will begins her melancholic cry. From across the pond comes the long warbling shriek of a screech owl. Then suddenly a coyote barks in the oaks to our north, joined by a multitude of yips and howls. Immediately the chorus is answered by a family in the western woods and then from a pack along Clay Creek. The coyotes have heard our subdued voices, or more likely sniffed the scent of strangers. The cacophony closes in, and we are surrounded by three packs of coyotes, hungry from a long day's sleep, curious to know what unfamiliar humans have invaded their domain.

Mingled with barks and howls are the yips and squeals

of the recently born. Like their domesticated counterparts, coyote pups are full of life, unrestrained, their curiosity and exuberance transcending instinctual fear. The voices come closer. Suddenly all is silent; we know that somewhere on the dark fringe where prairie meets woods they are watching us. The three-part symphony erupts again, intelligence of our presence and perhaps some evaluation of our potential for food or harm is communicated, and then the music fades back into night.

In the silence that ensues there is only the whisper of human voices, the hum of insects and the whip-poor-will's incessant, plaintive call, punctuated now and then by the blood-curdling trill of the screech owl. We pick our way down the dim prairie path to the broad trail home.

This will be a good year for the boldest predator on the bluff, the wily mammal Lewis and Clark called the prairie wolf. The several deer carcasses I have found in the woods in the past long winter have fed them well, and the nighttime choruses reveal a healthy crop of pups. The meadows of tall-grass prairie are rich in mice and voles, and cottontails thrive in the brush piles and the woods. The coyotes I have chanced to spy are sleek and strong. And they will need both strength and cunning to survive. Not all fellow humans share my love for the coyote's call. In the winter a monster pickup with Sioux Falls plates idled our county and township roads, looking for coyotes to blow away. Even a few neighbors still delight in senseless killing, or perhaps they simply fail to appreciate the vital role of the ruler of the bluff in keeping our ecosystem in balance.

May 28: Magical Morning at the Pond

Hidden behind a cedar I watch the resident pair of wood ducks swim to the northwest corner of the pond. The female flutters up to the wood duck house and enters, presumably to deposit an egg. The male stands watch below, his brilliant array of colors glinting in the sun—amber wings ringed with black, white and blue, green pin-striped head, white throat, white-speckled cinnamon breast, orange behind his bill.

The air is filled with song, a melody that from my vantage point on the hill overpowers the steady roar of clashing calls from frogs: leopard, chorus and tree. I strain to distinguish the competing and blended songs of the Baltimore oriole, orchard oriole, red-winged blackbird, gold finch, house finch, robin, red-breasted grosbeak, bluebird, brown thrasher, catbird, song sparrow and mourning dove. A broad shadow floats across my shadow, then across the water. A great blue heron is sailing in. He seems to pause in mid air, then settles effortlessly to an overhanging willow from where he can survey the clear depths of the pond. Birds continue to sing, but amongst the communities of frogs, word of the new arrival spreads and their croaking subsides.

The sun that warms my shoulders highlights the luster of rippling jewels that adorn the water, the cottonwoods and willows and the air between. So intoxicating is the moment that I forget myself until my legs begin to ache from lack of movement and I become aware of the awkward position in which my body is frozen. But dare I shift? Any movement might be detected by more than one perceptive eye. Even if I, in my camouflage and cover, were not detected, would movement itself break the magic of the moment? Mere self-awareness has interrupted a heightened level of communion, but no moment so special can last forever. Otherwise, we would cease to marvel when the extraordinary comes.

JUNE

June 2: Waiting for Rain

Last night I dreamed it rained. A long, pounding, soaking rain. I slogged through soggy meadows, shoes and jeans soaked, flesh drenched and cold. I awoke to a moonlit sky and a whispering wind. Not a single drop of moisture on the window glass.

For many days I've been preoccupied with rain, or the lack thereof. Weeks ago Norma and I planted this year's plot of native prairie, seven native grasses and twenty-nine flowering forbs on the hilltop that knew only cedars and brome before it was denuded in October by the fire accidentally set by a pipeline crew. Regardless of how often I check, the seeds still lay dry in the furrows, awaiting rain. Could this year replicate the drought of 2012? In the longest dry spell in recorded history, 1930 to 1937, average annual precipitation here was nearly seventeen inches. Everybody with roots in the Great Plains has heard the terrible stories of the thirties, when dry weather, dust and the Great Depression converged to drive thousands of farmers and other residents off the land. But in 2012 our total precipitation was three inches less than the 1930s average.

Coinciding with our arrival on the bluff, the *Yankton Press and Dakotan*—the oldest newspaper in Dakota Territory—published the record of annual precipitation in Yankton for well over a century, beginning in 1874. That record shows cycles of wet years and drought, but the annual average was about twenty-eight inches. Inspired by this documentation, I began maintaining my own record of precipitation on the bluff, twenty miles east of Yankton.

I can't swear to the complete precision of either the newspaper's records or of my own; my process is to dump the rain gauge after each precipitation event and record the date and the amount in my notebook. In winter, I bring the rain gauge in and substitute a tin can. When there is snow or ice I bring the can in to thaw and measure the level with a ruler. But despite possible imprecision, I am confident that my annual record is accurate within an inch or so. Over the past few decades our precipitation averaged almost thirty inches per year, a substantial increase over the previous hundred years, whether an aberration, or an effect of climate change.

In our first years, the early and middle 1980s, we averaged thirty-five inches, well above the historic twenty-eight. When leaves on vegetables and trees began to curl, rain would seem to come. But in 1987, little rain fell, and each of the next two years was drier than the year before. Nineteen eighty-nine matched 1936 and 1956, the two driest years in 116 years of record keeping. We received thirteen inches of snow and rain, less than half the annual average. Gardens withered and refused to yield. Trees hunkered down, faithfully producing leaves each spring, but failing to grow, marshaling resources in their roots and hanging on for better times. In those years our world turned to dust.

In April of 1989, I threw a shovel in the pickup, and I and our son, Walter, then nine years old and big enough to help, drove to the Missouri River. We dug up fifty cottonwood saplings and a dozen small redcedars and brought them home. "You're planting trees in the middle of this drought?" Norma asked, in the tone of deep skepticism the plan obviously warranted.

"It's an act of faith," I said. "Maybe it will rain again." Walt and I planted three rows of trees, two of cottonwoods and one of cedars to their north. And then it rained. Today the tallest of the cottonwoods exceeds sixty feet.

For as long as records have been kept, drought has visited the Great Plains about once per human generation, and in 2012 I feared we might be facing another extended dry spell. Yet in most of the twenty-eight years since we planted the cottonwood grove, and in the years since 2012, we have received precipitation above the historic average. Dry periods like this one make me nervous, but I cling to hope. I still plant, I still pray for rain, and I still dream of slogging through spongy soil, both when I'm asleep and while I'm awake.

June 4: Serpents and Voyeurs

Once long ago in Oklahoma, Norma and I awoke to see a rough green snake, *Opheodrys aestivus,* clinging to an oak branch outside our window, peering in. Whether he was interested in our lifestyle, or perhaps even our naked bodies and mating habits, I couldn't say. But long he stared at us through the glass from not much more than arm's length away, an unabashed voyeur.

He was in his habitat, of course; the rough green is among North America's most arboreal snakes. They spend most of their time in trees, where in summer months their color provides perfect camouflage. They crawl amongst branches and leaves, hunting for spiders, insects and other invertebrate food. At night they coil in shrubs or thick foliage. So perhaps like us, he had just awakened and had not yet set out in search of breakfast.

He was quite a handsome reptile, slender, bright green with a whitish belly, nearly three feet long. So we returned the stare. He was on the other side of glass, and even if he'd been on our side as a garter snake once was, he would have posed no threat. After a time, he'd apparently had his fill of window peeping, and slowly slithered out of view amongst the leaves.

Our South Dakota bluff is north of the rough green's territory, but here we also have our share of snakes. Garter snakes are most common, but our region also is home to fox snakes, lined snakes, smooth green snakes, racers and bull snakes, the latter of which is by far the largest. Adult bull snakes average twice as long as the rough green and can reach eight feet in length. I have finally mastered my reflexive leap off the trail when I encounter garter snakes, but I'm still working on the bull. Beyond their size, bull snakes also resemble the western diamondback rattler that is common in western Oklahoma where I grew up, brownish yellow with blotches of brown, black, white and sometimes red. Bull snakes, *Pituophis catenifer sayi*, are non-venomous, but they can certainly be fierce, especially if you are a rabbit, gopher or mouse. They have also evolved to imitate rattlesnake behaviors as a defensive strategy. They form their bodies into the classic rattlesnake S, rear their heads and lunge repeatedly at perceived threats. They even hiss and rattle their rattle-less tails against vegetation or the ground.

My encounters with bull snakes are rare and usually brief. Generally, one or both of us is quick to retreat. So on only two occasions have I had the leisure to truly inspect the finer points of the bull. Both times a pair of snakes were mating, and I was the voyeur. The first opportunity was in the wooded hills across the Missouri in Nebraska; the second was in our front yard. Norma, my brother, Paul, and his wife, Cindy, were on our way to the garden when we came upon them, a coiled

pile of two huge snakes locked in what seemed like battle, but was actually only intercourse. His body was entwined with hers, their sex organs engaged. But what was most striking was that the male gripped the female in his jaws, just behind her head.

It did not appear to be the gentlest of matings, and on some level we felt a bit uncomfortable watching. But watch we did, even snapping a few pictures. They lay in their tangled coil for a good ten minutes, not moving in the least until we, like the rough green snake of long ago, had had enough of voyeurism and moved on. Then they quickly disengaged and glided away into tall prairie grass.

June 9: And the Rain Came!

Just a week ago I lamented what seemed continuing drought. Following last year's spotty rainfall, this spring was menacingly dry. May and June are supposed to be a rainy season, but until yesterday prospects looked grim. Subsoil moisture lay very deep. The lawn was already turning brown and flowers refused to bud. With a couple of waterings the garden still looked good in its bottomland, but for how long? The seeds of grasses and forbs Norma and I planted on the hillside still lay dormant and dry. We desperately needed rain.

I awoke at two a.m. yesterday to drizzle on the window glass, this time not just a dream. By noon we had four tenths of an inch. I was thankful, but it wasn't enough and the rain seemed done. Today I drove to our highest hill to cut down a string of cedars where prairie meets ravine. I'd left these five, hoping at least a couple would turn out to be males. All five bore blue berries, reproductive seed. I want no new cedars sprouting in restored native prairie, so they had to go. I finished the job, killed the chainsaw and began dragging cedars over the edge. That's when lightning hit.

The strike was a few miles away, half way to the Missouri River. I watched it sizzle for what seemed like seconds in a cornfield, imagining such a strike nearby. A hilltop was no place to be. I threw the chainsaw and earmuffs in the pickup and headed down the hill. Thunder crashed and rain struck as I closed the gate. When I reached the garage, the truck was streaming water. I raced to the house and filled my glass with water, then stood in the open door and watched more water fall.

When the downpour ended, we had over two inches in the gauge, enough to carry the garden for a week or two. More important, the next sun should germinate the seeds of bluestem, switch grass, Indiangrass, wheat grass, side oats grama, wild rye and a bouquet of wildflowers, the promise of another hillside restored to something resembling native prairie. I could not have been more thankful for the rain.

June 16: Patience and Survival

There's something invigorating about watching annual plants grow. Annual plants, from tomatoes to soybeans, corn and goldenrod, have one brief season in the sun; their Great Plains life cycle—from germination to death—must be completed in half a year. In hot, humid weather, corn may stretch an inch higher every day. Musk thistles develop equally fast, cause for anxiety and vigilance.

Not so with perennial native grasses and forbs. Tall prairie grasses, such as big bluestem, Indiangrass and switchgrass, may grow higher than my head, but compared to South Dakota's ubiquitous field corn, their beginnings are inauspicious, so subtle as to require careful searching on hands and knees. Many weeks have now passed since Norma and I sowed this year's native grass seeds. On June eighth rain returned, and in little more than a week we have been blessed with nearly four inches. The ground is soaked, and this morning I went to look for grass. Most of the plants have yet to emerge, but digging carefully into the furrow with a pocketknife confirmed once again the miracle of germination.

I unearthed sprouted seeds, ready to put down roots and then shoot slender filaments toward the sun. Here and there a discernible line of slender green hairs marked the furrows, the promise of success.

Even with abundant rain and with the sun that undoubtedly will follow, we don't expect the native seeds to grow this summer like thistles or corn. In their genes are centuries of experience about not emerging too soon or exposing themselves to wilting heat before they are ready. In fact, for the whole first season native grasses grow more volume below the surface than above. Only when a substantial root system is established, a system designed to ensure survival in baked summer soil and winter's frozen earth, will these grasses fully assert themselves.

That is the secret of their success, born of countless generations of struggle. They know that survival on the harsh northern plains requires patience, and from these grasses I learn the same. Not that I won't walk the prairie daily watching for progress; I will. But I know that the tiny slivers of green that I hope will define themselves as rows and eventually as a jungle of grass that waves above my head are mostly a token of promise, now little more than a symbol of the waving restored prairie that grows in my mind.

June 19: Streamlined Kitty with a Fluid Drive

There is nothing more endearing than a mother nursing her babies—even if that mother is a skunk! We were privileged to watch our black-and-white-striped inhabitant feeding her young this week. The striped skunk's Latin name, *Mephitis mephitis*, is appropriate; Mephitis was the Roman goddess associated with poisonous gases emitted from the ground—from swamps and volcanic vapors. *Mephitis* is Latin for "smelly." Would you be surprised, as I was, to learn that an over-the-counter remedy for spasmodic cough is derived from the fluid secreted by the skunk's anal gland?

Our resident skunk—we call her Pepe le Pew for the Looney Tunes character of the same name—has lived near our house since winter. For reasons that should be obvious, I haven't followed her closely to learn exactly where she lives, but I think it's in a large brush pile east of the house, female cedar trees I cut down on that hill and pushed together with the tractor loader. I call such brush piles rabbitat, since cottontails are among the common residents of such safe havens. But possums, mice, voles and perhaps other creatures also find refuge and safety there from coyotes, foxes, owls, hawks and people. I'm not sure how these creatures feel about sharing a brush pile with a skunk, but they don't need to; I've left many a pile of brush— cedar and otherwise.

We first noticed le Pew traipsing across the front lawn in late winter. She had discovered the compost pile west of our house, and the front lawn was the shortest distance between bed and breakfast. Several times I stepped out and spoke to her, hoping that human presence might discourage her from coming so close. She was undeterred. So to accommodate her and to reduce the chance of undesirable close encounters, we began carrying our biodegradable waste down the driveway, closer to her home.

For a time, moving the food scraps seemed to change her behavior; her front yard visits declined. When she did  show up, I stepped out and clapped my hands and she scampered away. Once we surprised each other in the back yard, each spotting the other from thirty feet apart. Startled, she spun around and showed me her tail. I slowly backed away, and she withdrew the threat. Only twice in the months she's lived in close proximity did she find occasion to foul the air, and the clouds soon cleared.

A couple of weeks ago, I realized I hadn't seen le Pew for several days. I guessed that she had given birth and was busy with her young. I can't say that I really missed her frequent appearances. Attractive and entertaining as she is, I admit that I breathe easier without her around. So we were surprised to see her again Sunday, lying calmly in a clump of grass, a passel of babies rooting and nursing and tumbling like any litter of kittens or pups. She either didn't notice us, occupied as she was, or in her motherly bliss she chose to ignore us. I'm not sure how many babies she has. I didn't venture close enough to count.

Summer

June 21: How Sweet It Is!

What better day to harvest honey than summer solstice. On this longest day of the year, the bees are as busy as they will ever be. The prairies are dappled with the colors and exude the aromas of summer; a dozen or more forbs are reaching their fluorescent prime. The bees have been busy for the month they've been here, and the hives are heavy with honey. The weather is warm, and the bees will be too busy with their work to pay much attention to ours. That is, we can rob the fruits of their labor even as they fly far afield to gather pollen and nectar to replace the honey we take.

I have cleaned the garage, spread a plastic tarp to catch honey that we will inevitably drip or spill, and arranged the tools and equipment for extracting honey. The centrifuge is cleaned and ready, a stainless steel barrel in which two honey-filled frames at a time can be fitted and spun with a hand-operated crank. A three-gallon canning pot waits to catch the honey that will flow from the spigot, its top covered with cheesecloth to strain out debris that may cling to the frames—bits of foreign matter and dead bees or parts thereof. The electrically-heated knife used to scrape the waxy seal of the honey comb into another pot is ready to be plugged in.

The other set of tools we load into the wheelbarrow, things we will need for removing the honey-laden frames from the hives and bringing them to the centrifuge. The smoker is stuffed with dried sumac berries and ready to fire. There's a flat bar for breaking loose the hive cover and separating frames from the super, frames that the bees have firmly sealed with wax. The dripping frames will be quickly slipped into an oversized heavy-duty black plastic bag in the wheelbarrow to isolate them from the bees that otherwise would cover them and ride with them to the garage. We don heavy white shirts, bonnets and cotton gloves and wheel our load down the hill to the hives.

 The sun is already hot, which is good, because the hotter the weather the more active the bees, and thus, the less likely they are to pay heed to our enterprise. I light the smoker and give the bellows a few pumps until the smoldering seeds produce a cloud of smoke. I insert the flat bar under the lid and pry. When the wax seal pops, bees come swarming out. Norma pumps a cloud of smoke into and around the hive, and instantly the attention of the bees is diverted from us. It is thought that smoke masks alarm pheromones that would normally be released by guard bees. It also appears to produce a feeding frenzy as bees perceive the threat of fire to their hive, and it is more difficult for a bee with an abdomen full of honey to sting.

 The super, the box that sits above the brood hive, is stuffed with honey and wax, so a bit of prying and joggling is required to dislodge the first of a dozen frames, the vertically inserted casings upon which the bees have built the waxy comb of cells they've filled with honey. I lift out the first frame and brush off the clinging bees with a soft-bristled brush. Norma opens the plastic bag and I stuff it in. She closes it quickly to prevent bees from entering, though it is not possible to exclude them all.

 When all the frames are removed from the first hive and the wheelbarrow is full, I push the now much heavier conveyance back up the hill, followed by a swarm of bees. Norma opens the garage door, I rush the load in and she quickly shuts it again. A few bees manage to enter, and they will continue to threaten us as we work unless we can trap them—or in a few cases smash them—and put them out. We remove our protective gear and begin phase two, extraction. I lift out the first frame, and holding it over a large pot, scrape off the waxy seal with the hot knife. Honey begins to flow. Quickly as I can, I deposit the frame into the centrifuge, turn the cage half way and drop another frame into the other side. I close the lid and crank away, the centrifugal force slinging the honey from the opened cells where it drains to the bottom of the barrel and thence to the waiting pot. A couple of hours pass in this monotonous labor. Each time the honey pot fills, we take it to the utility room sink and pour the honey through a funnel into waiting quart and gallon jars.

When we finish extraction from the first hive, we head back down the hill, redeposit the empty but still dripping frames into the super where we hope the bees will fill them again, remove the frames from the second hive and repeat the process. By early afternoon, we have collected ten gallons of honey. But before we can take a break for lunch, we squeeze remaining honey from the waxy comb and begin the cleanup phase. Even when everything is well drained, honey does not wash readily from the many surfaces to which it clings—centrifuge and other equipment, tarp, floor and of course shoes and hands.

Speaking of hands, we had managed to complete the operation with only one sting. When I reached blindly into the plastic bag for another frame, an unhappy bee had retaliated by inserting its stinger into my index finger. No big deal, I thought. I had been stung many times by honeybees, and even by yellow jacket wasps and bumblebees, but never had the effect been long lasting or severe. But by the time we finished cleanup, it had become obvious that this time was different. My right hand had swollen to resemble a baseball catcher's mitt! Apparently my immune system had been compromised by leukemia, or by the chemotherapy I was undergoing or by some combination of the two. The phenomenon was alarming, but equally troubling was the question of whether I would have to part company from bees.

June 23: Eating What Bugs Us

Somewhere I saw a bumper sticker that read, "Birds eat what bugs them." Come to think of it, certain bugs also eat what bugs me. I refer to the tiny insect that thrives on leafy spurge, the flea beetle. Why is that important? Because much of the Great Plains—both native prairie and converted grasslands—is infested with the highly-invasive imported weed.

Like smooth brome, the dominant pasture grass of eastern South Dakota, leafy spurge, *Euphorbia esula*, is "exotic." That is, neither is native to the Plains. Brome was imported intentionally, leafy spurge by accident, presumably mixed with crop seeds brought by settlers from Eastern Europe. In recent years these two non-native species have come to dominate much of the Missouri River bluff and vast stretches beyond. We are among a handful of landowners working to restore native prairie grasses in place of brome, but across the region farmers and ranchers have fought leafy spurge for decades.

When spurge produces its pale yellow blossoms in early June, it's time to attack. For years I faithfully applied the herbicide 2,4-D from my backpack sprayer, with little long-term effect. But early experiments taught me that tallgrass prairie can somewhat control this noxious weed—and others—by shading and crowding them out, so spurge was high among my motives for native prairie restoration. But like prairie grasses, the roots of spurge grow deep, and complete eradication is very difficult to achieve.

That's where the flea beetle, *Aphthona nigriscutis*, comes in. Eventually it became obvious to range management specialists that the fight against spurge could not be won through chemical warfare. Every few years a new chemical might come online, but by the next year the range of spurge had spread. New thinking was required. One February I joined fellow county commissioners and weed supervisors from across South Dakota in Rapid City for the annual Weed and Pest Conference. I went with some reluctance, expecting two days of indoctrination on the latest agents in chemical warfare against invasive species that threaten natural ecosystems and agricultural vitality of the Northern Great Plains. I was delighted to learn that times are changing.

Yes, chemical companies and dealers were well represented, and yes, I and other delegates did find information on new formulations and new equipment and techniques for applying chemicals. Like all else in modern America, fighting weeds has gone high tech. On Prairie Bluff I will continue to engage thistles and other weeds with my hoe where possible, and with my backpack sprayer where necessary. But for the scale of ranches and roadside ditches, new technologies include GPS mapping to systematically record and monitor where various invasive species grow, what chemicals are used, when and in what quantities, and what progress toward control can be observed. Besides making the work of applicators more systematic and efficient, mapping and precise targeting of chemicals saves money and reduces potential contamination of water and soil.

Important as new chemicals, information and technology might be, what impressed me most about the conference was that in the past decade, a sea change in attitude has occurred. From weed supervisors to entomologists to department of agriculture extension agents, there is growing recognition that fighting invasive weeds with chemicals alone is an expensive and losing battle. The new approach is "integrated pest management," and the rising tool is bio control.

Bio control begins with the recognition that not all answers come from the chemistry lab. Instead, we must turn for answers, as our ancestors in every culture have done, to nature herself. In the case of leafy spurge, various thistles, salt cedar, purple loosestrife and a dozen other imported species that continue to spread despite decades of chemical attack, bio control begins with patiently observing what insects eat the plant in question in its Old World region of origin.

What follows is a rigorous scientific search for answers: Does a particular insect effectively control a particular weed where they have evolved together? Does the biological agent feed exclusively on the target plant in question, or might the insect, if imported, soon turn on our native or other desirable plants? And can the insect from, say Eastern Europe, survive a Northern Plains winter? The process of approval for importation is necessarily painstaking; most of the problem plants, insects and animals we fight today were imported from abroad by accident, ignorance or a lack of thought, and we shouldn't repeat those mistakes.

After years of controlled experimentation, researchers concluded that flea beetles eat only leafy spurge. Adult beetles feed on the leaves of spurge, then lay their eggs in soil around the stem. When the eggs hatch, the larvae feed on the stem and roots, which critically weakens the plant. In ensuing years, the same investigative process has led to importation of other controlling insects from the native regions of other imported weeds.

Flea beetles are not new to me or to our land. For two decades, the tiny insects have assisted my struggle against leafy spurge. In 1998 I drove to an experimental plot near the North Dakota border where the SD Department of Agriculture had designated a hundred-acre patch of out-of-control leafy spurge as a nursery for flea beetles. Every year since, I have collected more of the tiny black bugs closer to home and released them in various infestations of spurge on our land. As of today, every known patch of spurge on our property has insects nibbling away toward control, and one of the worst infestations seems virtually liberated. Each June for several years I have joined neighbors harvesting from a pair of local pastures where Clay County weed supervisor Dennis Ganschow had established colonies. But summer before last, I found enough beetles thriving on our land that perhaps in the future I can collect all I need without leaving home.

Our more comprehensive tool in the fight against noxious

weeds has of course been restoration of native prairie. In ever-broadening experiments since 1993, I have learned that tall grasses like big blue stem, Indian grass and switch grass not only overgrow, shade and choke out invasive weeds, but also provide the necessary habitat for insects and other organisms that evolved here as essential parts of an ecosystem in balance. Yet prairie grasses alone haven't completely solved the problem of invasive weeds.

So today, as I have most years for at least a decade, I joined other landowners interested in bio control to gather flea beetles in a pasture three miles up the bluff. The temperature was in the nineties, hot sun and no wind, ideal conditions for adult beetles to feed. The South Dakota Department of Agriculture and county weed supervisors handed out sweep nets (similar to butterfly nets but made of sturdy canvas) and off we went to walk the hills, sweeping the nets from side to side through leafy spurge, gathering beetles. A Clay County weed management staffer roamed the hills on an all-terrain vehicle, collecting our caches in a pillowcase, then hauling them to a home-made separator, a funnel-shaped device in which solar heat encourages beetles to jump out of the plant debris into a collection basin. The flea beetle harvest was good.

The dozen farmers and property managers each took home thousands of beetles to distribute in other spurge-infested pastures. I hauled mine to two patches of spurge that remain in prairies we returned to native grasses in 2006, prairies I must not spray because the sixteen-seed mixture we planted includes nine native forbs. There, the tiny insects will join previous generations of their kind, feasting on the most persistent weed I fight, the one that bugs me most.

June 27: Chilling Out in the Cool Tub

Years ago, a rural neighbor maintained a hot tub in his back yard. On a cold January night, Norma and I were invited to join a small party for a dip. We changed to swim suits, turned off the house lights and stepped out the back door into near zero air. We rushed to the tub and plunged in, our bodies shocked by the hundred-degree difference between the winter air and the steaming, roiling water.

It was a brilliant night, calm and clear. Snow reflected the light of myriad stars. We immersed ourselves to the chin in the comforting churn, inhaling deeply of the thick atmosphere of steam that rose from the super-heated water. Jets churned against our backs, and for a time, there was no place else on Earth we would rather be. But the human body can tolerate only so much of a good thing; eventually we had outstayed our time. Our host, a man of Scandinavian descent, leapt from the tub and prostrated himself in the snow, rolling and screaming under the stars, reenacting an ancient ritual of his tribe—or perhaps merely showing off for his guests. The rest of us climbed reluctantly from the embryonic fluid and dashed toward the house.

Later that night, I lay in bed thinking what a fine addition to our country home a hot tub might be. But the pleasure we had experienced was heavily laced with questions about how much energy would be required to maintain hundred-degree water—even in a well-insulated vessel—from winter cold. Given that our electricity comes mostly from non-renewable and climate-changing fossil fuels, including coal, I concluded before I drifted off to sleep that this was a moral compromise I could not further consider.

At about the same time, some quarter century ago, our neighbor Roy passed on, and his son Gilbert bequeathed upon our children, Walter and Laura, Roy's two aging Shetland ponies. Our kids called them Skeeter and Mama Pony. This gift meant work and expense for me. I had to build a small barn and corral, mow grass for winter hay, and carry buckets of water every winter morning to the thirsty beasts. I poured the water into an oblong galvanized steel livestock tank, two by four feet and two feet deep.

Skeeter and Mama Pony were well past their prime when they moved in with us. They provided delightful entertainment for the whole family when the kids were small, but at about the right time—when Walt and Laura had outgrown barebacked rides on sagging spines, the ponies conveniently died of old age. I emptied their water tank, dragged it out of sight amongst the trees and turned it upside down. There it remained, unused for the next decade.

One sweltering early summer day my eye fell on the tank, nearly hidden in tall grass. And suddenly I knew that it held yet another life. I dragged it out, brushed out spider webs and dirt, and found that its condition was still good. There were minor spots of rust, but mostly the galvanizing had protected the steel from deterioration. I dragged it up the hill to the house, scrubbed it with soapy water and a steel brush, set it upright under ash trees on the patio west of the house and turned on the hose.

This afternoon the air is humid and calm. The thermometer reads ninety-two. I have just returned from hoeing rows of potatoes, carrots and beans. Norma and I strip off our clothes—our backyard is completely private, so no need for swim suits here—and step into the cool water. No rushing jets, no steam, no energy beyond the sun, just the cooling elixir that so refreshes a heated body on a summer afternoon.

So why did it take a decade to see a body-invigorating cool tub waiting patiently behind the barn for a new life? Lack of imagination, I suppose. A failure to connect the dots, to pair an obvious problem with an obvious solution. Yes, the cool tub will require occasional draining and refilling—it holds a hundred gallons or so—but there is no waste involved. I will simply attach the garden hose to the drain valve at its base and let the water flow downhill to the flowerbeds. Changing water should occur during very warm days, of course, since the water at our faucets runs about fifty degrees. The first plunge into new water would be as shocking as that into a hot tub on a January night, but with the opposite effect, instant chill. I can still live quite well without a hot tub, but now we wonder how we ever endured sweaty summer days without the cool tub.

June 30: Calling Coyotes

Twice I sat for hours beside a coyote's den on moonlit nights, waiting fruitlessly for my spirit animal to appear. Possibly they had already emerged for the nightly hunt before I arrived, or more likely, they smelled my presence and simply waited me out. We do hear my favorite mammal most any night we invest time outdoors, but I long for more frequent encounters, face to face. So sometime last spring I visited a local hunter's supply store and bought a coyote call. The device consists of a three-inch hard plastic tube with a flexible joint and a mouthpiece. According to instructions on the package, one can blow into the tube as though it were a bugle, and through various contortions of the flexible tube and varying degrees of closure of the open end, produce a variety of screams and wails that are supposed to resemble the cries of a rabbit or other small animal in distress. Instead of waiting patiently for coyote's call, a hunter, with or without a gun, can theoretically initiate a conversation that will bring the wily predator of the plains to him.

My initial experiments produced a variety of snorts and squeaks that I guessed would more likely amuse a coyote than fool one, or perhaps even provide comic relief for a rabbit in distress. Eventually, after Norma had sent me outside for further rehearsals, I did produce what I thought might sound like a wounded bunny, though in truth I've never actually witnessed a coyote-cottontail encounter, so I couldn't be sure.

Next full moon I took my new toy to the hill west of the house, settled into a cushy clump of Indian grass, and reproduced my limited repertoire. No coyotes came, nor did I hear so much as a yip. Maybe my timing was off, perhaps the coyotes were on vacation or simply well fed, or possibly my rabbit imitation was so implausible that no coyote of even average intelligence could be duped. But it was a pleasant late spring night under the full moon, there were other night sounds to enjoy, a whip-poor-will in the woods and somewhere on Clay Creek a great horned owl, so though I wondered if the $6.95 I'd spent on the coyote call had been wasted, I considered my investment in the night well paid.

Tonight, when the past-full moon had not yet cleared the horizon, I sat in t-shirt and moccasins on the patio sipping a cold drink and watching stars define themselves in the darkening sky. Suddenly the communication I had sought came—from the valley west of the house, not more than a couple hundred yards away. I put down my glass and crept to the brow of the hill. No coyote was visible in the fading light. I thought of returning to the house for the plastic tube, but instead cupped my hands in a V and inhaled through pursed lips, producing a squeaking sound that I imagined might sound something like the illusive rabbit in pain, a cry at least as authentic sounding as any I'd produced with the store-bought device.

To my surprise the coyote answered, three short yips and a howl, not from the valley, but now from the hilltop beyond, where I'd recently waited under the full moon. I crept as quietly as I could down the hill, pausing now and then to cry like a dying cottontail. And each time the coyote replied, though each time the call came from the dark the same 200 yards ahead. Whether it occurred to the carnivore to wonder why a wounded rabbit would be pursuing the thing it most feared I don't know, but the conversation ensued. When I reached the hilltop, the coyote replied from the next valley west. When I arrived in that valley, the coyote answered from the next hill. And so it went as darkness fell.

Half an hour later I was lying in the grass on a distant hilltop, my lips growing numb as a rehearsing bugler's. Apparently my counterpart's curiosity wouldn't allow him to give up the novel encounter, but neither was he foolish, fooled or hungry enough to come closer. By now the only light was from the stars, and I had half a mile of rough terrain to cover in moccasins, including crossing a creek. Reluctantly I headed home. But now and then I would stop to utter my best squeals and groans, and to my great surprise, the curious coyote followed me at his usual safe distance toward home!

Only when I passed the pond and started up the final hill where the living room lights dimly dispelled the dark did my canine correspondent sign off and abandon his pursuit. But for an hour our curious calls had filled the night sky with wonder and fun. I can't say whether the coyote thought I was other than a strange, easily-amused human, or perhaps a deranged human, but I hope that our conversation entertained him as much as it did me.

JULY

July 1: Harvest Time

The months of eating daily from the garden have come. We enjoyed our first lettuce, spinach, onions, cilantro, oregano and strawberries in late May, and thanks to abundant rain in June we have harvested more than ten gallons of lettuce in recent weeks. We have luxuriant salads of green and red leaf lettuce every day, and we've pushed bulging bags of greens on a dozen friends. But lettuce doesn't tolerate the hot, dry weather of July, so we've move on to other delights.

We planted two varieties of bush beans, and both are weighted down with growing pods. For the next few weeks they should produce all the beans we can eat. Our first tomatoes are red and juicy, with scores of others in various stages of growth. The corn is tasseling and should be ready by the end of the month. Potatoes are blooming, which means we can dig the first tender new tubers. The first bell and chili peppers could be picked any day, but I'll try to resist and let them reach full size. We will gather the first crookneck squash this week, and the zucchinis, butternut squash, cucumbers, cantaloupes and pumpkins are setting fruit. The apple, plum and cherry trees are sagging low with abundant fruit.

The season of life at this latitude is nearly half the year, and growing longer with climate change. For four of those months, there's something new to eat most every week. Okra and eggplant love the hot, dry weather of mid summer, and won't produce until August. Unlike cucumbers, zucchinis and crooknecks, fellow vining plants like cantaloupe, pumpkin and buttercup grow slowly, and won't be ready until late summer. Pumpkins may continue to grow larger until frost, just in time for jack-o-lanterns and pumpkin pies.

From last frost to first, I visit the garden almost every day. In April I scoop up handfuls of earth, testing the soil for the dryness necessary for tilling without clods. In May we plant, and if we're lucky, eat the first greens. In June the garden reaches its glory, but so do invading weeds; June is the month of the hoe. After weeding and tilling, I mulch with oat straw or lawn grass to conserve moisture and block the emergence of more weeds.

In July and August we harvest and eat—and hope for rain. By late September, signs of death are everywhere and decay is in the air. Most crops have been dug, gone to seed or withered and died. Yet equinox should find us still eating squash, potatoes, onions, tomatoes, eggplants, peppers, pumpkins and cantaloupes. When frost is forecast, we will harvest the last peppers and ripe tomatoes to freeze. Green tomatoes we'll wrap in newspaper and store in the cellar, where they will continue to ripen. We may eat the last as candles flicker in the patio jack-o-lanterns on Halloween, or who knows, perhaps with Thanksgiving dinner!

July 4: Independence Day: Protecting Natural Land
 Today is Independence Day, a day when Americans celebrate freedom from the tyranny of foreign rule. We conveniently forget that we are also a nation built by invaders, by non-natives on this land. Here in southeastern South Dakota, that invasion began when white settlers displaced the Yankton Sioux, beginning in 1859 and rapidly accelerating with passage of the Homestead Act three years later. Homesteaders brought vigor and hard work and many admirable values and skills to the land they possessed, but they also brought non-native seeds, sometimes inappropriate land use, and in some cases disregard for both the peoples they dispossessed and for the long-term needs of the land they claimed. A century and a half later, little is left that might remind us of the rich cultural and natural world they inherited. Given the tiny fraction of native prairie that remains, prairie is perhaps the most degraded ecosystem in North America.

 Norma and I and our children are well aware of how blessed our lives have been in our country—and on this scrap of prairie bluff and woods, where remnants of that natural world remain and where we have had the opportunity to work at restoring some of what was lost. After thirty-five years of walking trails, listening to birds and sitting in meditation at the spring, I have not stopped asking myself, "What did I do to deserve this?"

Yes, we lived frugally and saved money so that when the opportunity to buy land arose, we could act. Yes, we actively pursued opportunities that helped make things happen as they did. And yes, we have invested thousands of hours of labor—building our home, rescuing land from the encroachment of invasive grasses, weeds and cedar trees, and to the best of our abilities, rehabilitating abused soil through the restoration of native grasses and forbs. But there was also a huge element of good fortune; more than once we were simply in the right place at the right time.

But the work continues. Every year we make the rounds, cutting down young cedars that have sprung from seeds deposited by female cedars I removed years ago. Many springs we have gathered friends to burn selected meadows to enhance and maintain the prairie's health. Every June I walk the prairie with a sweep net, gathering leafy spurge-eating flea beetles to release in yet another area threatened by the persistent weed. Every July we scour the prairies and woods, loppers or hoe in hand, removing other invaders that refuse to die. We are under no illusion that our land has been—or could be—restored to its truly natural condition. We are aware that our work has, to a large extent, been an artificial exercise; it is the paradox of conservation that the best human efforts to truly restore natural conditions will not be adequate. We simply have done what we could do as we had the insight and energy to act.

But for how much longer can we wield these tools, climb prairie hills and perform these tasks? If we are fortunate, and health holds out, perhaps a decade or two. Or perhaps not. These days my thankful meditations are often clouded by these questions; indeed I am sometimes gripped by anxiety when I ask myself who will carry on these vital responsibilities when we cannot? I find no obvious answer.

Perhaps these feelings are not so different from those experienced by women and men who have invested their lives in building institutions or even successful businesses.

Certainly I understand the angst of aging farmers who have carefully nurtured their land in the midst of an agribusiness revolution that has turned every farm around them into a profit-driven sea of monoculture, land that in many cases is managed by someone who neither owns nor lives upon the land, but is driven solely by the amount of profit that can be squeezed from this year's crop of corn or beans. And yet, our blessing and our commitment are different. Norma and I have been entrusted with what is an increasingly rare island of diversity, an irregular swath of water, woods and prairie hills that has grown in health while most surrounding land has been neglected, abused or turned into a medium for the annual injection of chemicals and engineered seeds.

So what to do? Years ago we began to discuss this question with our friend John Davidson, founder of the Northern Prairies Land Trust. Over many years of work, Northern Prairies has undertaken the protection of thousands of acres of ranch land, wetlands, riparian areas and other special lands through a legal framework that allows landowners to dictate future land use decisions and practices, and to incorporate those stipulations into the property deed, stipulations that will bind future owners to certain principles of conservation or preservation. Increasingly, this seemed like the best option for us. Thus, over a two-year period of consultation we discussed issues, drafted plans and eventually produced a document that has now been legally executed, a perpetual conservation easement that will preclude most future development on the 150 acres of Prairie Bluff. The easement requires that the land shall be maintained as near as possible in a natural condition, a mix of forest, native prairie and flowing springs.

Strangely enough, every year in recent memory, a group of state representatives have introduced a bill in the South Dakota Legislature to outlaw perpetual conservation easements. The leading sponsor is a rural person who believes mightily in individual rights and property rights—except when she doesn't. Exactly how she reconciles her fierce defense of the right to exploit one's land with efforts to prohibit others from protecting their land I do not comprehend, but there are many in the Legislature who follow her lead. Thus far, more rational heads have prevailed, and the option of protecting land from inappropriate development has survived.

But no legal document can alleviate my worries and fears. Yes, the conservation easement will prevent our land from being plowed and planted to commodity crops. The bluff land will not sprout a housing development. There will be no feedlots or livestock confinements, and grazing will be restricted in ways that promote rather than harm prairie health. The "no hunting" signs will be maintained, and the forest will not be cut down. But those are only the things that the conservation easement prevents. What worries me is that no legal document can either require or inspire future owners to care as we do about the health of the land, to watch over the land with love, to appreciate its bounty, to detect its needs, and to do the hard work that caring demands. In short, is there any way to dictate from this side of our graves how those who will own this land in the future will oversee its needs?

Our wills state that legal possession will be transferred to our children. They grew up on this land, and they love it as we do. But they live in distant cities, they have careers, families, homes and obligations of their own, and we do not expect them to drop their chosen lives and take up the lives Norma and I chose for ourselves. We trust that our children would never sell to "the highest bidder," if that is somebody who does not love the land as we do. But how can they find or choose the appropriate next possessors of this land, persons with the curiosity, humility and devotion required to learn from nature, and to respond?

As I suggested, our dilemma is not unlike that faced by people who have devoted their lives to a life-enhancing institution or to a business founded on principles beyond the bottom line. And yet there is something far more permanent and far less ephemeral about land, about the particular aggregate of soil, flora and fauna that have evolved together and exist on a piece of "real estate," for land is a living organism, one whose health requires loving care—or in some cases benign neglect in deference to the hand of nature.

So perhaps there is not much more that we can do. We have offered our best, as we saw how and as time and energy have permitted us to do. I have even left my version of events, a draft or a blueprint of sorts for what I see as the gifts this land has to give and the gifts it should receive. My book *Waiting for Coyote's Call* describes how we and our land evolved together, and hints at what we have learned. This present book is a celebration of how the Prairie Bluff has enriched our lives, while showing us day by day what is required of us in our feeble efforts to learn and repay. These books cannot, of course, provide any simple formula or recipe to be followed by future possessors of the land. But I do hope they might provide some inspiration, in the root sense of that word, for "inspire" is to breathe in, to absorb the atmosphere in a way that maintains life and love. And then we must expire, and of course perspire…and transpiration is sure to follow.

July 8: Making Hay

The summer I was eighteen, I worked for a harvester of hay. From June through August, I handled 100,000 bales. When I went to college that September, I was the strongest I've ever been—including during the two grueling years in the Army. After all, carrying an M-16 and a forty-pound pack on one's back is nothing compared to lifting thirty tons of bales chest high on the average day. By the end of that long summer I had developed an aversion to bucking bales. Yet four decades later, the pair of aging Shetland ponies that Walter and Laura received from Roy's son wanted daily feed, so every couple of years we hired a neighbor to bale a couple of acres of grass to keep the ponies satisfied through winter. But hauling in a couple of pickup loads of light grass bales was more like a family picnic than work.

Not long after my brutal summer in the sun, the traditional rectangular bales that, depending on the contents—straw, prairie grasses or alfalfa, and the degree of moisture, might weigh anywhere from forty to eighty pounds, were gradually replaced by the huge round or rectangular bales that are loaded onto trucks by tractors, thus eliminating one more opportunity for boys to become men. Or from another point of view, replacing by machine one more hellish manual task.

Work aside, I always enjoyed making hay. There is no aroma quite like that of freshly-mown grasses and legumes. If cool season grasses are harvested after prairie-nesting birds have fledged their young but before the brome and bluegrass seed matures, the quality of the hay will be good. Haying is less disruptive of natural processes than plowing under the stubble of wheat or the stalks of corn, and in years of normal precipitation, grasses, clover and alfalfa all regrow quickly. If the goal is to take maximum yield from a given plot, a good summer will yield three or four cuttings of hay. But more important for our purposes, is that cutting one early crop of hay hinders the competition of early season grasses that, if not removed, will inhibit the growth of native grasses and flowers. Ours is not a "working farm," and the ponies are long gone, so we rarely make hay these days. But this summer we incorporated haying as one more feature in our prairie management plan.

Today the same two-generation family farmers whose cattle graze our largest prairie each spring mowed hay on hilly land that couldn't be grazed because it wasn't fenced, and can't be burned because the grasses grow amongst scattered trees. When we replanted native prairie on these particular hills, we left existing deciduous trees and numerous male cedar trees to provide diverse habitat for everything from prairie birds to rodents, rabbits, coyotes and deer. Mowing and baling hay amongst scattered trees presents a challenge—a project that probably would not interest farmers with huge equipment and hundreds of acres of land. So we invited these neighbors to harvest the hay for free. After all, what benefits them also benefits the vitality of native grassland.

If weather holds dry, they will bale the hay in a few days, and within a week, shoots of native grasses will reappear. In a month the grasses will reach my knees. And with timely rains, by summer's end the heads of Indiangrass, big blue stem and switch grass will wave above my head—ideal habitat that will feed and shelter many a mammal and bird through the long winter to come.

July 12: Welcoming Walnuts

On February 9, I wrote about the excitement of discovering mature native walnut trees I didn't know we had. Before that date, I knew of three black walnut trees on our land, all of which we'd planted some three decades ago. But in the past week I have discovered, to my delight, that those walnuts are propagating! I found two saplings south of the barn, no doubt descendants of the tree Norma and I planted below our home site even before the house was built. Today I found another healthy sapling a quarter mile to the east, far from any adult walnut tree. Perhaps a walnut was squirreled away by a squirrel last fall, a squirrel that then forgot to return to his cache.

Until recently, when friends asked me to name the native trees and shrubs on our land, my list included burr oak, green ash, hackberry, American elm, box elder, eastern redcedar, mulberry, plains cottonwood, peach leaf willow, red-osier dogwood, choke cherry, wild plum, basswood and black walnut, the latter two of which we'd planted. But as of February, I could include naturally-occurring mature black walnuts—and now walnut reproduction!

The growing diversity of native deciduous trees is especially critical as two key species, American elm and green ash, fall victim to spreading diseases. Once the dominant tree along the ravines in our woods, most of the American elms have already succumbed to Dutch elm disease, the scourge spread across the country by bark beetles in the twentieth century. Today the forest floor is littered with their decaying trunks. The handful of American elms that remain die at a rate of several each year—good for a continuous supply of great firewood, but a sad loss of a great native tree. The breadth of this tragedy is well known; the beetles are believed to have arrived in the United States from the Netherlands in 1928, and by 1989 three quarters of American elms were dead.

Another key component of our forest is green ash, but this magnificent hardwood is also seriously threatened. The emerald ash borer is not here yet, but it is eating its way across the border states of Minnesota and Iowa, and presumably will someday arrive here. Meanwhile, we are already losing mature ash trees, possibly to native pests such as the ash/lilac borer, the roundheaded borer or the flatheaded apple tree borer, all of which attack drought-stressed or otherwise unhealthy trees. So to discover that another native hardwood is multiplying is comforting, more evidence of growing natural succession and diversity on the bluff.

To paraphrase the common rhetorical question, "which came first, the chicken or the egg?" one might ask, which came first, the walnut or the squirrel? Near our house, the answer is clear. We saw squirrels in and near oak groves in the woods, but we rarely saw a squirrel near our house before the walnuts and oaks we transplanted matured to the point of producing fruit. Now the nuts keep squirrels fed each fall and busy storing winter food. And there is little doubt that for the emergence of new walnut trees we can thank the squirrels.

Yet the discovery of new walnuts and the inquiry it prompted bring to my attention another troubling reality. Thousand Canker's Disease is also spreading our way, killing black walnuts in its path. Already walnuts are quarantined in neighboring Minnesota and Nebraska. Like the green ash, the American elm and many other species of animals and plants, the walnut's future is in question. Perhaps our walnuts' relative isolation will keep them safe, at least for now. The squirrels and I share that need.

July 17: The Valley of Ashes Blooms

On April 22, Earth Day, I wrote about planting prairie on the spot where I had burned hundreds of cedar trees killed by the pipeline fire. Today we stroll across a riot of color against a hillside of green. It is far from an orderly flowerbed. Those who prefer formal gardens where lovely flowers are manicured in distinct patches or rows and where colors are coordinated to avoid clashes might find this scrap of prairie the antithesis of order. But I'm with nature. Her notion of order is not tidy, nor is it organized in a way that might qualify for garden of the week.

I had roughly planted two native mixtures—four grasses and twenty-nine flowering forbs. By "roughly," I mean that I raked the surface clear of leftover debris, broadcast the seed, raked it in and tramped the area down by foot. Such a method is far from perfect, and I knew that I should not expect a high percentage of the seeds to take root. In such circumstances, my rule of thumb is to overplant and hope for the best.

The first heavy rain cut a tiny rivulet down the center of the patch, which I closed with my rake. The second rain sprouted many of the seeds, and some had produced sufficient roots to hold them in place when a third downpour came. But many sprouted seeds and most of those still dormant washed to the lower edge of the patch, where grass formed a dam that held them in place. The outlook for the new bit of prairie was far from ideal. But as spring progressed, tiny blades of grass pushed up, a pledge that roots were also thrusting down. Since the seeds of most native wildflowers are tiny, so are the first leaves, but soon those tiny promises unfolded too, and some degree of success seemed assured. At that stage, another gully washer could have borne the vital half inch of topsoil away and all the life it held, but that did not occur.

Now in mid July, prairie flowers are in their prime. Established forbs are blooming across the prairies, purple coneflowers, snow on the mountain, black-eyed susans, varieties of coreopsis, prairie clover, sunflowers and more, their degree of prominence amongst the grasses dependent upon the degree of competition present in the particular site, how heavily the grasses were grazed in spring, or whether the particular meadow had been mowed for hay. In this first-summer prairie garden, competition from grasses is still minimal. Native grasses grow much more underground the first year than above, so two months into their lives the blades of the short grasses I had planted—blue grama, sideoats grama, little bluestem and buffalograss now stand no more than two or three inches tall. By next spring the grasses and forbs will compete on an equal footing, and another year down the road the grasses will limit space available for wildflowers. But today the insurgent broadleaf plants glory in their dominance.

Of the twenty-nine forbs I planted, I did not expect to see a high percentage emerge. A few of the species in the mixture were represented by a finger pinch of seeds. Every site will welcome certain species and reject others, depending on soil type, tillage, slope, moisture level and orientation to the sun, and this was a less than hospitable slope. Some seeds germinate best if covered by a quarter inch of soil, some by a half inch, and others might take root on the soil surface if moisture and temperature are ideal. Some seeds are so light and ephemeral that the heavy rain probably floated them completely off the plot. But of the thirty-three, at least a third have already made themselves known.

Among the toughest and most reliable—as tough as many "weeds"—are the black-eyed susan and the blanketflower.

Throw in a few purple coneflowers and hoary vervain, and you have all the beauty some folks can handle—purple, yellow, gold, brown and red. But there is so much more, the reddish gold of California poppies, the lavender of lemon mint, the delicate blue of flax, the brilliant reds of dwarf coreopsis and Mexican red hat, the white of yarrow and snow on the mountain. Who needs twenty-nine flowers in bloom? Lover of wild and discordant beauty that I am, I can settle for ten or twelve—especially when you throw in the brilliance of honeybees and bumblebees and various butterflies that come for nectar and pollen.

In another month, most of this beauty will fade. Black-eyed susans and snow on the mountain will remain, and given enough moisture, perhaps a handful of other blossoms. But otherwise it will be the season of prairie grasses. Rooted down, they will reach toward the sun, produce seed and prepare for frost. In autumn they will replace the frost-faded flowers with their own more subtle pink and purple hues.

Next summer, not all of the flowers will return. A few are annuals, and their persistence will depend upon whether they produce seed and whether those seeds find space and fertile soil in which to sprout. Most, however, are perennials, and given proper conditions, they should grace this cemetery of incinerated cedars for generations to come.

July 21: Holiday in San Antonio

This week, Norma and I are in San Antonio, Texas, where the afternoon temperature hits 100 degrees in the shade. Obviously our timing is bad; the time for a South Dakotan to head south is January, not July. Yes, we strolled down the San Antonio River Walk one night, and last night we enjoyed Tejano, the Latino festival of music, food and drink in Market Square. But mostly we are here to work, not play.

Our son, Walter, and his wife, Lizzy, have bought their first home. The century-old house is on the fringe of the historic King William neighborhood, near the River Walk south of downtown. When the elderly owner died, her daughters couldn't agree to sell the house, so it stood empty for eight years. Fortunately the roof was good, so there was no water damage inside. But pretty much everything needed rehabilitation, from the ground up.

When we arrived, the foundation was repaired, and Walt and his hired handyman, who calls himself Silver, had gutted the interior and restored drywall on the eleven-foot ceilings. Over the next few days, Walt, Silver and I sheet-rocked the walls, and soon they'll be ready for paint.

There were floor boards to replace and holes to fill, and floors will soon be ready to sand and varnish. Electrical wiring has been replaced, but major plumbing repair lies ahead. Cabinets arrived today, which we will install after the kitchen is painted. And that's just the interior; when we are shivering in South Dakota next winter, Walt will scrape and paint the exterior in comfortable San Antonio weather.

Why would anybody undertake such a project? We ask ourselves that question every day. But the answers are evident. First, the price of a restored house in this historic neighborhood—even a two-bedroom house such as this one—would be prohibitive for a young couple like Walt and Lizzy. Restoring the house to its original grandeur is a good investment that will pay off in the long run. But more important, the house will be a lovely place to live, grand on a small scale, with its large, high-ceilinged rooms, columned wraparound porch and mansard roof. And perhaps most important, restoring an old house instead of tearing it down and throwing up a modern replacement with inferior materials is an act of sustainability—not unlike our own work back home to restore damaged soil and native prairie.

Our ten-hour days in sweltering heat aren't exactly fun, but they are satisfying, seeing at the end of each day a few more steps toward restoration. It's also gratifying to see that our son has learned the values of maintenance and repair, of conservation and care, and that he is willing and able to do the hard work that they require.

July 27: Living High Off the Hog

Yes, we still eat meat. It is with some measure of guilt, or perhaps regret, that I have not transcended this practice. Henry David Thoreau also ate meat with his beans, but perhaps he was right when he observed in *Walden*, "I have no doubt that it is a part of the destiny of the human race, in its gradual improvement, to leave off eating animals, as surely as the savage tribes have left off eating each other when they came in contact with the more civilized."

No cannibals in our house, but like Thoreau, we have not yet reached the lofty plateau of civilization he envisioned. We have not achieved the status of vegan, or even vegetarian. Though Norma and I now limit our consumption of beef, pork and chicken, we continue to eat—and enjoy—limited quantities of meat. We are omnivores who believe in the value of moderation in all things. Yet in harvest season, that has not always deterred me from gorging on vegetables and fruits. I can afford this indulgence only because high metabolism allows me to eat more than most of my friends without gaining weight. Even so, unless the fruits and vegetables are particularly exquisite, I try to refrain from gluttony. But today was not such a day. Our garden has gone wild, producing far more of the best food imaginable than any glutton could consume.

I grew up on a very small farm in Oklahoma, where we raised most of what we ate. My mother invested countless hours every summer canning excess summer vegetables for winter consumption. But she also killed and I helped her butcher enough chickens every summer to have Sunday dinner for the coming year. All the eggs and milk and beef we ate were produced on our farm. It was a healthy, balanced diet, totally organic long before any of us had heard the term.

I enjoyed every chicken, hamburger, steak and pork chop I ate—even though as a boy I did not know that there are other ways to cook meat besides well-done. Poor though we might have been, we lived "high on the hog."

But in July, the need or even the desire for meat grows thin, especially in a summer when every seed we planted in the garden is producing an abundant harvest. Today, it occurs to me, we might have set a Guinness book record for the variety of vegetables eaten in a single day. Breakfast was the usual, yogurt, cereal and fruit—strawberries from the garden and plums from the orchard. For lunch Norma stir fried onion, green pepper, yellow squash, snow peas, green beans, jalapeño, okra and scraps of a not-home-grown vegetable element, soy tofu. For dinner we had corn on the cob, tomatoes, cucumbers, potatoes and chives. That adds up to two fruits and a dozen vegetables eaten in a single day, and all within hours after they were picked! Yum.

As every resident of northern climes—including the Great Plains—knows, fresh fruits and vegetables are almost impossible to come by for half the year. We of course eat the pickles and jellies Norma has made with extra cucumbers and fruits, and we gradually empty the freezer of the previous summer's excess produce. Our grocery stores display all the foods we ate today and more, sometimes disingenuously advertised as "picked ripe," but fresh? Out of the question. Most were harvested long ago and far away—in Florida, Texas, California or Mexico, and some on other continents. Most were unripe when harvested, and many—tomatoes for example—are bred for uniformity and shelf life, not for flavor. No vegetable, whether picked unripe and shipped to us or frozen for months, retains either its full flavor or its complete nutritional values like a tomato or cucumber or bean that was still on the vine minutes before it lands on our plates.

So in summer we live well, eat well, enjoy the exercise of working and harvesting vegetables and fruits, inhale the oxygen they exude even as we pick them, soak in the sun that provides the full complement of vitamin D, and incorporate them into our bodies as an almost spiritual exercise. In summer we live high *off* the hog.

July 29: My Toady Friends

One of our children's favorite books was Arnold Lobel's *Frog and Toad are Friends*. The book of course anthropomorphizes the amphibians, investing in them the best of human qualities, as well as a dose of human foibles. But mainly the book celebrates friendship, even the friendship between two creatures whose needs and habits are quite different from each other.

Actually, seven thousand species of amphibians have now been identified, and it would require lots of anthropomorphizing to say to what extent any two species are friends. The sad news is that amphibian species are going extinct about as fast as we discover new ones. Of all those diverse animals, I have identified only a handful on the bluff.

Whatever similar traits evolution has bestowed upon these diverse amphibian species—and there are no doubt more similarities than differences—I have yet to encounter a convention, much less friendship, between our few homegrown frogs and toads. Yet each frog, toad and other amphibian I have encountered appears to be enjoying its own brief time under the sun, carrying out the functions endowed to its kind by its genes. Our frogs and toads do eat similar foods—mostly insects, though because they generally inhabit different environments, their menus are not necessarily the same. Toads have even been known to dine on the eggs of their distant cousins.

Our frogs—leopard, chorus and tree—live around the ponds, where they herald spring with their raucous croaks. In a favorable year, toads might be encountered in the woods and in prairie grasses and around the fringes of the ponds, but I am most likely to meet them in the flowerbeds and lawn around the house. This year, conditions were good for a big hatch of toads. Suddenly a few days ago I noticed that I needed to watch my step to avoid smashing one, especially in cool mornings and evenings. They were not yet the big warty creatures they will become an infinite number of insects from now. Today they are downright cute—like most other baby animals. They are less than an inch long, and close examination shows them to be beautifully camouflaged until they hop, a subtle, earthy brown with irregular but distinct patches of tan across the back.

I watch one crouching at the edge of the patio, sheltered by a two-inch-high forest of bluegrass. With an action so fast that I completely miss it, his tiny tongue apparently flicks out half his body length. All I can say for certain is that a passing ant disappears. He remains in ambush until dusk falls, then advances from cover, hopping, stopping, hopping again, until he has positioned himself in the path of a small black beetle that lumbers slowly toward him until it reaches striking distance. This time I watch more carefully, and I think I do see the sliver of tongue flash again, and the beetle disappears.

But what kind of toad am I watching? *A Field Guide to South Dakota Amphibians* published by SD State University indicates that four species of toads inhabit southeastern South Dakota—the Great Plains toad, the American toad, the Canadian, or Dakota toad and Woodhouse's, or Rocky Mountain toad. The guide pictures the toads in color, but as adults, so I'm not immediately sure to which species the youngsters busily hunting insects on the patio and in the lawn and flowerbeds belong. Only hundreds of insects later will they achieve full toadhood, and thus more closely resemble the pictured adults.

I pick up one of the youngsters for closer examination. He immediately urinates on my hand, as frogs and toads are apparently required to do. Holding him next to the photographs of his elders, it appears he bears the features and coloration of the American toad, *Anaxyrus americanus*.

His back is olive brown, mottled with irregular but distinct patches of lighter tan. The belly is white with black flecks.

Frog's friend and mine seems eager to return to his pursuit of insects, so I set him gently back on the patio stones. He hops twice, then freezes when he sees an ant emerge from the grass. The ant moves closer, likely on its own hunt for something to eat. When the ant reaches striking distance, some two feet from the baby toad, Captain America leaps. Out flicks the tongue again, so thin I'm still not sure whether it is my eyes or only my imagination that perceives it. In any case, the ant has disappeared. The toad hops again, pauses briefly to excrete the remains of his previous meals, then hops into the forest of grass and is gone, leaving me to ponder a question of great import: the bald eagle is our national bird, and on November 1, 2016 the bison was designated our national animal, so shouldn't the American toad qualify as our national amphibian?

July 30: Rescued Robin

I was sprinkling the flowers when I heard the sharp thud. The corner of my eye registered dual movements, movements about to converge. A robin careened from the windowpane toward the sidewalk, and Luna the cat leapt into action, moving as fast as a sixteen-year-old feline can. As if by instinct, I yelled at the top of my lungs "CAT!" and simultaneously redirected the spray from my hose toward the flash of yellow. Luna screeched to a halt, reversed course and beat a quick retreat as I dropped the hose and rushed to scoop up the fallen bird. Our cat lacks front claws and wears a bell, and rarely catches a bird unless it is stunned by a collision with glass. But research indicates that house cats and feral cats are responsible for the deaths of far more song birds than windshields or wind turbines or any other adversary, with estimates of cat-caused casualties ranging from half a billion to a billion birds each year.

But back to the robin, a juvenile *Turdus migratorius*, its sides below the wings already bearing the amber of a mature robin, its breast still white but speckled with splotches of black. I clutched the immobilized body in my palm for closer examination. Neither its wings nor its neck appeared broken, and no blood seeped from its eyes, ears or beak. Its eyes were open, glazed and crazed, madly blinking. The talons of one foot gripped my finger. Its heart beat wildly and its beak was opened wide for gasps of air. It is just such a bird that more than once has ended up in Luna's belly, its feathers and head scattered across the mat at our back door. Had I not been in the right place and responded quickly, this bird would have been cat food.

For several minutes I held the heaving robin in my hand. Gradually I eased my grip and opened my palm. Periodically its eyes began to droop, but when I stroked its head they opened wide. Whether they focused on me—and what they saw—I cannot tell. It seemed that stimulation kept them open and bright. I felt around the little body, and could find no injuries. I guessed that like other crash victims I had rescued, it was severely stunned by the collision, but might regain its senses. On the other hand, like a human football player who has sustained punishing clashes with opponents, the robin might have suffered a concussion from which it would never fully recover. But for the moment it was alive, and while I held it in my hand and applied the stimulation that kept it conscious, seemed somewhat alert.

But I needed to finish my watering and then weed the flowerbeds. After a quarter hour or so, in which the robin seemed to get no better or worse, I carried it to the big maple in the center of the driveway. Making sure the cat was not watching, I nestled it into the crotch between two trunks, a place where it would not be seen from the ground, and a place where it could recover—or die in peace.

Half an hour passed before I finished my work and came to see. There was no apparent change. The body was immobile, and the eyelids still drooped. I feared that the damage was too severe for recovery. Of the numerous birds of several species I have retrieved from a crash into the windows, most recovered within moments and flew away. I returned the young robin to its resting place and went to pick tomatoes.

Another hour passed before I returned to the maple. The bird was gone. I scoured the surrounding area for the telltale sign of feathers, but there were none. No signs of foul play. The cat slept peacefully in the patio sun. Apparently after two hours of rest the juvenile robin had recovered the ability to fly, and hopefully had resumed its search for the insects and worms that would quickly transform it to adulthood. I wondered whether the experience had implanted any memory of what occurred, a memory that might make the older bird a wiser bird. Or maybe the opposite occurred, a complete loss of memory of what preceded its arrival on the maple crotch and of the huge creature that brought it there. Or perhaps such speculation is merely the anthropomorphizing to which humans are prone. In any case, it is one more robin to sing in the treetops, one not down the hatch of a carnivorous cat.

AUGUST

August 3: Buffalograss Lawn

Though we have planted tall prairie grasses and forbs as close as thirty feet from our house, we maintain a strip of citified lawn around the perimeter of the cedar-clad walls. It is a barrier between us and the wild, a bluegrass lawn where we can lounge or walk barefoot by moonlight, and more important, a defense in case of prairie fire. Yet by August I'm as weary as my neighbors of maintaining this strip of civilization. Especially in rainy summers, I grow tired of mowing the lawn. In dry years I don't like watering and paying the bill just to keep this exotic strip of green alive. That's why we have converted two areas of our lawn to buffalograss, the sole grass of the genus *Buchloe*.

If this hardy perennial native of the western and southern Great Plains was indigenous on our tallgrass bluff, I have found no remnants. Possibly the buffalograss I have planted is the first to grow on this land. On native prairies of the more arid central and southern Plains, buffalograss is a common species, and in areas that have been overgrazed, it often dominates. In the northern Plains, and especially on the less arid eastern edge, this shortgrass species does not compete favorably with taller grasses such as Indiangrass, switchgrass and bluestem, so it is rarely prominent.

Though no buffalo graze our land and few roam the other grasslands of the region, buffalograss has grown in popularity for low maintenance lawns. My first experiment with the short prairie native began in 2007. On the eroded slope where we built our house, topsoil is in short supply, especially west of the house. After years of coaxing bluegrass to grow, the chalky clay soil was still exposed and there was too little vegetation to hold the rain. I ordered five pounds of Cody buffalograss seed from my supplier in Murdock, Nebraska, disked the west lawn, and raked in the seed.

Like its tallgrass relatives, in their first summer the seedlings concentrated on putting down roots, forming a dense sod that ended the threat of erosion. Next summer, each plant sent out above-ground stems called stolons, which rooted and filled blank spots. By the third summer the patch resembled the fur of a pale green, wooly mammal, the fine stems and curly, hairy leaves forming a dense mat. Today the ground is completely covered by a carpet four to six inches deep that discourages invasive weeds.

Besides its beauty, tenacity and utility, the buffalograss lawn is self-sustaining. I rarely mow this piece of lawn, and except for its initial season, have applied no water. Granted, six inches might be a little deep for lounging, for barefoot walks and for an effective firebreak, but for areas less occupied, I have concluded that buffalograss is the perfect maintenance-free lawn. I like it so well that this spring I planted another patch on the hill behind the house.

August 4: A Killer on the Loose

From the front window I saw what appeared to be a pile of dirt on the sidewalk. I knew it wasn't there last night, so some creature somehow deposited a mound of something on the stones. I went out to investigate.

Yes, it was earth all right, neatly stacked in a mound perhaps a foot long and half that wide, about four inches high. And sure enough, at the edge of the grass was a perfectly-rounded hole the size of a penny. What creature of that size could have dug a burrow at the edge of the lawn, and why?

Three clues were obvious. First, rather than finely-textured grains of removed earth, the pile consisted of tiny globs. Apparently the digger had used a miniature shovel—or more likely paws or claws or feet—to remove eighth-inch balls of dirt. Second, the removed soil was of two distinct colors, the lower level of the pyramid the brown of topsoil and the upper layer the reddish hue of clay. Obviously the digger had dug beyond topsoil to the subsoil below. Third, down the middle of the mound was a neatly rounded trench exactly the size of the hole, apparently the runway the creature had used to move soil away from the mouth of its burrow.

I called Norma

out to see. She was as flabbergasted as I. Without the benefit of several moments of speculation, she began to throw out possibilities—a gopher? No, way too small. A mouse or other rodent? No, too small for that too, and what mouse or mouse's cousin digs dens in the ground? A snake? No, a small snake might slither down such a tunnel, but so far as we knew, none of our snakes is equipped to dig.

Norma was for researching rodents. I leaned more toward insects, since I knew no rodent that small. We headed inside and turned to the Internet. Googling "burrowing insects," we found half a dozen insects and their respective holes in the earth. One matched exactly what we had found—the *Sphecius speciosus*, the Cicada Killer Wasp!

And now I knew that I had met this fellow creature in a different context. One summer day a few years ago I was working on the lawnmower under the shade of the spreading maple when I heard something pop. I glanced up to see that a large, colorful wasp, well over an inch long, had hit the gravel with a struggling cicada in its grasp. I watched as the wasp plunged its stinger in the cicada's abdomen, and within moments the cicada was still. And then it was the wasp's turn to struggle. It had somehow to get off the ground carrying its victim, which was perhaps twice its size and weight. It wasn't a pretty flight, but eventually they were airborne, off to an undisclosed location.

And now I know where the hairy reddish and black wasp with yellow stripes on its abdomen was taking its prey. Research tells me that what I saw under the maple tree was a female; it is the female cicada killer that digs soil with her jaws, then pushes the dirt behind her with the spines on her legs. She digs one or more nesting chambers off the tunnel, then flies off in search of cicadas. After the kill she stuffs one or more cicadas into the nesting chamber—two cicadas if the egg she is about to lay will be a female, since females are larger and require more food. Once food is provided and her eggs are laid, she closes the cell with earth.

Within two days the egg will hatch and the larva will begin to eat. After two weeks feeding on the cicada, the larva will develop a sheltering cocoon. The creature remains dormant until the earth warms; when spring comes, the pupa will emerge from the cocoon and dig its way to the above ground world to become the next generation cicada killer wasp.

That is, unless it is itself eaten by the larva of a cow killer, a large, furry black and red creature with a powerful sting. Cow killers, also known as velvet ants, are really not ants, but wingless female wasps. The female cow killer lays eggs on the pupae and mature larvae of ground-nesting wasps and bees, including cicada killers. When velvet ant larvae hatch, they feed on their host.

But if the cicada killer survives, have no fear—unless you are a cicada. Big and scary looking though she might be, this solitary wasp will sting humans only if her space is violated. And the males, hovering nearby and sparring with rival males to mate with females, have no stinger at all. Unlike yellow jackets and other aggressive wasps that use their formidable stingers to defend their nests, the cicada killer is only looking to provide breakfast for its offspring.

August 6: Nature's Plan B

Drinking from the spring deep in our woods, I give silent thanks, and I remember how I learned from this perennial spring that nature is not bound by man-made calendars.

The greatest flood in modern history swept down the Missouri River in the summer of 2011. Record rains fell across much of Montana and North Dakota in spring, adding to the much above-average snowpack in the Rocky Mountains. By May, it was clear that trouble was on its way for the Missouri River Valley, all the way to its convergence with the Mississippi River in Missouri. In June, flow from the last dam on the Missouri, Gavins Point above Yankton, SD, by far breeched previous records at 160,000 cubic feet per second, more than doubling the US Army Corps of Engineers' long-standing projection that any future peak flow might reach 79,500 CFS.

The Missouri and Mississippi rivers most dramatically demonstrated that year's extraordinary precipitation and flooding, but excessive spring rains were widespread across much of their drainage basins. On Prairie Bluff, our 2010 precipitation totaled over forty-one inches, thirteen inches above the annual average. It was the second highest rainfall since we arrived, in fact the second highest since records were first kept in Yankton in 1873—even slightly higher than the great flood year of 1881. And significantly, 2010 was the sixteenth consecutive year of moisture exceeding our annual average of twenty-eight inches.

So in May of 2011 the soil was soaked, most ponds were full, creeks and tributary rivers were flooding, and farmers were unable to plant crops across thousands of acres of river bottom and potholed upland. The pond below our house filled almost to the spillway and maintained that level well into fall. For the first time in thirty years on the Bluff, the runoff creek by the garden, which in drier years flows not a drop, ran through summer and autumn and until ice stopped its flow in the dead of winter. Even then a trickle continued under the ice.

But perhaps the most remarkable aspect of that phenomenal year was that while the Missouri raged from May through September and our little intermittent stream seeped until it froze, local rains came to a near halt by late June, the last rain of more than an inch falling on June 26. The drought of 2012 had begun in the midst of the 2011 flood! It was as if a faucet that had gushed for years was suddenly turned off.

Rarely does a weather pattern change so suddenly and dramatically. While rivers flooded and ponds filled, the rest of the world dried in drought—drought that continued for two years until the summer of 2013 when "normal" precipitation returned. For eighteen months a great region of the Plains was under severe drought; by late summer of 2012 southeastern South Dakota had reached the National Weather Service's most extreme category—"exceptional" drought.

Though climate change will likely produce more radical swings in the future, we have always endured cycles of excess precipitation and drought. But here is the part that amazes me: in years of average precipitation, the spring-fed pond in the woods sometimes ceases to overflow in August, and outflow does not resume until cooler temperatures return. The larger of the springs that feed the pond is ever faithful, still producing at least fifteen gallons per minute in the worst of times, but not quite enough to counter losses through seepage and evaporation in hot dry summers. However, during the exceedingly dry August of 2012, after more than a year of drought, the outflow was continuous and strong.

How can that be? Obviously a substantial reserve of ground water was stored in the fifty to 100 feet of soil that overlies the chalkstone bedrock from which our springs emerge, enough water to carry those springs through a year and a half of drought and the severe heat of summer and still run strong, stronger than in some years with twice the rainfall of 2012.

Why is this important? It illustrates nature's capacity to reserve and to disperse in times of need. The pond and its feeding springs live on a different timetable than what happens on the surface and in the atmosphere. The life of the spring is disconnected from the cycle of the seasons, and it is not governed by short-term precipitation. Thus, the spring and the pond it feeds are able to extend life that otherwise might wither, to water plants that might otherwise die and mammals and birds that would have to migrate to other shrinking sources to survive.

June and July rains allowed us to hope that the drought had broken, and that proved to be the case. But we know too much about historic cycles and about climate change to make predictions. And for how long a drought, we wonder, might the stored ground water keep the springs flowing at replenishing rates? That I cannot say, and I hope we don't have to find out. But our neighbor Roy Johnson told us before he died three decades ago that the big spring flowed faithfully throughout the parched 1930s. Like our neighbors, we rejoice that normal rains seem to have returned. But when drought recurs—and it will—we can gather for reprieve at the ever-faithful springs, thankful for nature's Plan B.

August 10: Canoeing the Missouri

It's been a busy summer. Prairie management, gardening, writing and other tasks have left little time for recreation. That's why I was delighted when our friend, Clarence, called last week and invited us to float the Missouri with family and friends. Summer was slipping away and we had only floated the Missouri once!

It wasn't a long or demanding trip; we launched the canoes at Myron Grove in the southwest corner of Clay County and floated to Clay County Park, seven miles of the spectacular fifty-nine-mile stretch of free-flowing National Recreational River between Gavin's Point Dam at Yankton and the beginning of channelization near Ponca, Nebraska. We've done this stretch at least once each summer for as long as I can remember, so the route is familiar. Yet our eyes were open to whatever the river might offer that was new.

The only significant decision was whether to skirt three-mile-long Goat Island on the north or the south. If water had been low, we might have gone south so that those in our party who had not seen her could visit the remains of the *North Alabama*. The skeleton of the 160-foot steamboat still lies where she went down in 1870, her bow embedded in the sandbar that still anchors the cottonwood snag on which she was impaled so long ago. But with the Missouri reservoirs full, the Army Corps of Engineers was releasing lots of water, and the *North Alabama* was safely hidden in her watery grave.

We steered to the South Dakota side of the island.

I was ready to go with the flow, but actually I prefer the South Dakota side. Half way down the island, a growing sandbar funnels water into a narrow and swift channel. Where that opens wider near Goat's foot, a marsh had formed. We guided our craft through a narrow passageway, scattering dragonflies, blue-winged teal and red-winged blackbirds and rousing huge carp and gar from apparent slumber in the shallows. Once past the island, we floated quietly past two large flocks of Canada geese relaxing on sandbars.

But the biggest change from earlier years is that the 2011 flood changed the river in dramatic ways. Deep holes were gauged by the record flow, and dislodged sand was redeposited in great sandbars up to half a mile long. On those new formations, we found debris that had lain in the river bed since before Lewis and Clark poled their way up the river in 1804—ancient buffalo ribs and femurs, the vertebrae of giant fish, skulls and bones we could not identify. Our friend Nancy found the antler of a long-dead elk. New backwaters inside the sandbars provided ideal spawning for many fish, and the long stretches of sand provided nesting habitat for endangered piping plovers and threatened least terns. Fortunately researchers with the Army Corps of Engineers still sign nesting areas off-limits until chicks have hatched and fledged.

After roaming unrestricted sandbars, it was back in the canoes. Canoeing is great exercise, that is if you paddle as if you have someplace to go. But at this flow, the river's current will carry a canoe seven miles in a couple of hours with little exertion required beyond dragging a paddle to rudder the craft. We didn't break a sweat, so there was no particular need for our occasional dips in the water, beyond the sheer pleasure of wading or floating or swimming, or just standing in the cooling current and sipping a cold brew.

Summer would not be complete without excursions down the Missouri. From the water, we could see our distant bluff to the north, where the lawn needed mowing and the corn and beans and tomatoes picking and where thistles still lurked. But work, I've found, will wait, unlike the constant flow of the river. Already it's calling me back.

August 14: Beyond Our Horizon

As much as I love life on the bluff—where I live rather simply in spite of living amongst interactions more complex than I will ever understand—I have sometimes found it necessary to engage other challenges. Yet, I surprised myself a few years ago by running for a seat on the Clay County Commission. Most of the work was routine, studying reports, approving contracts, considering permit applications, paying bills and occasionally mediating disputes. But those are not the things I will remember, and that is not why I ran.

County commissioners in neighboring Union County had approved rezoning several thousand acres of prime farmland for a 400,000 barrel-per-day refinery for Canadian tar sands crude oil—without requiring the basic safeguards of a social and environmental impact study. I was alarmed that decisions of such import could be made without thorough consideration of the consequences. I wanted to ensure that if such a proposal came to our county, at least one commissioner would demand that pertinent questions be addressed.

When I took the oath of office, I uttered the usual promises to uphold the public good, but I also made promises to myself. I would do my best to develop a good working relationship with my colleagues. I would do my homework on every issue, ask every question I thought should be asked, choose carefully any battles that should be fought, and always reserve the right to vote no.

The first issue came soon. A group of land speculators bought 565 acres of land—a mile of undeveloped riparian terrain on the Missouri National Recreational River known as North Alabama Bend for the steamship that went down a few miles upriver—the land we hiked on April 10. The developers approached the commission with a full-blown plan to sell 468 building lots in an area that I knew to be a historic floodplain. To make a long story short, I consulted with river experts and natural resources conservation officials and procured an extensive study of the property, including elevations, old river channels and soil types. It became clear to me—and with this information in hand, to fellow commissioners—that the development should not proceed. Eventually the US Army Corps of Engineers bought the land through a program designed to offset or mitigate environmental damage caused by the Missouri dams. I was able to help facilitate the process, and today the land is open to the public and is protected from development. The wisdom of stopping this scheme was quickly borne out; for the entire summer of 2011, the greatest flood in recorded history inundated the old river channels that bisect the property.

From June through September the Missouri River raged through Clay County at 160,000 cubic feet—or more than a million gallons—per second. All along the river, homeowners were rocking shorelines to prevent erosion. But some landowners went a step further—simply bulldozing truckloads of broken concrete paving, including exposed reinforcement bars and lots of junk, into the river. I complained to the Army Corps of Engineers, whose regulations clearly prohibit the use of such materials. I was assailed by an angry crowd at a commission meeting, simply for asking regulators to ensure that erosion control measures were in compliance with the law. My efforts failed, but once the waters receded, I was surprised and delighted when the National Park superintendent came to a county commission meeting and presented me with a miniature canoe paddle inscribed with the words "River Stewardship Award."

My next challenge was to help modernize the Joint Jurisdictional Ordinance that regulates development on property adjacent to the city limits of Vermillion. The existing ordinance was ill-conceived, seriously out-of-date, and a long-standing source of friction between city and county officials. The issue had smoldered beneath a blanket of ill will for years. Commissioner Dusty Passick and I persuaded fellow commissioners that we should try again. After two years and dozens of meetings with city counterparts, we achieved that goal, and today, county and city officials meet in a friendly atmosphere to work out issues of common concern.

My fourth and last year was devoted to updating the Clay County Zoning Ordinance, including top priorities of protecting the county from inappropriate industrial development and increasing building setbacks from the erodible banks of the Missouri National Recreational River, a unit of the National Park System. Finishing touches were applied just as my term expired.

There were disappointments, of course. For example, I failed to convince fellow commissioners that we should transition the county vehicle fleet to more fuel-efficient models. Each year when the sheriff requested authorization to replace an aging cruiser, I requested a statistical analysis to demonstrate how much fuel—and money—the county could save by buying a mid-sized sedan, rather than Ford's biggest model, the long-time favorite of law enforcement. When Ford finally phased out the Crown Victoria, I saw what I thought might be the opportunity that had eluded me. But I was wrong. Instead of the gas-guzzling Crown Victoria, commissioners authorized purchase of equally thirsty sport utility vehicles.

When I ran for office, I asked the retiring commissioner I hoped to replace what major issues I would face. "Agricultural drainage," he said. He was right. In an era of seven-dollar-per-bushel corn, many farmers sought every opportunity to maximize profit, including plowing grasslands, bulldozing groves of trees and installing drainage tiles to ensure that they could farm seasonal wetlands in rainy years. The results of such actions are well-documented. Wetlands are critical for controlling flooding, recharging aquifers, filtering water and providing habitat to waterfowl and scores of other wildlife species, and much of that is going down the drain. Agricultural drainage is also a major contributor to nitrate pollution of rivers and city water supplies, and to the production of a massive and growing dead zone at the mouth of the Mississippi and other rivers.

In my first year, I did convince fellow commissioners that before we issued a drainage permit we should require a wetland determination from the Natural Resources Conservation Service. This modest step proved unpopular with many farmers, and particularly with the tile drainage industry, both of whom strongly expressed their disapproval of the policy in public meetings. But that revision of the drainage ordinance allowed commissioners to monitor developments, and in some cases impose permit conditions, such as the maintenance of grass filter strips along drainage courses. Yet as my term wound down, it was clear that once I was out of the way, fellow commissioners and my replacement were ready to throw out the entire ordinance, greatly reducing their workload and headaches, but throwing the floodgates open to unregulated drainage. Furthermore, a new push soon emerged to remove all limits on the size of concentrated animal feeding operations (CAFOs), and even to allow CAFOs of unlimited size over the Vermillion and Missouri River aquifers. The proposal drew strong opposition from many citizens, who successfully derailed the worst features before the revised ordinance was adopted in 2017.

No question, my service was a mixed bag. I made lots of friends, and probably alienated as many people. I understand clearly why many elected officials refuse, or more likely simply fail, to take a stand on issues they know are right or wrong. Many hope to be reelected, and others simply find remaining popular much easier than standing up to opposition. When I filed to run for office, I promised myself that I would serve a single term, and that I would never remain silent on issues that in my judgment threatened the natural environment or the public interest. My goal in the public sphere was the same as on our bluff—a sustainable future. In cooperation with good fellow commissioners, we achieved many of the goals that prompted my run, and I retired from my final paying job with few regrets.

August 17: Swallow Symbiosis

I love to watch the swallows that are rearing their young below our second story roof. True, they've made a bit of a mess, first by constructing a nest of mud—delivered from the pond a beakful at a time—on the rough cedar siding six inches below the overhang, then by pooping on the wall and occasionally on the patio and the window glass. Any day now, the fledglings will begin contributing their offal to the mix. But these are minor annoyances compared to the benefits we enjoy from sharing our home with these feathered friends.

Recent rains have produced yet another hatch of mosquitoes. We discourage mosquito reproduction by disposing of old tires or cans or anything else that might hold standing water, but the pond is 400 feet from the house, and we are surrounded by trees and head-high native prairie, so mosquitoes we have. The pesky insects lie low most of the day and most of the night, but at dawn and dusk they swarm in search of blood. That's when we go out to enjoy the morning and evening cool, and when our barn swallows come alive. But even if they weren't performing a function vital to our summer quality of life, simply watching their aerobatics would be recompense enough for any mess they make.

The mosquito, our nemesis, is apparently the fledglings' favorite food. Since I can't see into the swallows' adobe nest, I'm not sure how many offspring the parents have to feed, but at least four mouths gape over the edge, and apparently the young are always hungry. I have no idea how many dozens or scores of insects a growing swallow can eat in a day, but for

an hour in the morning and perhaps two each evening, the adults soar and dart and streak across the front lawn, their widening circle telling me they have effectively eliminated prey close at hand. That means I can safely relax on the patio without myself becoming prey.

The barn swallow, *Hirundo rustica*, is distinguished from its cousins by its blue head, amber breast, rusty red throat and deeply-scissored tail. But the barn swallow is but one of half a dozen swallows that migrate north and nest across the United States each summer. Cliff swallows, bank swallows, rough-winged swallows and tree swallows are also common in our region. Bank swallows create cities of nests carved in exposed banks along the Missouri River. I've seen scores of cliff swallows inhabiting a single overpass on Interstate 90, and last year a pair of tree swallows raised a family in one of our bluebird houses. All swallows enhance the lives of humans by living up to their name, by swallowing as many insects as they can catch.

When summer ends and our swallows fly south to Mexico or beyond, I may be tempted to get out the ladder, pull down their nest and clean up the mess. But I will resist the urge. Autumn rains will clean the wall and the nest will remain, protected by the overhang. The nest will remind me on frigid winter days of a time when mosquitoes were worse than cold, and when visiting swallows served as alarm clock, pest patrol and aerobatic delight. When spring comes and the swallows return, minor repairs will ready their home for another nesting season. I only hope that next summer they will need to work harder to find mosquitoes.

August 24: Living with Irony

I should pitch my tent in the woods, or maybe go live in a cave. Something to reduce my negative impact on the ecosystem of which I am part. But in the woods I'd likely need to kill other animals to eat, and in a cave I'd disturb the bats. It seems that however hard we try, we humans find ourselves a negative force to fellow creatures, a liability in the natural ecosystem.

As I worked at my desk this morning, a sharp thud registered in my consciousness. I vaguely acknowledged that another bird had probably struck a window, but I was engrossed in my work and did not go out to check. Such collisions are not so uncommon, after all, and most of the birds that crash into the house survive. Only later when I went outside did I find the fine long body of a yellow-billed cuckoo, *Coccyzus americanus*, lying dead on the lawn with a broken neck. One of our less common birds had flown smack into a window of our passive solar house. Cuckoos sometimes nest and hunt around the pond in summer, but they tend to be reclusive. In more than three decades I'd never seen a yellow-billed cuckoo alive in our front yard, and now one lay dead at my feet. Presumably, it saw trees reflected in the windows and flew full speed into a death trap of glass.

The human impact on the ecosystem—especially in advanced industrial countries such as ours—derives principally from the mechanical and technological innovations that make our lives comfortable and convenient.

For example, we still power climate-controlled homes, modern transportation and all the high-tech wonders of modern life principally by burning fossil fuels, though we know we are altering our climate and polluting our planet in irreversible ways. Even solar homes require energy and resources to build, and obviously, they too can harm other life.

Our negative impact on fellow animals results in part from our evolved position in the food chain. As omnivores, humans have always eaten other creatures as well as plants to survive. It's such a part of our history that most English translations of Genesis attribute to God the injunction that we are entitled to "dominion" over fellow creatures. Some of us now reject that "God-given right," believing as Native Americans traditionally believed that we are all related—that we have ethical obligations to fellow creatures, even if we choose to eat them. Others of course eschew the very act of eating animals, choosing to nourish their bodies solely with fruits, vegetables, grains and other plants.

As I noted elsewhere, I have not evolved beyond my inherited habits as omnivore. I continue to eat meat with my vegetables. But I do respect fellow creatures, and it pains me when, through carelessness or through some action of mine, another living thing needlessly dies. I remember the birds and mammals I shot as a youthful hunter. I grieve for the birds, mammals and butterflies I've accidentally struck with my car. But the truth is that every lifestyle choice, even building a geo-solar house, has repercussions for other species.

With all the abilities bestowed upon humans by our technological prowess, we lack the power to restore life to a yellow-billed cuckoo. I hold in my hand the body of a beautiful and mysterious bird, but never again will I hear its long descending cackle, nor will it return to its life work of consuming insects and caterpillars. This beautiful bird has fallen victim to my effort to reduce my negative impact on Earth. That's an irony from which I see no escape.

August 29: River Trail Flotilla

We're back on the river again, but this time we are far from alone. Summer is winding down, so *carpe diem*. It's Saturday morning and the Missouri River is dotted with boats. Eighty-seven people from four states and many locales, including a couple with their dogs, Sparky and Emma, have launched kayaks, canoes and other non-motorized crafts at Mulberry Bend south of Vermillion. We will paddle twelve miles to Bolton, also known as Chaney's Landing, west of Elk Point. With this event, the Missouri River Water Trail is officially inaugurated.

The idea of a designated "trail" was in the works for years. But now, through the efforts of the National Park Service, the University of South Dakota's Missouri River Institute, the Living River Group of the Sierra Club and others, the trail is mapped and access points are defined, improved, and signed with information about the history, geology and ecology of each stretch of river. Besides these organizations, river trail sponsors include South Dakota Game, Fish and Parks, Nebraska Game and Parks, Missouri River Futures, the South Dakota Canoe and Kayak Association and the Izaak Walton League. Actually, we are perhaps a few millennia late in designating the trail. People have moved themselves and their goods up, down and across this great river for thousands of years. When Lewis and Clark followed the water trail from St. Louis to its head in the Rocky Mountains in 1804, the river was already a major thoroughfare, not only for many Native tribes, but for Euro-American explorers, trappers and traders.

It is fitting that this float trip begins on the Nebraska shore and ends in South Dakota. The Missouri forms the boundary between the two states for over a hundred miles, including the still-free-flowing thirty-nine-mile stretch from Fort Randall Dam to Running Water and the fifty-nine miles from Gavins Point Dam at Yankton to Ponca State Park. The downstream segment that we float today was designated a National Recreational River and added to the Wild and Scenic Rivers

System in 1978, the upper reach a few years later.

Though the Missouri has been a transportation corridor for thousands of years, perhaps never in history has this stretch of river seen so many boats at one time. The majority are one-person kayaks, but they share the river with two-cockpit kayaks, canoes, foot-peddled kayaks, even a home-built sailboat, crafts of many a shape, color and size. But all are people-powered, aided by current and wind. No motors drown the bird songs this crisp late summer morning; the blue blue sky is punctuated by great blue herons and a bald eagle.

Even after the Corps of Engineers "engineered" the river by damming it most of the way through the Dakotas and straightening and channelizing it for barge traffic from Sioux City to St. Louis, thus shortening it by many miles, the Missouri remains North America's longest river, 2,320 miles. So, after this summer's floats down twenty-five miles or so of river, we'll have other stretches to explore next summer. But today there is little doubt that the eighty-six other people with whom I share the river are grateful that this stretch remains relatively wild. May that remain true for future generations.

SEPTEMBER

September 3: How Not to Fell a Tree

For this task, as with many others, my concentration was narrowly focused on the series of steps involved. It began with the logistics of felling a huge tree, an American elm that in life had dominated the west edge of a several-acre grove. My chain saw has a sixteen-inch bar, and the trunk was more than three feet thick. That meant that even if I judged the drift of the giant tree correctly and began on the down-weight side, then cut all the way around the tree, a core of several inches of wood would remain at center, possibly enough to keep the tree upright.

So I had to begin as an axe-wielding woodcutter would have done, cutting away wedges of wood around the circumference until my chain could slice what remained. But things don't always go as planned. I began the final cut on the north, what I felt sure was the lighter side. I hadn't cut far when the tree shifted my way, and the chain came to an abrupt halt. The bar was pinched between the stump and the many tons of a gigantic elm. I had misjudged the balance of limbs, and gravity was pulling the tree north instead of south.

On a much smaller tree, and if the weight was only slightly shifted the wrong way, or if the wind had been favorable and able to help, I might have succeeded in rocking the trunk enough to free the saw. But with this monster, with its forty-inch trunk and four massive branch trunks that reached above the forest canopy, there was no way. No use even trying.

I headed back to the house for the tractor and all the chains and ropes I own. I threw a heavy rope over the biggest branch on the south side, tied a loop and pulled the noose tight. I stretched the rope its full length south, then attached two lengths of log chain. The rope and chains together stretched a good eighty feet beyond the trunk. Standing at the end of the chain I stretched one arm toward the pinnacle of the dead tree. It appeared that the angle of my arm from the earth was less than forty-five degrees. If I succeeded in pulling the tree my way, I and the tractor should not be struck by the upper limbs when they fell. The necessity of making this field calculation I had learned the hard way long ago, the day I dropped a tree that was supposed to miss a friend's truck, but didn't. But that is another story, one I'm trying to forget.

I hooked the chain around the tractor's drawbar, put the Ford in first gear, and began to pull. The tires quickly dug holes in the soil; the tree shuddered a bit, but stood firm. The saw remained locked in its jaws. Only one thing to do: call for help.

With my friend Clarence to the rescue, I set the tractor on

fresh earth a few feet over and prepared to try again. But this time Clarence had a firm hold on the chain saw, ready to yank it free when and if I could rock the trunk enough to loosen its grip on the saw. This time I popped the clutch for a fraction of a second, disengaged, popped again, disengaged, and gradually set up a rocking motion, the treetop now swaying from south to north to south in a barely perceptible arc. Then as the tree rocked my way I engaged the full power of the little tractor, and Clarence fell away from the tree, saw in hand.

Now I was back where I'd started a few hours earlier. But this time I cut away at the south side of the remaining trunk, and soon the century-old tree crashed to the ground, trunks cracking, limbs splintering, branches flying free, twigs shattering into kindling lengths. Now all I had to do was spend the rest of the day cutting the tree into the sixteen-inch lengths our stove can receive, loading them into the pickup and hauling them to the house. I would stack the burnable sizes in the garage, and pile the chunks thicker than our stove's nine-inch mouth to be split on a cold January day.

September 7: After Apple Picking

In his 1915 poem, "After Apple Picking," Robert Frost describes the troubled dreams of one who has passed a long day on a ladder amidst apple boughs, harvesting a bumper crop of fruit:

> I have had too much
> Of apple-picking: I am overtired
> Of the great harvest I myself desired.

When Norma and I planted an orchard in 1983, we imagined some future day when we would fill buckets and baskets with apples, plums, peaches and cherries. Three times I replanted the Reliance peach trees recommended by Yankton's Gurney nursery before I gave up on my favorite fruit. The first saplings were destroyed by deer, the second by rabbits, the third by drought. The last died a mysterious death. For us, the Reliance proved unreliable.

But the plum, cherry and apple trees survived. Today we have two large kanga plum trees that provide blossoms in spring, shade and bird nesting in summer, and a couple of buckets of juicy, yellow-fleshed plums each July. The meteor cherry is another story. Except for a couple of springs when late frost nipped its buds, this hardy tree has provided all the fresh cherries we could eat, as many as we could stow for winter pies, all we could induce friends to pick and some for the birds.

We planted three apple trees, Harolson, Red Baron and Lodi. Only the Lodi survived the attacks of deer and other calamities, and for the first two decades it bore little fruit. But when the tree reached its twenty-first year and we had long since written it off as another flowering shade tree, it unexpectedly exploded into plenty, and has produced almost every summer since. Already this month we have picked three bushels of large, crisp apples, and we have yet to deploy the ladder. I have not reached the tiredness of Frost's apple picker, but the fruit bin of the freezer is full, we're peddling apples to friends, and best of all, we're enjoying the most delectable deserts of the year.

For a recent potluck dinner, I made apple cockaigne. (Yes, it's pronounced like the evil drug, but it produces only a sugar high.) Cockaigne has been around since thirteenth century France, when it was a favorite cake at country fairs. Its name comes from the medieval mythical land of peace and plenty, a fantasyland of luxury and ease imagined by overworked peasants. It was popularized in America by Marion Rombauer Becker, who explained in the foreword to the 1975 edition of *Joy of Cooking* that she had added the word "cockaigne" to her favorite recipes, the same name she'd given her country home in rural Ohio.

The joy of fruit cockaigne depends in part, of course,

on ample quantities of brown sugar and butter. But more important yet is the fruit—which can be peaches, apples or plums. And cockaigne is at its best when the fruit is freshly picked, cells still dividing and bursting with juice. If I dream of apple picking tonight, I hope the climax is another piece of cake.

September 14: The Monarchs Have Flown

Only a few stragglers remain, prolonging this bittersweet late summer season when weather is perfect, the prairie is in its glory, trees are heavy with apples and leaves are turning gold. On early September nights ten years ago, clusters of monarch butterflies by the hundreds clung to cascading willow leaves around the pond, resting for the next day's flight. A dozen or two might huddle together for warmth on a single twig. By this date most would have sailed south, still 2,000 miles from their winter sanctuary in the pine and oyamel fir trees of the Biosphere Reserve in the mountains northwest of Mexico City.

Every year the number of congregants at our pond grows smaller. This year, even at its peak, the migration was a shadow of a decade ago. What is happening to the monarchs, *Danaus plexippus*, should give us pause. Though their winter sanctuary in Mexico has been reduced by illegal logging, the primary cause for the monarch crisis is the loss of milkweed, upon which their larvae feed during their four-generation journey north and south. Sadly, both their required habitat and food are being destroyed. Fencerows are removed, road ditches are sprayed, prairie is converted to row crops, and agricultural herbicides like glyphosate kill every plant except those engineered to survive its application, for the most part the monoculture crops of soybeans and corn.

According to the Center for Biological Diversity, the Center for Food Safety, the Xerces Society for Invertebrate Conservation and several leading scientists, over the past two decades the North American population of monarchs has declined by ninety percent, a shocking number that suggests the species could disappear. The rapid decline spurred the U.S. Fish and Wildlife Service to consider recognizing the monarch as endangered, triggering protection under the 1973 Endangered Species Act, a designation that would require states to work with the federal government on measures to protect the monarch from extinction. In recent years hundreds of private property owners have responded to the crisis by encouraging milkweed growth, but time is short, and the future of monarchs, both continentally and locally, is far from assured.

A cold-blooded creature, the monarch's body temperature dips with the thermometer. To fly, they must warm themselves to about eighty degrees Fahrenheit. At dawn they turn their black and orange wings toward the sun, solar collectors that transfer heat to their thoraxes and abdomens for flight. If we move quietly, especially once the evening chill falls, we can approach very close to the now rare clumps of fiery gold. But don't fool yourself that you're fooling the monarchs; the eyes that watch your approach are much more complex than ours. Thousands of lenses peer in all directions at once.

If long life is good, monarchs of this generation are the lucky ones. Of the four annual cycles that each pass through four stages of life from egg to larva to chrysalis to adult, this generation, the great-grandchildren of those that left their Mexican mountains in early spring, will live longest. Their nectar-fueled flight will end in and around the monarch colony at El Rosario in November. In February they will emerge from hibernation, mate, reproduce and die, and the four-generation cycle will again begin.

Recently a group of naturalists gathered a few miles down our bluff at Spirit Mound to capture and tag butterflies, part of the ongoing effort to understand the monarch miracle. Some other species of *Lepidoptera* (butterflies and moths) travel long distances, but usually in one direction, seeking food; no other butterfly travels so far. How could these almost weightless creatures fly from the northern Great Plains, the Great Lakes and the northeastern states, across Mexican desert and the high Sierra Madre mountains, to find their winter home in the exact spot their great-grandparents left months ago, sometimes even to the same tree? That marvel has yet to be fully explained, and given the tremendous reduction in monarch population, it is possible we will never fully understand.

The casualty rate of migrants is high. Thousands are smashed on the windshields of cars and trucks, and some fall victim to poisons and other machinations of man. Fortunately for monarchs, birds know better than to eat them; their milkweed diet contains toxins, cardenolides and resinaids, chemicals that makes birds sick. Before I learned that milkweeds are the milk and honey of monarch larvae, I sometimes chopped them down; now I welcome their fleecy seedpods and encourage their spread. But in a world of monoculture, some migrating monarchs simply can't find bed and breakfast—food and a place to rest—in a world that little values biodiversity and habitat for fellow creatures like butterflies.

All too soon, leaves will turn the color of monarchs, though not so bright. The leaves too will migrate, but only down to earth. The long season of barren branches and twigs will come, reason enough to cache memories of monarchs while they are here, images to recall on long winter nights cheered only by the fluttering golden flames of blazing wood. And reason enough to exert the political will to save this magnificent creature from joining the dinosaurs.

September 15: To Bee or Not To Bee

This was a good summer for flowers, for bees and for making honey. By late summer the beehive supers had again grown heavy, so we decided to take a second harvest, though we would leave enough honey to sustain the bees over the long winter months. This time we harvested only four gallons. We were now veterans of the process, so things went more smoothly—except that I was stung again, this time on my left hand. And this time not only my hand, but my arm all the way to the elbow swelled to what looked like the bursting point. I reported this to my oncologist of course, but it was now abundantly clear that I should retire from keeping bees.

Two years after I was diagnosed with chronic lymphocytic leukemia, the disease had progressed to the point that my doctor told me in the spring that it was "time to pull the trigger." Between June and November I underwent intravenous chemotherapy for two days in every twenty-eight-day cycle. I had completed the first treatment the first time I was stung, and the fourth treatment days before the second harvest. It was undeniably clear that my tolerance for bee stings had come to an end. Either the chemotherapy drugs, or the disease itself and the toll it took on my immune system, had changed my body's ability to ward off the minor infusion of poison that a honeybee can deliver. I would have to return Grace's hives when she got home and henceforth keep my distance from bees.

When spring rolled around, a commercial beekeeper inquired about setting up hives on our property. He would bring forty hives and place them between the Severson log house and the barn, and each fall we would be compensated with two gallons of honey. Happy that we would still have all the honey we could use and a little to share with family and friends, we agreed. Busy bees generally ignore humans, so I was pretty sure that the bees that visited our flowerbeds and garden would pose little threat. We would still have the services of pollinators for the garden and the native prairies, and still have the pleasure of watching bees at work. Yet there was a certain sadness in the recognition that no longer were bees and I meant for each other.

Today I stand at a safe distance between cabin and barn

and watch the bees at work. A few feet above my head, a continuous hum accompanies the flow of bees south and north between the hives and an alfalfa field beyond Clay Creek. The farmer's crop is enhanced, the bees have everything they need to sustain themselves, and I am imagining one of Norma's pecan and rhubarb muffins fresh from the oven in January, dripping with honey.

September 16: River Appreciation Day

Today a group of friends—veteran river lovers all—gather at Clay County Park on the Missouri River to celebrate our regional treasure with sixth graders at the annual River Appreciation Day. Sun glistens across the rolling river, cardinals and red-bellied woodpeckers call from the cottonwoods and geese lift noisily off the river and head across the fields to feast on still-standing corn. A yellow school bus pulls up and disgorges the first of several batches of excited scholars, delighted to be at a riverside park instead of in a classroom.

More buses arrive, and soon a hundred students from across Clay County have gathered near the river bank to hear greeting songs from local musicians, Ed, Michelle, Terry, Bruce and Cindy. The standby song for this event of course is "Shenandoah": "Oh Shenandoah, I long to hear you. Away, I'm bound away, 'cross the wide Missouri."

Formerly as a Clay County Commissioner and now as a nature writer, I have been invited for several years to welcome the kids. "How many of you have been to Clay County Park before today?" I ask. Many hands go up. "How many have floated the Missouri in a canoe or other boat?" Fewer hands. "Ever camped in the campground? Hiked the trails through the woods?" Fewer yet. Believe it or not, there are kids and parents who have lived for years in Vermillion or Clay County but have never experienced this great river up close.

I explain to this year's crop of twelve-year-olds some of

the features that make our country's longest river special, and in particular our fifty-nine-mile reach of free-flowing river. Almost 2,000 miles of the Missouri have been either channelized for barge traffic or dammed for flood control, recreation, navigation and power generation, and in South Dakota only ninety-eight miles still resemble the river that Lewis and Clark navigated over two centuries ago. Perhaps best, the six miles of river south of Vermillion between Clay County Park and the Newcastle Bridge remain free from development.

The kids are assigned to trail groups and begin a circuit of eight camps, each of which provides a fun glimpse of river life and ecology. Kids stroke and identify the skins and skulls of beaver, fox, coyote, skunk and other local mammals and learn about their lives. They learn about soil conservation and about the importance of the water cycle, the river and its tributaries and how to keep our water clean. They play a game that teaches them about water safety. They are introduced to kayaks and canoes and build miniature sail boats that will race the river before they go home. They sketch a river scene and write a river poem. Before reboarding the buses they gather around the Oyate Drum group for a song and dance and a Native American perspective on the natural world of which we all are part.

Why is River Appreciation Day important? Because some people stumble through life without recognizing the beauty of our natural world. They fail to comprehend the degree to which we, our fellow creatures and our ecosystem are at peril. If they are oblivious to their places in the natural realm, they may fail to protect and enjoy the biodiversity that remains. If nothing else, I hoped the sixth graders would go home with a sense of joy that the great and historic river that graces their home county still flows free.

And perhaps they go home with the seed of conservation planted, the beginning recognition of a truth so well expressed by Aldo Leopold: "We abuse land because we regard it as a commodity belonging to us. When we see it as a community to which we belong, we may begin to use it with love and respect. There is no other way for the land to survive the impact of mechanized man." Perhaps they leave the river aware that they are part of something worth protecting—and that their inheritance involves responsibility to preserve this relatively undeveloped piece of the Missouri River for the children they haven't even begun to imagine to enjoy.

September 21: My Axis of Evil Burs

On this last day of summer, the tallgrass prairie is in its glory. The meadows we burned in April are heavy with seed, heads dancing in the breeze above my eyes where amber and rust meet horizon blue. Though our prairie culture is far less diverse than that once grazed by bison, of the sixteen species we planted in 2006, most have found their place in a rewoven tapestry of native grasses and forbs. Yet, while investing hundreds of hours encouraging biodiversity, I and my hoe have waged war on an axis of evil burs—sandbur, buffalo bur and cocklebur.

Nobody knows how many grasses and forbs grew along the Missouri River bluff when white settlers arrived about 1860, but in her book *Prairie: A Natural History*, Candace Savage estimates that at least 140 species of grasses and thousands of forbs took root and evolved somewhere on the post-glacial Great Plains. Though diversity has greatly declined, our hillside remnants of unplowed prairie still support many of the natives that once thrived here. For decades, cattle overgrazed the hills, eliminating some species that depend upon seeding for perpetuation, and allowing plants of more abundant foliage—including exotic imported grasses and weeds—to crowd them out. Trees encroached on the slopes, squeezing out plants that require full sun.

Alongside our efforts to replant native prairie, we've also worked to rehabilitate these unplowed scraps, where we have identified more than three dozen native survivors, including big and little bluestem, sideoats grama, Indian grass, switchgrass, needle-and-thread, Canada wild rye, witchgrass, tall dropseed, leadplant, purple coneflower, gayfeather, showy partridge pea, purple and white prairie clovers, yarrow, cornflower, showy and plains milkweeds, cudweed sagewort, heath aster, wavyleaf thistle, stiff sunflower, skeleton plant, goldenrod, hoary puccoon, bracted spiderwort, snow-on-the-mountain, woodland sedge, shell leaf penstemon, wild onion, meadow anemone, wooly verbena, prairie violet, groundplum milkvetch, smooth scouring rush and bittersweet. And yes, buffalo burs, cockleburs and sandburs.

Every plant in the rich native tapestry fills some niche; each of these—as well as many imported and invasive species—is used by humans or other mammals, insects or birds. And each has specialized mechanisms for dispersal; some spread by roots, while the seeds of others are transported to new locations by mammals, birds, water or wind. But few exotic intruders are as well-suited for self-perpetuation as the triumvirate of native insurgents listed above, the burs that top my enemies list—my axis of evil burs—buffalo, cockle and sand. Perhaps these are the "thorns and thistles" with which, according to *Genesis*, God punished Adam and Eve for eating the forbidden fruit of the tree of knowledge. "Cursed is the ground," God allegedly told Adam and Eve when he exiled them from the Garden of Eden. "Thorns and thistles shall it bring forth to thee."

Every surface of the buffalo bur will sting your hand, not just the abundant burs themselves, but the stems and leaves. Only the seedpod of the cocklebur produces pain, but the plant also poisons animals that eat its immature seeds. And the sandbur? Well, let's just say that you haven't lived until you've stepped barefoot on a healthy head. I'd challenge you not to scream.

I have found no uses for these pests, besides clinging to the fur of animals and the pant legs of people. Yet I have no doubt that the handful of natives I don't encourage fit somewhere in the natural scheme; otherwise, they likely would not have survived. Fortunately they are opportunistic invaders; they cease to thrive once native grasses are well established. In the meantime, I spend late summer hours collecting and burning their fruits to restrict their spread. Proponent of natural diversity that I am, these prickly pests test the limits of my creed.

Autumn

September 22: The Season of Letting Go

There's a bright side to every dark cloud. Granted, the bright side is generally above the cloud, and thus not visible to Earth-bound viewers, but it's always there. The last flowers of summer are showing their age, the garden is shutting down for the year, and the hours of daylight have shrunk half the distance from seventeen in June to nine in December. So where's the bright side? The toil of summer is over. No more weeds to chop this year, no more sweat, no more gnawing insects, more hours to read and to socialize with friends, and not least, the ripening breath of autumn to inhale on trails through prairie and woods.

As the calendar turns toward the season of death, a certain sense of foreboding is inescapable. Any day now, and almost surely within a month, a killing frost will descend and all the glory of summer will wilt, fade and fall to the earth, where it will decompose and add a millimeter of richness to the soil. Not that the work is over. Now instead of chopping thistles I will fell dead trees and cut them into firewood. I'll clean out the bird feeders and lay in a supply of sunflower seeds. Soon we'll dig the last potatoes and onions and store them away in the cellar, pick the last of the tomatoes and peppers and put them in the freezer for winter casseroles and soups, and before long, harvest the pumpkins that Norma will bake in pies or we'll carve for Halloween.

Fall on the bluff has its own beauty, perhaps not so dramatic as in regions of aspens or more varied hardwoods, but a subtle palette of yellows, golds and browns, accented by the brilliant reds of sumac and maple leaves and the glossy orange berries of bittersweet. Another bright side is that once the killing frost comes, the leaves will fall and we can once again leave well-worn leaf-littered paths and wander aimlessly across hillsides and down ravines recently hidden by underbrush. It is after the leaves fall and before the snow that one can best explore those hidden places, not only because we can again see more than a few feet before our eyes, but because the insects have died along with the weeds, impediments to navigation are removed and we will now be wearing jackets that armor our arms and bodies from low hanging branches and thorns. It is the season for finding dropped antlers, for examining the lichens of summer-hidden boulders, for locating the bird nests that we knew were there in summer but that no amount of searching would reveal.

In the Northern Plains, autumn can prove as brief as spring, so it must be savored while its glories reign. In part, that means that I should hike the prairies and woods without carrying a lopper or a hoe. When I bring tools I always find use for them, but in this season I can steal a few hours of leisure without feeling negligent. This is a time for gathering last fruits instead of first, for laziness, for loafing in the sun like the slothful grasshopper, for soaking up the last warmth of summer to carry us through the frigid time to come, for wrapping the soul in the peace that this time of transition brings. It is a season of both completion and contemplation, not only of the physical world of which we are part, but of our own being. For those like me in the autumn of their individual lives, it is a time for letting go, for being thankful for the spring and summer we have lived, for the growth, the degree of maturity and the longevity of our personal journeys, and for the calmness to face the next and final season with dignity and hope.

September 23: Heron and Wood Duck Heaven

Many times I heard my grandmother say that equinox would likely be greeted by a storm. Last night brought another good rain in an already bountiful summer. With three months left on the calendar, we have already received most of the rainfall of an average year. Not that it equals the summer of 2011 of course, the first summer in three decades when water ran continuously down the intermittent creek below our house for months on end. The pond was deep then, almost up to the spillway, the fullest it had been in the years since native prairie restoration began to retain most of the water on surrounding hills. The ring of cottonwoods and willows that circled the pond stood waist deep in water that fall, and the pond was full of life. Frogs that might have hibernated in the mud until spring emerged and croaked endlessly on warm fall evenings. Birds that nested in nearby trees and had not yet migrated south feasted on abundant native seeds, insects and frogs.

But this fall, too, has brought a remarkable sight to the pond, the congregation of perhaps fifty of the continent's most colorful waterfowl, *Aix sponsa*, the wood duck. They arrived in early August and still remain. Food has been plentiful, and overhanging willow branches provide ideal roosting places, surrounded by water and safe from predators. The wood ducks' unique whistle is counterpoint to the croak of frogs. I jot a reminder in my notebook that when the ponds freeze in December, I will move one of the wood duck houses from the big pond in the woods back to this pond where it once hung, in hopes that come spring some of the fifty will return and raise their young here, as they do every spring in the woods.

The abundant life that plentiful rain brings is not welcomed by all. When the Vermillion River spreads across the floodplain, county commissioners scrounge for money to repair flooded roads. Some farm fields were too wet to plant in spring, and once late-planted crops were up, wetlands and river bottom flooded again. The Vermillion River, usually docile and low in late summer, has flooded once more.

One recent afternoon, Clarence and I set out on a driving tour of the county's flooded fields and roads. East of Highway 19 and south of the Clay Rural Water wells and treatment plant, we counted sixty great blue herons, *Ardea Herodias*, on a narrow strip of vegetation that protruded from the flooded valley. It is common to see a heron here and there in summer along the rivers and creeks or fishing at the edge of our pond, but neither of us had ever seen a flock this large, concentrated for some common purpose. We stopped to investigate.

The flooded floodplain began at the edge of the road. When we stepped from the car, a dozen long, green leopard frogs leapt for water. With every step we took, the grass exploded with more. The flooded bottom must have hatched millions of frogs. Binoculars brought close the distant grassy strip and its congregation of herons. We couldn't be sure what it was they plucked from the water at their island's edge, but we guessed it was frogs that also laced their strip of heron heaven.

Heaven or Hell? It depends on whom you ask. Many a Clay County farmer was at wits end, preparing to harvest beans and corn, and now another soaker on already soggy fields. Those who recognize the reality of climate change see the fulfillment of scientific prediction; the year was headed toward another global record of heat and precipitation, so perhaps this is the future we face. But frogs and herons and wood ducks and the plethora of mammals from coyotes to voles, oblivious as some humans to how climate change might alter their future, have proliferated. They have fed on plenty, and couldn't be happier.

September 25: Fifteen Flitting Flickers

The northern, or yellow-shafted flicker, *Colaptes auratus*, is among my favorite woodpeckers. They are not common here except during their twice-a-year migration. Otherwise we see the non-snowbird only occasionally at the feeder in winter, and now and then hear their loud, shrill "flick flick flick" call or see them beating and drifting across open spaces in the flight pattern common to woodpeckers—flap flap flap glide, flap flap flap glide, rising on beating wings, resting on graceful downward arcs and flapping up once again. Their colors are subtle, yet dramatic, seven hues in all—rippled gray back, a torso tan with black cravat, yellow under wings, white on the tail and a three-colored head—tan, blue and red.

When a flicker calls, I always search the trees, hoping for at least a glimpse. In spring there will likely be a mate nearby, but more often these solitary visitors make their presence known by their flash of color, their hammering peck or their raucous call. But rarely have I seen an entire flock of flickers, as I did a couple of days ago. Just past the barn, the first flew up from feeding on the ground and flapped toward the pond. A moment later, up came another, then another—an entire tribe of flickers, at least fifteen in all, sheltering, resting and feeding amongst the boxelders, mulberries, hackberries, sumac and plums that line the creek. Such serendipity that I should encounter them here, that they should choose this trickling stream and its surrounding ecosystem for an evening snack, perhaps of ants—a mainstay of their ground-feeding diet— and perhaps a night of rest on their long flight south.

So now I realize that the few flickers I saw last week were trailblazers, the avant-garde who migrated ahead of the flock, perhaps marking the path for others to follow, or perhaps the outliers who will be first to arrive and settle in on winter feeding grounds far to our south, likely in Mexico. Now I watch for them everywhere I go. And sure enough, today the woods near the big spring are also full of flickers, feasting, drinking, resting, enjoying a perfect fall day before the next northern blast carries them on its crest to warmer winter lands.

Should I go with them? But then who would be here to witness tomorrow's gifts? What new delight might go unseen?

September 28: Prairie Rumination

What could be better than strolling amongst the first purple coneflowers, black-eyed susans, Mexican red hats and all the other flowers of a luxuriant native meadow in June? But if spring on the prairie is wondrous and perfumed, late summer is magnificent and awe-inspiring. On a recent Sunday, the Living River Sierra Club invited the public to hike our hills. Thirty people from many walks of life, from a toddler to a retired biologist, wandered and wondered the trails together. We explored the mysteries and identified myriad grasses and forbs that thrive on reestablished and rehabilitated stretches of the Missouri River bluff.

As much as I enjoy sharing this realm with others, I equally enjoy going alone. This afternoon I sprawl in a world ruled by beetles, ants, mice and voles, the bottom of a food chain that includes the red-tailed hawk and the turkey vulture that sail the updrafts in search of food. I lie in a tangle of mixed prairie grasses in their mature glory—big bluestem, Indian grass and switch grass waltzing in the wind above little blue stem and sideoats grama—and contemplate the cosmos. The pitches and tones of the moaning wind are an orchestrated harmony played on grass heads and stems above, but not a breath of breeze touches my face on the floor of this forest of grass. I understand why the Zapotecs, the Maya, and other indigenous peoples of central and southern Mexico saw grasses and other plants as the spiritual link between heaven and Earth. I inhale pure air and exhale body moisture and heat, my breath rising to meet the floating clouds, expiring in the cosmos. Whatever my transgressions, I find atonement in the archaic sense of the word, reconciliation and concord with the universe.

Below my elbows and thighs the prairie roots reach down, both system and symbol. Each June, restored prairie and remnants of unbroken sod reawaken along our bluff, even here and there in pastures of brome where native grasses and forbs somehow survived decades of plowing, overgrazing and chemical warfare. Roots of the same big blue stem and pale purple cone flower that fed bison and elk for centuries resume their above-ground life.

The miracle of survival is simple; the roots are unfathomably deep. By weight, more than two-thirds of many prairie grasses is subterranean; the roots of big bluestem may reach twelve feet down. In the 1930s, Nebraska plant ecologist Frederick Clements excavated a small patch of prairie grass, and from a half-square-yard of earth, extracted 150 miles of root! And modern man thinks his fiber optic filaments complex.

But it would be a rare half-yard of earth that would contain the roots of a single plant. More likely, any place one sprawled in healthy native prairie would be within arm's reach of at least half a dozen grasses and forbs. That, of course, is the sum of thousands of years of post-glacial evolution. "The old prairie lived by the diversity of its plants and animals, all of which were useful because the sum total of their cooperations and competitions achieved continuity," said Aldo Leopold in *A Sand County Almanac*. In the modern world of monoculture, the rich diversity of native prairie fills me with a sense of wholeness like nothing else. Anytime is a good time for a prairie hike—or to cease hiking, sprawl on the earth and surrender one's self to peace.

OCTOBER

October 1: The Ecology of Native Prairie

The Prairie has visitors again. For many years, my former Mount Marty College colleague Jim Sorenson has brought his ecology students to our bluff each fall for a lab on native prairie restoration. But before they visit our prairie, he takes them to what, sadly, is a common "prairie" these days, a forty-acre plot along the Missouri River west of Yankton. That prairie still supports native burr oaks and eastern redcedars and a variety of other trees, grasses, mammals and birds, but is dominated by non-native smooth brome grass.

Most of the students come from cities, small towns or modern row-crop farms, and few have experienced native prairie. Though most are majoring in one of the sciences, typically chemistry or biology as preparation for teaching or for work in medical fields, few are familiar with, or can identify, many native species of prairie life. To come from a meadow of drab brown brome that reaches to their knees to walk a tallgrass prairie where a sea of big bluestem and Indiangrass towers above their heads is an eye opener for some.

I begin the tour with a bit of history—describing the condition of these hills and meadows when we assumed responsibility years ago and showing them an area that has not been revitalized. I also point out that the entire prairie we are entering was grazed to the ground in May, so the six-foot growth they see has occurred in the summer months. We begin our ascent of the bluff, identifying individual species of grasses and forbs as we encounter them. When we reach the crest, they have admired big and little bluestem, switchgrass, Indiangrass, sideoats grama and wild rye, along with shrubs such as smooth sumac and western snowberry and the now-dried flowers of many forbs—purple cone flower, purple and white prairie clover, leadplant, Illinois bundleflower and others. Frost has not yet come, so a few forbs are still in bloom, an occasional black-eyed susan, ox-eye daisy or coreopsis.

In the upland meadow, students assemble homemade one-meter-by-one-meter frames to sample the populations of plant communities. Working in teams of four, they lay the squares on random sites, identify the species present in that square meter, count the individual plants of a particular species, and estimate the percentage of surface each covers. They proceed in a chosen direction two meters and sample again. After five such samples, they are able to draw from the data tentative conclusions about the plant diversity of a particular area, and which species seem dominant there. As we work, a red-tailed hawk and a pair of turkey vultures circle overhead, the former looking for rodents we might dislodge, the latter for something already dead. "Keep moving," I tell the students. "Don't give the buzzards any ideas."

Learning a simple application of scientific inquiry into plant communities is useful for ecology students. But what is perhaps more important is their encounter with a native prairie ecosystem, their amazement at the diversity and vitality of the prairie, and their realization that though they may have lived for two decades in what was nothing but native prairie 150 years ago, for many this was the first opportunity to admire its beauty up close, and to view the distant horizon through its waving heads. Thus they become aware of how much has been lost, perhaps of the importance of preserving the tiny scraps of native grasslands that remain, and of the work required to restore prairie or rehabilitate isolated remnants that have somehow survived abuse, overgrazing and the encroachment of invasive trees, grasses and weeds.

Following the plant population survey and a hike to the far edge of the prairie, we descend from the plateau to woodland and water. In the forest, I point out the diversity of native trees and shrubs—elm, hackberry, mulberry, burr oak, cottonwood, box elder, cedar, choke cherry and dogwood, along with invaders like buckthorn and various weeds. But what a dozen people moving through the woods mostly miss are encounters with the mammals and birds that thrive in the trees and underbrush. Rooted prairie grasses and forbs remain stationary for examination, but mammals and birds hear talk and laughter before we arrive and rush to cover. Also, October is not the best season for viewing birds. Nesting and fledging are long over, some migrating species have already departed, and most winter migrants have not yet arrived. Yet, if we had more time and could wait quietly and watch intently, we would find evidence in the prairie and woods of mice, voles, squirrels, raccoons, possums, skunks, foxes, coyotes, badgers, deer, and easily a dozen birds.

In spite of the advance warning we telegraph, we do spot one red squirrel, and while gazing across the pond we first hear and then witness a rare encounter, a falcon, probably a merlin, in hot pursuit of a northern flicker. The squawk that draws our attention is from the flicker as the falcon strikes, the only time I have heard such a scream of alarm from a flicker. Through a series of dodges and maneuvers, the woodpecker manages to evade the pursuer and escape to the safety of cedars and oaks. The disappointed merlin glides away to seek other prey. Perhaps this flicker is one who will not fly farther south this fall. Perhaps we will meet again, if he avoids the talons of merlins, prairie falcons and sharp-shinned hawks.

I look forward each fall to the opportunity to share our prairie and woods with another group of young people, and I think they enjoy it too, if for no other reason than to escape the confines of the classroom for a couple of hours. Perhaps some will long remember not only the experience, but also the names of grasses and forbs and trees. And perhaps in a few, a spark of recognition may be ignited. Perhaps they will never again view grasslands quite the same as before, and the innate human need for wildness and diversity will manifest itself. Perhaps they will have taken a step on the essential path of conservation, preservation and renewal that is necessary to the sustainability of our planet, and in particular of our homeland, the Great Plains.

October 6: Prairie Fire

I wrote on April 22, Earth Day, about replanting prairie where an unplanned fire had ravaged a steep bluff hillside the previous October. It happened on this date, and this is how

it unfolded. We had just sat down for lunch when the phone rang. "Did you know your woods are on fire?" our neighbor Terry asked.

"What? Our woods are on fire? Where exactly? We'll be right there!" Norma hung up the phone. We left our food untouched, pulled on boots and jackets and rushed outside. The moment I opened the door I heard the sirens. The firefighters were on their way. Above the tree line the sky billowed with smoke. We ran to the bike barn, pulled out our three fire-fighting flappers, my backpack sprayer and leather gloves. We filled the sprayer and a couple of extra jugs with water, threw everything in the pickup, and tore out the driveway and down Frog Creek Road.

At the Bluff Road intersection we saw the flames. We parked at the Severson log house, grabbed our gear and ran toward the blaze. Driven by a brisk north wind, the fire had already raced down the hill and was eating ravenously at the tall, dry prairie grasses. One fire truck was working the east end of the inferno, another was just arriving at the western front. Wailing sirens told us that more were on their way.

There was no question how the fire had begun. For two days, a crew from Missouri had been clearing the right-of-way of a petroleum pipeline that crosses our land, a pipeline that moves gasoline and diesel from San Antonio to Yankton and east to Iowa. The fall grasses were as dry as they would ever get, so it seemed a strange time, after forty years of neglect, to send heavy machinery to do such a job. I had watched carefully as they worked their way across our land, particularly where they crossed Boulder Creek and made their way up a steep hill between a pair of beautifully mature burr oaks. I had made it abundantly clear that these trees were not to be harmed.

Perhaps the contractor had submitted the lowest bid. Suffice it to say that the company's investment in equipment was minimal. The giant machine that inched its way up the hill, chewing up cedar trees and underbrush in its path, clattered and stuttered and belched black smoke. It had seen better days. At the prairie edge, the machine caught fire from a diesel leak, we later learned, and in moments the grasses were ablaze.

Norma, Terry and I took our places on the unmanned northern flank, upwind from the blaze but where the fire ate into the wind and the head-high grass. Working against withering heat with our minimal hand tools and spray from my backpack tank, we were able to slow the spread, but no way would we put out the flames. But within minutes, units from four fire departments had arrived—Vermillion, Yankton, Gayville and Wakonda. A crew of more than a dozen volunteer firefighters—those from Vermillion having been pulled away from the festivities of the Dakota Days parade—fought the fire valiantly. Trucks now raced up the hill to attack the line we'd been laboring to hold. With well-equipped fighters and proper equipment now working every front, I left the line and began crawling through brush where the trucks could not go, spraying water on fire that was creeping through leaves and accumulated debris on the forest floor.

Two hours later the fire was extinguished, though old brush piles and fallen trees continued to smolder or burn. Firefighters gathered on the blackened hillside, where we thanked them profusely for their help, and they washed and packed their gear and prepared to go home. Norma and I remained for a couple more hours, walking the perimeter and mopping up smoking spots. Before we headed back home to wash up and eat a belated lunch, we climbed the bluff once more to examine the smoking remains of the machine that had started the blaze. It was now a hulking ruin, its giant tires burned to the rims, pools of melted rubber and burned fuel and oil seeping into the ground.

The immediate damage was evident, some fifteen acres of prairie and woods burned at the worst possible time, with winter coming on. Winter wildlife habitat was destroyed, a steep hillside was laid bare to potential erosion, and brome and weeds would have the perfect environment to thrive come spring. The next day I made a closer survey and found that the blaze had also killed at least fifty hardwood trees, most of them green ash, but also including mulberry, hackberry and elm. Cedar trees too numerous to count were also casualties of the blaze, though for them I did not mourn. However, I would have to hire the removal of the corpses before we could begin prairie restoration on the devastated hill.

I gathered information about fire department expenses and the costs to remove burned trees and to restore prairie and woods, and submitted a damage claim, which the company promptly paid, probably happy that they would escape without a lawsuit. And thus would begin two years of work before the health of this piece of the Prairie Bluff Conservation Easement could be restored.

October 13: Ready for Winter?

It is Columbus Day in some states, Native American Day in South Dakota. The first flurries are in the air. Am I ready for this? I've removed the tomato cages and uprooted the garden plants so decomposition can begin. I've drained the garden hoses and put them away. I've cleaned the chimney and cut some firewood, though surely not enough.

Enchanting as it is, snow induces uneasiness about what lies ahead—and about how much we have yet to do. The first snow also brings to mind the cycle of human life, in my case now positioned in an unknown part of autumn. But am I ready for physical winter? The real answer is yes. I don't exactly look forward to cold and snow and the season of death, but I intend to enjoy it with bundled-up hikes and cross-country skiing across the prairies and through the woods. And those fall details left undone—I'll get to them next week. I will face the coming season with confidence, partly because I finally followed my father's advice.

Not about how to live one's life, or how to prepare for its ultimate end, but how to be sure my tractor starts when the big snows come. Years ago he told me I should convert the electrical system of my now fifty-eight-year-old Ford from six volts to twelve. I was always too busy to get it done, but the real reason is that compared to my father and brothers, I'm mechanically challenged. I wasn't sure I was up to the task. So for decades I limped along, hoping the old beast would start when I awoke to a blizzard, the crankcase and its contents were below zero, and the 500-foot driveway had to be cleared. Usually it did start, groaning and straining and coughing before finally catching fire. But sometimes it didn't, and that meant driving the pickup down the hill to the barn, jump-starting the tractor, then hoping I could get the pickup back up the hill. It was time for more certainty in life.

I went to the local farm store for a twelve-volt battery, found a Delco-Remy alternator salvaged from a 1982 Chevy pickup, bought strap iron from the local welding shop and set about building new mounting brackets to eventually bolt the new charging apparatus in place. Then came the hard part—wiring the new system so it would function. I called both of my brothers, Jim and Paul, and even a technician at Delco-Remy, and eventually I got the wiring figured out. Imagine my delight—and surprise—when it worked!

Now the old Ford fires up so fast that the mice that build nests above the radiator have little warning to leap for life. The ignition is hotter too, so the engine runs better than it has for years. So let it snow! I am ready. Maybe not mentally for either of the coming winters, and certainly I share the trepidation of my neighbors. But I am more confident than ever that I'm prepared for the most dreaded task of winter, moving snow. Now I'd better tune up the chainsaw, because if you can believe the lore about the wooly caterpillar, we'll need lots more wood. It is said that the fierceness of winter can be predicted by the width of the wooly caterpillar's fuzzy black stripe. As always, the stripe is wide.

October 19: Stones, an Eagle and Red-tailed Hawks

Laying stones is solitary work. Whether you're building a wall or a walk, it's one stone at a time. Eye the pile, choose one rock for color and possible fit, try every angle, then more than likely put it back and choose another. Stones have no odor, and nothing is more silent than stone, but sight and touch are fully engaged. That was my task this afternoon: in this case building a pathway of basalt to the upper room, the space above the dug-into-the-hill garage that is accessible only from up the hill. On hands and knees, I concentrated myopically on the task at hand, oblivious to everything overhead—until the air was pierced by the scream of a red-tailed hawk, *Buteo jamaicensis*.

Any birdcall is a signal to stop whatever I'm doing, take a break and scan the trees and sky, even if it's a robin, a dove or another common companion. But of all our birds, the red-tail's cry is perhaps most dramatic, splitting the air like a steam locomotive's shriek. True, blue jays are capable of a fair imitation; they've fooled me more than once. But this cry came from high in the firmament. I had no doubt what I'd heard. It didn't take long to spot the hawk circling directly overhead.

I set my tools aside and sprawled on my back in the grass for a better point of view, a perspective that would not strain my neck. Now I saw that there were actually two hawks, a pair gliding together on the updraft above the bluff. Round and round they sailed, drifting up the bluff on the wind. Focused intently as I was on the pair, I didn't see the eagle until he entered the red-tails' arc.

The bald eagle was engaged in the same activity as the smaller birds of prey, riding the updraft in search of dinner. But then I realized that the eagle had something else in mind. Each revolution brought him closer to the hawks. His circle was wider, but his flight was faster and he was closing in. Presumably the eagle saw the smaller raptors as competitors for whatever rodents or rabbits might be flushed, and he was the biggest bird on the block.

Yet with greater size and speed comes diminished agility. The four-foot wingspan of the red-tails enabled them to easily evade the advancing eagle, which though not fully mature, had a wingspan a third wider than that of the hawks. The buteos didn't seem especially concerned about the larger bird, but neither were they eager for a confrontation with the ruler of our skies. Gradually the eagle pushed them with the wind, and up the bluff they drifted, leaving behind any unlucky mammals the eagle-eyed monarch of the sky might spy.

October 21: Skull and Bones Society

Some people consider me weird, or perhaps morbid. Perhaps I am a society of one—unless you consider the many creatures, both living and dead, that share my world. It is true that our house and yard are full of skulls and bones, but to me they are more than curiosities. They are the remains of many a beautiful creature from whom the spirit has flown. Or has it?

Norma long ago drew the line at displaying skulls and bones in the living room. But animal effigies are permitted, and in fact, Norma and various artists and friends have contributed to a collection that rivals Noah's ark, though none of our animals requires food or the cleaning of stalls. A mobile of nine tropical African birds that daughter Laura gave us hangs in the window. Two other windows feature an owl and a bluebird in the process of flying through the glass, their front and back halves held together by magnetic attraction. A carved wooden jaguar from the Mexican state of Guerrero shares a wall with a beaded jaguar from Sinaloa, a mythical bird from the Yucatan and a bouquet of feathers dropped by many real birds. There's even a human skull, actually a Mayan depiction thereof, made of clay, an amazing piece that contains three faces, three phases of life in one. A cabinet top is guarded by a black bear carved by a retired Lutheran pastor.

What to some might be a China cabinet is instead decorated, or cluttered, by a range of fauna, created in a variety of artistic modes: a coyote carved on the surface of an emu egg; an ironwood duck; turtles of clay, pipestone and onyx; a stone-carved menagerie from a Zimbabwean friend that includes two rhinoceroses, a family of hippopotamuses, and two lizards. A wooden camel my parents brought from Israel shares space with the exoskeletons of scores of creatures from two oceans and many seas. Like all other available horizontal surfaces, the piano has its own menagerie, a steel hummingbird, colorful lizards from the tiny Oaxacan village of Arrazola and ceramic frogs from Panama and the Mexican state of Quintana Roo.

Though the remains of actual fellow creatures are banned from the living room, we long ago reached an informal truce that permits such riches in the sunroom. On that wall hang the skull of a cow, from whose horn is suspended a colorful molded parrot we bought in Puerto Vallarta. On one side of the cow is the well-worn skull of a prehistoric bison, long ago dug from the bed of the Missouri River when water was low, and on the other side an antlered deer. Above this trio, a Texas longhorn skull and its massive polished horns span five feet of wall. Amidst flowers and plants on shelves and tables rest the antlers of three buck deer, the femur of a great bison bull and the tailbone of another ancient bison, long buried in the depths of the Missouri but dredged to the surface and deposited on a sandbar by the great flood of 2011. There are numerous smaller bones, a raccoon skull, a cow vertebrae, the shells of many creatures from the sea, bison teeth, a cow horn converted to an Alpine bugle that I bought in Switzerland in 1969 while on a weekend pass from the Army in Germany, and the bone of a sea turtle's fin that washed up on the beach in San Agustinillo, Mexico. Even a cicada's discarded hull and two scraps of bones from dinosaurs that once roamed the edge of the inland sea near what is now Lemmon, South Dakota.

Lest some might suspect foul play, I hasten to add that no animals were harmed in the process, or should I say obsession, of collecting these artifacts of the former lives of fellow creatures. Each bone or fragment represents the remains of a lived life, one which I imagine was in its own way happy and fulfilled. I can only hope that, if any consciousness still adheres to these bones, their owners will understand that I display them in daily view because their beauty fulfills me, because I respect the lives they lived and because they remind me that I am simply an insignificant part of the ecosystem they shared.

But the bones and skulls of fellow creatures are not alone in the sunroom, and here Norma and others are complicit. The bones are accompanied by many an effigy of yet other animals in many mediums besides bone: a cast iron lizard, a clay pig shaped by Norma's own hands, a collection of Mexican creatures made from seeds and shells—a turkey, an armadillo and several species of turtle. There's a plaster frog, a coiled snake carved from a root that grew in the village of Boquillas on the Mexican side of the Rio Grande, and ceramic planters resembling burros and frogs. Even a pellet regurgitated by a great horned owl, a tight bundle of everything the bird could not digest, principally the hair and tiny bones of mice or voles.

And that is just the beginning. Step outside, and the collection sprawls across the yard, hangs from trees, even graces the doors of barns. Here the rougher items reside, other skulls, femurs and pelvic bones, ribs, antlers and vertebrae. A few non-natives share the yard, including the armadillo shell I picked up in my native Cimarron River country in Oklahoma. Some creatures lived and died in the waters of the Missouri, a few in other places our rambles have taken us. Most died in our prairies and woods, including two old Shetland ponies that our kids rode when they were young. There's the still-furred head of a coyote, all that was left of an animal apparently consumed on the spot where he fell. What besides a cougar, I wondered, might have taken our usually top predator down? In spite of the variety, many of the creatures that share our bluff are not represented. Partly that is because the skulls and bones of the smallest creatures are not readily found and are quickly consumed or otherwise returned to earth.

But in all the years of roaming, of admiring and occasionally picking up a skull or a bone, I was not prepared for last Sunday's find. Norma, Clarence and I were out for a typical goalless ramble across the native prairie bluff when we spied in the trail a collection of bones—a well chewed spine and ribs, bits of flesh and sinew still red as in life. What might it be? Each offered speculation, but our musings merged in the notion that we had found the skeleton of a small deer, a fawn. Yet logic quickly called that hypothesis into question. It was late October, half a year past the birthing time of deer, and this animal had recently died. What else could it be?

Then Clarence glanced down the trail, and there laid the

skull. A large skull, perhaps five inches long and three inches wide. But the prominent feature was the teeth. Two pairs of long, orange incisors dominated the visage. It could be only one thing, *Castor Canadensis*, an American beaver. The beaver's front teeth, we knew, are like sharpened chisels, harder than bone, ever growing to replenish what is worn away by the task of gnawing wood. The upper teeth in this skull were more than an inch long, the lower teeth a good inch and a half. But we were seeing but the tips of the teethbergs. The beaver's teeth are actually several times that long, firmly planted in the strongest and heaviest bone of the skull, from which in life they perpetually grow. And the orange color? The pigmented enamel of their teeth contains iron.

It was certainly the remains of a beaver we had found, but why here on this dry prairie bluff? For answer we had only to look south. Half a mile across the valley flows Clay Creek, or Clay Creek Ditch as some have called it since farmers straightened, dredged and diked it to drain their fields more than a century ago. But nobody told the beaver that Clay is no longer a creek, or if they did, the beaver paid no heed. They continue to inhabit the creek, much to the chagrin of farmers, since the dams they build impede the flow of their drainage ditch.

I had seen beavers in the creek, but I had never seen a live beaver on our land above the valley, nor any evidence that one had visited. It seemed unlikely, then, that this unfortunate fellow came to visit of his own accord. It was more likely that a coyote caught him away from his den along the creek and brought him to this protected southern slope for dinner. In any case, my collection of skulls and bones has increased by one more, another species to admire and study, another fellow creature whose spirit I wish to make part of my own.

October 24: Reflections in a Spider's Eye

Some things I've learned in unanticipated ways. Partly that's because for everything I know, there is a universe of things I do not know. It's also because of the limitations that ignorance places on my fields of inquiry. It's hard to be curious about something to which you are oblivious. Take spiders, for instance. I have never been a fan of spiders. As a boy tasked with repainting the soffit of our family home, I did reach accommodation with the dozens of daddy long legs that lived there. At that time, and for most of my life, I erroneously believed that daddy long legs are spiders; instead they are *Opiliones*, an order of arachnids commonly known as harvestmen. In any case, instead of killing them or encasing them in paint, I lightly brushed them off, leaving them dispossessed of home but with the opportunity to continue their lives elsewhere. Strange as longlegs are, I recognized them as non-threatening fellow creatures with a right to life.

Like rats, snakes and skunks, spiders in general have a bad reputation. It's not deserved, of course, but discrimination is sometimes triggered by generalized prejudice rather than by true distinctions between the qualities of an individual or a species. We sometimes lash out at whole classes of people or animals or insects based upon imagined threats or the capacities of a few. See a spider in the corner, smash him before he has a chance to hustle away or before you have a chance to think about how many flies and box elder bugs he might consume. If we stopped to think, we might just scoop him up and carry him outside.

For whatever reasons, like many fellow humans I had failed to make a close study of arachnids. I have encountered numerous tarantulas on hikes in arid southwestern states, and scary though they appear, I have convinced myself that they will do me no harm. I think I would recognize a black widow if I saw one, based on pictures I've seen of the red hourglass on its glossy abdomen, and perhaps a brown recluse, the fiddle back, by the image of a violin on its head. But in a thoughtless moment, any black or brown spider might be suspect. I admit that I have killed my share of spiders I find sharing my home, and especially living under my bed, on the grounds that I'm not sure which ones might enjoy crawling under the covers and perhaps tasting my flesh.

For those that reside out of doors, I easily embrace the principle of live and let live, but that doesn't mean we must be best friends. That is a long-winded explanation of why I have failed to familiarize myself with arachnids, as I have with mammals and birds. So it was largely a matter of chance, and thanks to a gift bestowed by a friend, that I discovered a marvelous aspect of at least certain spiders that share the bluff.

Last night brought a crisp fall evening, one that tells us that frost is falling fast. There was time for a starlit walk before bed. I slipped on a jacket and donned a cap Clarence had given me, a cap that looked rather ordinary, but which actually had imbedded at the outer rim of the bill a tiny LED, a light emitting diode.

I was walking up the path from pond to barn, my headlight casting a narrow beam aligned with the bill of my cap, which is to say directly in front of my eyes, when I noticed a sparkling crystal in the grass beside the trail fifty feet ahead. What could it be? Surely not a diamond, though its glitter was certainly as vivid. Perhaps a shard of glass? Keeping my head properly positioned to maintain contact, I advanced toward the brilliant spark. I approached the shimmering object, eventually on hands and knees, my eyes inches from the glint that had drawn me. And what should I find, but a spider's eyes! The spider returned an unblinking stare. For a long moment neither of us moved, but we had connected. I wondered whether my new friend was as curious and surprised as I, whether the spider surmised that he had encountered a new sub-species, a human with a blazing Cyclops eye. At last he flinched, or perhaps grew tired of the spotlight, and employing all the speed his eight legs could muster, rustled off into the grass.

So what do I do with this piece of information, this reflected insight into another facet of my natural world? Perhaps nothing of external value. I recognize that I had lived a lifetime of natural interactions without discovering this phenomenon as it relates to spiders simply because all the other flashlights I have carried have been wielded at arm's length from my eyes. Apparently the necessary geometry is a perfect 180 degrees reflected from a spider's eye to mine. Though for decades I had marveled at the reflective eyes of cats, coyotes, raccoons, deer and other mammals, I had not pursued the question to its answer: The eyes of many nocturnal mammals reflect light because of a layer of tissue behind the retina called *tapetum lucidem*, tissue that increases the light available to the photoreceptors, thus enabling the animal to see better in what we consider dark.

But now I can add certain spiders to the list. Unfortunately, at the moment I was so stunned by my "discovery" that I paid insufficient attention to the particular spider I had met to confirm his identity. Later research suggests it was probably a wolf spider, *Hogna lenta*. Of the estimated 4,000 species of spiders in the United States, many are nocturnal. A few families, like the night roaming mammals mentioned above, have eyes equipped with *tapetum lucidem* to enhance available light, enabling them to find their prey and escape their predators in the dark. The wolf spider actually has eight eyes, and is so equipped.

Another natural marvel revealed. But as with the acquisition of any new insight, I am prompted to wonder what else I have missed, what other pieces of the puzzling tattered fabric of which I am part I have yet to discover. Sadly, the vast majority of these vital scraps will likely remain unassembled when I go to my grave. But one thing is clear; discovery requires a proper point of view.

October 26: The Season of Death

The Grim Reaper is stalking us once more. The farmers have reaped most of their corn and beans, so even the fields seem void of life. We've flirted with frost for most of October, though the killing freeze has been held at bay. Until today. This morning the bluff is glazed with ice. Not the kind that falls from above, but the sort that creeps up from the earth as warmth and accumulated moisture from the passing season meet frigid air from the north. The result is astoundingly beautiful: millions of miniature crystals coating every exposed surface from blades of grass to rooftops and still-clinging leaves.

Despite its beauty, the effect is deadly. Except for bluegrass and brome and other cool season grasses that are able to withstand temperatures below thirty-two degrees, the grasses and forbs are dormant or dead. The garden is finished, and the only homegrown food we'll eat for months besides the cilantro that grows in the sunroom is stowed in freezer bags or jars or cached in the cellar. A few petunias and blanket flowers and a rose protected by our south overhang still bravely bloom, but all other flowers are finished. Sweet aromas have given way to musty wilt and decay. For the next six months, hopes and illusions of revival are futile.

Yet the sun has risen warm, and its reach through south-facing windows is strong and long; this afternoon we'll be toasting in t-shirts and socks without fossil fuels or wood. And there are other trade-offs and benefits to enjoy. Yes, I'll be cutting and splitting firewood, but no more weeds to chop. I may soon be shoveling snow, but I won't mow the lawn until May. The house may need touch-up stain, but I can't do that until spring. There's less daylight to enjoy, but when winter sets in for good, more time to sit by the fire with friends or a good book. Maybe I'll even get more sleep. Songbirds that depend on insects and nectar have flown south, but they are replaced at the feeder by a diverse assembly of winter birds.

And there are less tangible things. Autumn and winter are

seasons for reflection and appreciation. Our country long ago set a special day in November to be thankful for friendship and bounty, though I hope that every day, even in my darkest day, I will remember to be thankful for all that is good. On cold winter days we may long for blossoms and for the fresh cherries and apples they bring, but we can heat the oven and bake a pie from frozen fruit without overheating the house. The colder the night, the clearer the sky and its million stars, and the more distinct the coyotes' howls. I too prowl the woods more silently on decaying leaves, and through the opened canopy I gaze on distant hills.

In this season, the daily loss of light accelerates, moving inexorably toward the longest night. With winter solstice less than two months away, can we hold our breaths until the faithful Earth resumes her tilt back toward the sun? Hope does spring eternal in the human breast as poet Alexander Pope reminds us, and the coming winter will give us ample time and good reasons to cultivate our capacities for hope. The opposite of hope is despair, and there may be nights in the long winter ahead when we must fight its grip. But let us keep our eyes on the crystalline frost below our feet and the constellations overhead. Despair is a state of mind, as is hope, as is the capacity to enjoy the beauty and promises that each moment brings.

October 28: Outwitting Coons

We are not the only species that prepares for winter. Among the luckiest are those equipped with wings to carry them south. The rest of us, earthbound creatures, prepare as best we can in our own ways for the dark, cold days ahead. Squirrels find hollow trees with squirrel-sized openings, or they insulate nests high in the cottonwoods with extra layers of frost-browned leaves and cattail down. Coyotes refurbish grassy mattresses in their hillside dens. Mice cushion shallow burrows in native prairie with milkweed fleece. Raccoons make similar plans, reclaiming hollow trunks where they were born, or if the family has grown too large, another trunk or log safe from larger predators but near sources of water and food. Few mammals are as adaptable or inventive as raccoons; any protection from the elements will do. For many years that included winter refuge in the attic of the 1869 Severson log house.

When we purchased more bluff land two decades ago, we also inherited responsibility for the historic house. The prevailing odor in the house testified to residence by generations of coons who had made the attic their home. Lift the attic door even today, and the musty stench of their long-dried feces assaults the nose. In the decades of neglect before we acquired the house, the basement door blew away and the west foundation collapsed, providing easy entry to a quartzite fortress. But far more secure was the attic, where coons gained entry by climbing the log walls to the roof, maneuvering fat bodies down the brick chimney to an upstairs room, crawling through the stovepipe hole and scrambling up to the open attic door. This I know from the deep claw scratches in the chimney plaster.

I have not ventured into the attic to clean out the generations of dung and other debris, but I did take measures to keep the raccoons out. By replacing rotten logs, I blocked gaping holes. Our son, Walter, and I rebuilt the basement wall and installed a new cellar door. I fashioned a sheet metal chimney cap. I assumed the coons would go back to the woods and settle for a comfy hollow tree or log. I was wrong.

In the first fall and winter, the persistent beasts dug a hole through the cedar shingles of the roof. They were foiled by the decking beneath, so they set over a few feet and tried again. When I discovered the damage, I dragged tools and a handful of shingles up the ladder and patched the roof. The next fall they returned and tried another spot, which I dutifully repaired, and then another. But the routine was getting old, so I tried another tack.

In the back of our refrigerator was a large bottle of a substance left behind by a well-meaning friend. The label called the murky liquid Kick Ass Hot Sauce. In large red letters that I interpreted as fair warning, the manufacturer promised that this was "the most fiery sauce on the planet." In a careful test I had confirmed that a single drop would make my eyes water. By extension, I figured a teaspoonful would be a lethal dose, so at the back of the fridge it had remained.

On my latest venture to the roof, I had the Kick Ass in tow. After making repairs I spread the toxic concoction across the roof as far as the quantity would reach. I climbed down with a sadistic chuckle, wondering how many nighttime hours I'd have to watch to spy an unwary coon take a sniff and likely a lick and come tumbling off the roof, gasping for water and air. But that night it rained. Not an ordinary fall mist or even a shower, but a downpour. By morning the Kick Ass was dispersed in the soil around the cabin. Whatever coon-deterrent powers it might have possessed were gone, leaving only the question of whether it would kill the grass.

And so it went. Each fall for longer than I care to admit, another failed attempt to break and enter was followed by another climb to repair the roof. I took to implanting sheet metal under the shingles in favored spots, but again this week a new hole appeared. As among humans, traditions apparently die hard in the community of coons. The current population must still harbor tales passed down through generations of ancestors about cozy nights in the spacious attic, protected from coyotes, snow and wind. For me, the long-standing custom of battling coons had become yet another ritual of autumn. Until today.

I was in the barn winterizing a lawn mower when my eye fell on a long unused solar-powered fence charger, a relic of Shetland pony days. For the first time, my feeble brain registered an obvious connection. If a mild shock could turn a pony, why not a raccoon? I dragged the charger out, dusted it off and set it where the sun's rays could strike the small photovoltaic panel. After an hour or so I touched the live and ground terminals, and sure enough, it still delivered a mild shock. I gathered a roll of light-gauge fence wire, dragged scraps of half-inch plastic pipe from my junk pile, cut them into twelve-inch lengths and notched a groove in the end of each. I headed for the log house with my assortment of junk in tow.

An hour later, I had screwed the plastic pipe insulators to the corners of the house, stretched the wire around the perimeter, set up the charger and turned it on. As when I had applied the Kick Ass to the roof, I considered sitting in the dark that night waiting for my unsuspecting raccoon friends to show up, nose the wire to see what was new and leap away from the wall, never to return. But the night would be cold, so I gathered my tools and headed home. I would satisfy my wicked impulse by imagining the encounter from my bed, the covers tucked warmly under my chin.

October 30: Blue-Tongued Deer

Last summer and fall were tough on our white-tailed deer, *Odocoileus virginianus*. An epidemic of epizootic hemorrhagic disease (EHD) was the apparent killer of hundreds of white-tailed deer across the region, and at least four on our land. Likely there were other victims we did not find. The first of the deer I suspect died of the disease I found south of the big pond September 8, a big buck that looked perfectly healthy—except that he was dead and his tongue lolled from his mouth. I have more than once found dead deer with arrow or rifle wounds during and after hunting season, and winter sometimes takes its toll on the old and infirm, but it is unusual to find a dead white-tail in early fall, when food is plentiful and deer are in their prime. I had heard about the spread of EHD, so I called the local game officer to report. He said that if the animal had been dead twenty-four hours it would be too late to sample tissues to determine the cause of death.

Research told me that deer are infected with EHD (similar to so-called "blue tongue" but slightly different) by an organism transmitted when the deer is bitten by a midge, a small gnat-like insect. The deer face death from internal bleeding and from a swollen tongue, which makes it impossible for them to drink all the water they need. The bodies are likely to be found near water. I mourned the loss of a magnificent buck, but also determined to follow this phenomenon in various ways. First, I fastened our motion-sensing camera to a nearby plum bush to see what the carcass might attract. Each of the next four nights, a lone coyote came to dine. By day he was replaced by a squad of turkey vultures.

The second carcass I found first with my nose, also dead near Boulder Creek south of the pond. Not until this doe was half eaten and decomposed did I find her with my eyes. It was far too late to determine the cause of death, but her location near water suggested she too had fallen to EHD.

Number three was the strangest case of all. Norma and

I were taking in the view from our observation tower when I saw through the brush a spot of white. Could this be the unique flag of another white-tailed deer? We climbed down and made our way to yet another carcass, this one a young doe with the signature distended tongue. The only other mark of death was a trace of blood seeping from the anus. Likely another victim of the spreading disease. It was too late in the day for an official inspection, so I determined that in the morning I would again call the game ranger for a look. But strangely enough, when we returned to the site next morning the deer was gone.

We followed a faint trail of bits of hair and drops of blood down the hill to where it crossed my mowed path. There the trail disappeared. No more bent-over grass, blood or hair. No evidence of the body being consumed, dragged or moved. The trail was not only cold; it had come to an unexplained end. What could possibly have become of the latest victim? That mystery remains unsolved. Could a human being have hauled the corpse away? If so, why, and more to the point, why would a rational human drag the body down the hill, only to pick it up and carry it back up the hill path? No single coyote could have moved the hundred-pound doe, and if a pack of coyotes had been involved, there would have been strong evidence of eating and dragging, eating and dragging—hair, skin, blood, an easy-to-follow trail of body parts. The only other animal that could have picked up the carcass and carried it away would be a mountain lion. It seemed unlikely that even a big cat would carry the deer away instead of consuming it on the spot, though they have been known to stash carcasses for future meals. We searched the whole ravine for over an hour, walking parallel strips a few feet apart. We found no sign whatsoever of the mysteriously disappearing deer.

If we discovered victims numbers one and three by sight and number two by smell, the fourth dead deer, another buck, I found this week by sound. I was awakened before midnight by the dissonant chorus of a pack of coyotes, surely not more than 200 yards south of the house. I searched the area next morning and found the latest victim in a plum thicket east of the home pond, already half consumed. Again I set up the camera, and over the next three nights and days recorded the dining of a coyote, a raccoon, a flock of vultures and a neighbor's dog.

Now that cold has returned, freezing nights have presumably killed off the offending midges. When I found the first victims, I feared that our local deer population would be devastated. But a light snow fell night before last, and next morning I threw out a can of corn by the garden. Before long deer began to arrive, four in all. Word apparently spread, since this morning ten came to feed, including three antlered bucks, a veteran and a pair of youngsters. EHD has reduced the local herd, by my guess perhaps twenty percent. But enough survive to support genetic diversity and to keep the herd strong. EHD is a recurring phenomenon, part of the natural cycle, but I hope it will not return again, at least not soon. In some way I am comforted by the fact that in nature nothing is wasted. As always, death feeds life.

NOVEMBER

November 2: Coyotes, Cranes and Day of the Dead

As we approach our longest nights, Americans and Mexicans alike countenance death. Halloween, "hallowed eve," is followed by All Saints Day and the Day of the Dead. On Halloween, North Americans feign fear, but the "holy day" has lost its spiritual aspect. Halloween is a night for costumes and masks, candy and outlandish acts. In Mexico the season retains a deeper meaning. On November 2, Mexicans eat skull-shaped cookies and taunt symbols of death, but they also connect with inhabitants of the spirit world. People gather in cemeteries to wash gravestones and decorate them with marigolds, and to commune with lost loved ones and offer them food.

Halloween night, a dozen friends sat with Norma and me around a bonfire beside the Severson log cabin. As the full moon cleared the eastern horizon, coyotes emerged from their dens and greeted the night. From then until midnight we were serenaded five times by choruses of coyotes, one pack claiming an unharvested corn field and the narrow strip of brush and trees along Clay Creek to our south, another on our prairie hills. The coyotes' call is a thrilling cacophony of yips, wails, barks and howls, the perfect accompaniment to the dark aura of Halloween. Exactly what they are communicating beyond demarking territory and keeping the family together I can't say. But the coyote's voice is the most dramatic on our bluff.

I readily recognize a lone coyote's howl, and the practiced ear can separate the calls of a pair. But when more than two voices merge, I hear discord that after years of straining, I cannot discern. Is it three or half a dozen wailing under the moon? But on this night, one voice, likely the alpha male, led the pack with sustained, hair-raising howls, while others added barks and yips. Whatever the makeup of the chorus or the reason for the cries, it brings joy rather than fright to my heart; the presence of large predators is evidence of ecological health, of an ecosystem and a food chain regaining balance.

Today, the Day of the Dead dawned calm and clear. Trimming trees after lunch, I heard the distant chortle of sandhill cranes. I dropped my loppers and craned my neck toward the sky. Migrating sandhills fly at nearly stratospheric heights, so on windy days and in noisy places they may pass overhead unheard. But this calm afternoon their trumpeting was distinct, and eventually I spotted them, perhaps a mile up, a flock of four dozen gliding lazily south. I say "lazily," because unlike geese, whose wings beat frantically and whose voices croak in what sounds like desperation, cranes sail calmly in circles, riding thermal updrafts, but with each revolution moving toward their southern winter home. The downside of their circuitous soaring is that a thousand-mile flight might require twice that many miles, but they have evolved to "go with the flow."

So what do the coyotes and I and other earth-bound creatures have in common with cranes, for which our cherished bluff is generally flyover country? Perhaps it is that Halloween and the Day of the Dead are mere figments of human imagination, rituals of death that have little to do with life. That said, perhaps the Day of the Dead does acknowledge another kind of migration that we, the coyotes and even the cranes must one day make, back to the earth from which we came. Accepting that fact, I hereby proclaim this a day, and this a world, of life. I raise a cheerful glass to Halloween and the Day of the Dead, and to coyotes, cranes and human friends.

November 6: Licking Salt and Locking Horns

For years we restored or rehabilitated a few acres of native grasses and forbs each spring and summer, but the zone surrounding our house remained primarily domesticated—bluegrass, brome and other non-native species. In recent summers we set our sights on bringing native culture closer to home. Now within a stone's throw of the house on every side, six-foot native grasses grow. That, of course, has brought wildlife closer to our doors.

Over our thirty-five years on the bluff, the populations of many wild creatures, from possums and raccoons to squirrels and whitetail deer, have expanded. Gradually our fellow inhabitants' apprehension concerning humans has been replaced by curiosity, and we have become close neighbors. Deer, for example, have long lurked by the garden gate and peered inside at forbidden fruits. They frequent the salt block under the mulberry tree, and on frigid mornings when I toss a can of corn on the snow, they quickly materialize to dine. In

#

recent years, a small herd winters within a few hundred yards of the house pretty much fulltime. Here they find cover and safety, water at the spring, and plenty of food—not just corn, but fruits, grasses and brush to browse.

So we know when rutting season comes. Among the telltale signs is bark freshly scuffed from young pine or ash trees, which tells us that testosterone is flowing and young bucks are testing their antlers. We find their jousting grounds in the woods, a pair of meter-wide spots a dozen feet apart, pawed bare of grass, often accompanied by marking scent. When a doe or a herd of does streaks across the valley before hunting season, we can expect a buck close behind. But second only to actual mating, the most dramatic manifestation of rutting season is the meeting of bucks, the locking of horns.

To watch a crisp sunrise last week, I had just settled into my recliner with coffee when a young buck strolled from behind a cedar tree. At this time of year they seem to fairly strut, heads and antlers held high, nostrils flared. As I watched, a second buck appeared, older and larger…and soon the two faced off. As if to complete the cast of the unfolding melodrama, three does arose from their beds in Indiangrass, a mother and last spring's fawns.

The presence of females brought the bucks to action. The older and larger, a ten-pointer with an off-balance rack, moved in on the younger foe, a fellow with a mere six points to his credit. The pair angled for position, pawed the earth a time or two and locked antlers. The younger buck was more aggression than thrust, the equivalent perhaps of a human teen with raging hormones. For the veteran, it seemed more ritual than challenge. Likely the two had met before, and the young buck was merely keeping up appearances—and announcing his candidacy for a future year.

Meanwhile, the doe and her teenaged daughters strolled demurely to the salt block and began to lick, apparently ignoring the valiant battle waged on their behalf. But their moment of peace was short-lived. Soon the older buck had pushed the youngster twenty feet down the hill, and the upstart gave up and ran. The old chap lifted his nose high, nostrils sniffing with enthusiasm, and the chase was on.

November 9: Canoeing Clay Creek

When we feel like canoeing, we usually think summer, and we usually head for the Missouri. The river is wide and swift, its scale dramatic. From time to time we have canoed the narrow, muddy Vermillion and James rivers, their tree-lined banks providing shade and harboring myriad birds. But Clay Creek? At some point millennia ago it was undoubtedly the mighty Missouri's bed. When long before recorded time the river shifted ten miles south to the valley's other edge, Clay Creek would have remained a quiet but no doubt luxuriant, wooded stream. But a century ago the creek was denuded, straightened and channelized to drain the hills and the northern swath of the valley for the benefit of production agriculture. Harnessed and maintained by man, it is now identified on maps as Clay Creek Ditch. I persist in calling it Clay Creek, though for longer than anybody alive can remember it has been less than a natural creek. Clay Creek does still support a range of mammals and birds, but it doesn't come to mind when one thinks of a recreational canoe trip.

Yet on this date, fellow County Commissioner Dusty Passick and I launched my canoe from the 459 Avenue bridge half a mile south of the bluff, and headed downstream. This was not a recreational outing; we were on official business. Among the most persistent and vexing problems faced by commissioners was the oversight of agricultural drainage. Landowners whose forbears long ago established a coordinated drainage district in the valley, and who annually assess themselves a tax levy to maintain the drainage channel their great grandfathers dug, want to be sure the former creek is straight, deep and clear of obstruction, capable of carrying flood waters away from their farms. By ordinance, the county commission also serves as the board of equalization, and prominent among the duties is to serve as the "ditch board."

The mission this November day was to check for obstructions that had been reported—beaver dams, logs lodged in the channel and anything else that might restrict the flow of water when snow melted in the spring. The sky was gray, the wind sharp and cold. But deep in our ditch and heading southeast with the wind, Dusty and I were warm.

Neither Dusty nor I had particular expertise in drainage. He had served for decades as the county sheriff; I had worked as a teacher and writer. So today's outing was part education and part investigation. But we determined that in spite of the rawness of the day—the last day of the year as it turned out that such a mission was possible, for tomorrow the surface would turn to ice and snow would fall—we would also have fun. Little paddling was required; the flow remained adequate to bear us along at one or two miles an hour. I'd brought my camera to photograph points of interest and my global positioning system to tell us where we were. We passed under three county bridges, inspecting them from below in a way otherwise difficult to achieve. We crossed the remains of several beaver dams, all in advanced stages of disrepair, none threatening the stream's flow. We determined that the slope of the bank was good, and that heavy sod held it in place. In short, we concluded that Clay Creek Ditch was in adequate condition to serve the purpose for which it had been altered.

Fortunately, nature retains the capacity to overrule human acts; in spite of periodic interventions by man, the ditch in many ways has remained a creek. Around most every bend a great blue heron rose from the bank and wheeled away. In a remnant grove of cottonwoods, a great horned owl roosted until our voices woke it from an afternoon nap and it fluttered away down the channel. Cardinals flitted amongst cedar trees, and a squirrel scaled a leaning box elder as we approached. A school of catfish stirred in a pool as we passed. Though straightened and channelized, and along much of its length stripped of its trees, this stretch of the creek still supports an ecosystem that would otherwise not exist.

And it harbors death. We counted half a dozen raccoons decaying along wooded regions of the banks. Possibly some had expired from natural causes, or possibly from some pollutant they had found. More likely they had been blasted from trees by coon hunters who sometimes roam the creek at night with dogs, spotlights and guns.

When we dragged the canoe up the muddy shore a couple of miles above its mouth, snow had begun to fall. We had accomplished our mission of inspecting a drainage ditch, at no cost to the taxpayers or the farmers the ditch serves, and we had enjoyed a leisurely float down the county's largest creek, still a lifeline of the fifteen-mile valley and a sanctuary of life.

November 11: The Time of Fire

Today is Veterans Day. Like many fellow veterans I may observe moments of solemnity, remembering those who lost their lives, but in their honor celebrate the fact that life goes on. The winter's wood is in—two cords of oak, hackberry, mulberry, ash and elm. If it's an average winter, there should be a little left when spring finally comes, or at least that's the plan. Trudging through ice or snow to cut and carry wood is not my idea of fun, though more than once in pre-retirement days I was reduced to that. Among the beauties of "retirement," of not reporting to work every day, is that jobs like cutting wood can be spread over time, and can actually be pleasurable instead of a chore.

That being said, a few cool days in October produced a familiar sense of urgency I might not otherwise have felt. Days of clouds or drizzle or below average temperatures always warn me that winter will be long and time to prepare might be short. In some Octobers we have already burned the wood that in other years might hold us to Thanksgiving. In other years the sun warms us and we need no fires before we head to Oklahoma to visit family for the holiday. This year has been mild, so in spite of past experience, through most of October I suppressed the sense of urgency I might have felt in working years when I relied on stolen weekend hours to lay in wood. Instead, I labored a couple of hours at a stretch, no longer than I could enjoy the job, then knocked off for a ramble or some less strenuous pursuit. Yet without breaking a sweat, by the end of October I had completed the annual task, and still no need for fire. Whether this year is an aberration, or whether we are witnessing a manifestation of climate change, it is impossible to know, but October weather extended into November, and dry, sunny days continued. The sun has heated our geo-solar home most every day, and the few cloudy days were warm enough that stored heat got us through the night until another dawning sun—until day before yesterday, when the north wind howled in and flurries filled the sky.

But I have no fear. The north wall of the garage is stacked to the ceiling with dry wood. A pile of ash and elm trunks waits outside to be split, but that is a job for mornings when the thermometer hugs zero, when wood splits readily and hard work feels good, when one tackles the wood that heats him thrice, once when cut, a second time when split and finally when we sit by the stove.

Our hardest firewood is oak, but fortunately our oaks rarely die. Ash ranks a close second in the British Thermal Units of solar energy packed into a cubic foot of wood. I like ash because its grain grows straight. On a cold January day, a seasoned chunk of twelve-inch trunk will split with a single blow of an axe-faced maul. But compared to the interwoven grain of elm, our other most common firewood, ash measures up poorly in heating thrice. I have sweated in shirtsleeves on a sunny zero-degree day splitting elm, while for ash I require a jacket or vest. The other woods we burn fall between ash and elm on the scale of heat and sweat that splitting generates. Three common native trees I don't bother to cut for the stove—cottonwood, willow and box elder. These soft woods produce lots of ash, not much heat, and more air pollution and greenhouse gas. If you forget to tend the fire, it dies.

It has been a long and lovely season in the sun, but all good things must end. The weatherman forecasts a deep freeze tonight, and tomorrow, a below-freezing high. The season of real winter is about to begin, but at least with regard to fuel, we are ready. Like our ancient ancestors, we will sit cozily tonight by the fire, staring mindlessly into the flames and glowing coals, luxuriating in the slow release of energy the sun has patiently stored for decades in the cells of living trees. The season of rest and contemplation has begun.

November 13: Drama at the Bird Feeder
When the days grow colder, our bird feeders gather the United Nations of birds—blue jays, cardinals, hairy, downy and red-bellied woodpeckers, house and gold finches, juncos, nuthatches, sparrows and more. But birds are not the only visitors at the feeders. A possum occasionally dines on fallen

morsels, and hungry deer rear on hind hooves and sweep up seeds with outstretched tongues. Last night at dusk, a mouse emerged from his tunnel in a small snow drift beside the patio to munch on fallen sunflower seeds. He glanced furtively about, perhaps aware of his exposure, a dark dot on brilliant snow, an easy target if Luna the cat might be lurking near.

We are not the only ones who watch the activity at our feeders. Besides Luna, a neighboring cat makes occasional visits, and prairie falcons, merlins and sharp-shinned hawks conduct periodic checks, swooping out of nowhere at magnificent speeds in the hope of snatching an inattentive bird. But the juniper beside the feeder provides quick refuge, and long generations of natural selection dictate that most birds keep an eye on the sky and take refuge in time.

Once, on a day when puffy clouds floated in a sky of blue, the kind of day when our solar windows mirror the world outside and a bird might crash into a reflection of its world, I sat in my recliner by the window reading. Suddenly came the too-familiar crack of a bird's skull on glass. But this was not an isolated collision; I glanced up in time to see two more small birds, a pair of finches, follow—bang—bang. But then came a much louder thud—a pursuing prairie falcon smashed headlong into glass. I rushed outside and picked up the stunned raptor. I held it for some minutes in my hands, carefully examining its features until gradually its talons tightened on my hand, its eyes focused on mine, and in a moment of recognition, it sprang away.

But today was different. This cold day I happened to be gazing through the glass at the feeding frenzy when in my peripheral vision, a larger shape appeared. In what couldn't have been more than a second or two, a dozen birds scattered, the hawk chose one, veered in flight, snatched its victim from a tangle of juniper and was gone. So quick was the dive of the sharp-shinned hawk that I was able to identify it only as it swooped away, a junco clutched in its fist.

Such are the vagaries of the natural world. Life feeds

life, and hawks and falcons live on flesh instead of seeds. Ironically, in setting the table for our many winter resident birds, we attract potential meals for cats and birds of prey. Our cat is aging, belled, declawed in front, and spends as many winter hours as allowed by the fire, so her impact as a catcher of birds is minimal. Even for raptors, the conquest is rare. But as much as I love watching the congregation of healthy birds at the feeder, I confess a thrill at witnessing a drama as old as life on Earth.

November 16: Blazing and Following Trails

From the beginning, I was lured by woods. As a child on our fifty-acre farm east of Oklahoma City, I followed the creek south from the house, crawled under a barbed wire fence and slipped into the woods my father rented for firewood and to graze his milk cows—eighty acres of oaks, hickories, willows, cottonwoods, persimmons, meadow and swamp. To a seven-year-old, an eighty-acre forest is infinity. Yet I learned the eighty's orientation to the sun, where the land inclined, where the soil was boggy or dry, where groves of various trees grew, when and where to find ripe persimmons and why to avoid those that are not.

I knew the trails made by cows and men, but a boy of seven can follow the trails of smaller animals too, and gradually I sketched ever-finer details on my mental map. I found the trails of raccoons and possums and deer, sometimes following, sometimes intersecting the more predictable foot-wide paths of cows. On hands and knees I followed the lower, narrower trails. Some tracks I didn't know, but I followed them all, ever deeper into brambles and underbrush. I found where the possum crawled into his hollow hickory log. I knew the tall cottonwood in whose rotting trunk the raccoon lived. I found the limb on which he dined, saw where he dropped his waste, learned what fruits and creatures he ate. I discovered the hollow oak where honeybees stored their goods. Following trails expanded my universe of mammals and birds.

But nature herself is not a fan of trails. Long before I read Rabelais' observation that "nature abhors a vacuum," I found it true. The height and width of each trail is no greater than that of the largest animal that regularly passes. A few large animals, moose for example, are equipped to keep trails wide, and deer help maintain trails by browsing brush. But of all the animals in the woods, only humans carry loppers or saws to efficiently counter nature's penchant for closing trails. I am such a man.

There are rational reasons for trails. They provide access to otherwise forbidden places and to fallen firewood trees. They allow fuller access to the woods, whether by foot or on skis. And on the Missouri River bluff, where eastern redcedars are invading every square foot not otherwise occupied, trail blazing keeps remnants of native prairie alive and exposed to the sun. So when autumn rolls around I take to the woods to make or maintain trails. That was my occupation this fine November week. The result is a pair of new cross-country ski trails, the longest a quarter-mile run from bluff to river bottom.

But truthfully, all my logical reasons for trail maintenance are on some level a rationalization for being in the forest. Perhaps my personal motive is not so different from that of the hunter who carries a gun instead of a saw and whose object is deer rather than firewood or fun. Given the ingrained work ethic of our culture, we seem to need an excuse for frittering away an afternoon in the woods.

In the end, perhaps a rational reason for cutting a new trail is to get closer to what lies in a tangle yet to be explored. Yet trail maker that I am, I admit there is a problem with trails. Once opened, whether by cows or coons or man, creatures may follow them without asking why. So perhaps I face dual conundrums; there is the paradox that in seeking adventure I tame the very wilderness I love, and if I cut a new path, I am likely to follow it instead of crawling through unexplored brush. I'm aware that far too often my feet take a charted course without consulting my head. But as for taming wilderness, I shouldn't be overly concerned. Nature is quite efficient at countering our every domesticating act, including closing our trails. And we live amidst cedar trees, one of her most efficient tools.

Now that the leaves have fallen and the weeds are losing their burs, I will make a point of venturing more frequently from the tracks of woodland creatures and men. Very occasionally, I might experience the delight of temporary disorientation, but on every venture I will find something I have not encountered before.

November 17: A Maddening Death

The woods and prairie of the Missouri River bluff are full of life—and death. No organism survives forever. The life of some, including many insects, is measured in days. Burr oaks can live hundreds of years. For annual plants, the growing season at our latitude is six months at best, and though native grasses are perennial, everything but the central roots dies away each fall. Each organism, including humans and raccoons, returns in its own way to the earth, our decomposition restoring the minerals and resources we have borrowed for a time.

So death in the woods is not new, and not necessarily a cause for sadness or concern. Frost ends the life cycle for annual plants, and even before frost, trees begin to shed their leaves. When fungi grow on an ash tree, I suspect its days are numbered. Animals that leave their sanctuary face greater threats. For example, many a raccoon fails to make it across the road from the cornfields along Clay Creek to its home on the bluff. But I also find dead animals in the woods, sometimes just feathers or fur and inedible parts of birds, rabbits and rodents that have fed a larger predator, sometimes the decaying bodies of creatures that may have died of injuries, disease or old age.

Now and then I find death that fills me with sadness or anger. Once I found the carcass of a red-tailed hawk cradled in the jagged top of a rotting cottonwood. I could not reach the hawk for examination, but a natural death on that pinnacle seemed unlikely. I had just read that two men in the service of a local pheasant-shooting preserve had been arrested for shooting protected birds of prey.

Today brought another discouraging find. Passing the pond, I saw something large floating near the north shore. I walked upstream and crossed the creek to investigate. It was what I feared I had seen—a half-submerged whitetail deer. I went home for a rope, paddled the raft out to the carcass and dragged it to shore, then up the hill to where the body could feed coyotes and other carnivores and scavengers without polluting the water. I examined the deer, a young antlerless buck. Just behind the front leg was a half-inch hole. I grasped a hoof and turned the body over. Opposite the hole was a bloody gash, ripped by an exiting bullet.

I do not oppose ethical hunting, and some winters we enjoy venison jerky passed to us by a friend. But our piece of the bluff is clearly marked as a wildlife preserve, no hunting allowed. The pond and the creek are not unusual places for wounded animals to die; they instinctively seek sanctuary and the water that a bleeding animal needs. The pond is well within our boundary, but a wounded deer may run that far, so it is quite possible that whoever shot the young buck and failed to follow the trail of blood fired from outside our fence. But what is more disturbing is that I found the carcass today, four days before rifle season begins.

There is nothing magical about November 21. A deer shot that day is just as dead. But those who disregard the law and the science behind it to kill animals out of season are among those who give ethical hunters a bad name, like those who kill hawks and owls, and those who, every fall, cruise county and township roads, shooting from vehicles and tossing beer cans in the ditch. And who might be inclined to ignore a "no hunting" sign.

I know hunters whose respect for nature and for fellow creatures is similar to mine. One friend, who ranked among the state's top archers, spent dozens of hours of archery deer season in his stand, but never released an arrow because he wasn't sure of a killing shot. Unfortunately some who hunt, and some who do not, have not learned to respect either the laws of the state or the higher laws of nature, or to recognize our essential kinship with other animals with whom we share our Earth.

November 21: Airborne Raccoon

Norma, our daughter Laura, her husband Sam and I descend the steepest slope in the most remote middle of the woods to the hundred-foot gulch from which our tallest cottonwood rises. It is rooted at the edge of a perennial stream, just below a spring, so it has grown tall and straight, a perfectly shaped tree that has survived the ravages of Great Plains wind because it is protected on all sides by the heavily-wooded slopes of the deep ravine. It stands at least 150 feet tall, its top limbs reaching sunlight above the lesser trees of adjacent slopes. Its four-foot trunk rivals those of the oldest burr oaks in the grove downstream, but it is taller than the grandest oak.

We are not the only residents who revere this tree. Nightfall often finds turkey hens flapping and scrambling to its upper limbs to roost in safety from coyotes and foxes and other risks of the forest floor. Various smaller birds nest in peripheral branches every spring. I have seen squirrels leap from limb to limb. But raccoons have reigned supreme here and made this giant cottonwood their home. High in an upper trunk where long ago a limb broke off and left a gaping hole, raccoons have long lounged, dined and raised their young.

We have watched them for years. Many a sunny winter afternoon I have called up to a coon sprawling in the doorway, trying to rouse it from apparent sleep. Their sleep is deep, or perhaps they simply ignore me, accustomed as they are to my staring. Or perhaps they simply live so far above earthly affairs that they see no reason to heed my summons. I once spent hours of a summer night watching for the spectacle of a plump raccoon descending the rough bark of the trunk seventy-five feet to the ground, which I presume he did each night in search of food.

On this day, approaching the cottonwood from the west, the raccoon's home is hidden from our view, but a rustling somewhere in the upper branches tells us a coon may be lounging in the sun. Probably he doesn't see us either, and perhaps our voices and our own scrambling down the slope have startled him. In any case, none of our party sees him on his lofty perch—until the small branch to which he clings cracks loudly and gives way, and suddenly we witness the strange spectacle of a fat raccoon tumbling through space toward the creek bed below.

How the coon perceives his fall I do not know. But to us it is in slow motion—not unlike a leaf floating to the forest floor, though gravity ensures that his trajectory is more direct, his descent more rapid. He drops like a furry rock. What happens next is the greatest surprise. His body hits the streamside mud with a splat, not like a cat landing on its feet, but more like a sack of flour. But immediately he is on his feet again, ambling down stream, and in moments he is gone.

One of the stranger dramas we have witnessed in our woods. Once in a lifetime a sure-clawed coon might lose his grip, but even then, how likely could it be that we would be there to see—if not precipitate—the fall, and that he would survive a seventy-five-foot plunge? If raccoon bodies are anything like ours, I expect that for the next few days his muscles and joints will be sore. Or perhaps his injuries are far more serious, broken ribs or punctured organs. When spring comes we may find a raccoon skeleton not far from the cottonwood. But if he does survive, he might seek a less lofty home.

November 25: Skating a Crystal Universe

Our spring-fed pond is slow to freeze, but even it cannot forever defy winter's icy breath. Yet with the Earth experiencing new record temperatures nearly every year, the day in which we can walk on water seems to come later each fall. That is not a good thing. Most of us recognize that climate change is occurring at a seemingly unstoppable speed, and that unless we take bold and decisive action now to slow our production of greenhouse gases, there will be hell to pay. Yet like most residents of the Northern Plains, even those who comprehend and fear the impact of modern man on the planet, I secretly harbor the hope each fall that winter will come late, and that tomorrow's dawn will bring another lovely day. This year, that selfish short-term desire has been fulfilled. In early November I worked outside in shirtsleeves.

But on November 10 it appeared that somebody had forgotten to close the north door. What meteorologists call the Polar Vortex had arrived, a skin of ice began to form on the ponds, and we dragged out winter coats. For two weeks, the ice has grown thicker each day. In most winters before we can enjoy the ice, down comes the snow, and the chance to skate is gone. That has not happened this year, and today the ice seems firm enough to support our weight. I pull on my ice skates and venture out. I bounce on the surface near the edge, and nothing cracks. A few feet out, where the water is still less than waist deep, I try it again. Seems OK. And so on, until I am satisfied that the ice is firm. Only then do I cast caution to the windless blue sky and glide away.

The woods pond covers about an acre, an oblong circle with necks that reach far up two ravines toward the springs that feed its life. It would be foolish to go far up those appendages today; the closer one gets to running water, the thinner the ice. Yet I venture first toward the smaller spring, then toward the other, stopping when the first splinter echoes across the basin. In this neck, protected from wind when the water first glazed, I find a placid surface on which to pump and glide. But I also encounter a marvelous canvas in the making, an unbelievably varied work of art. Even where the ice is thickest, I see straight through in places, down to the still-green vegetation on the bottom, the lens upon which I stand a kind of magnifying glass. Below the surface, usually-hidden logs are well-defined, as are multiple shades of vegetation, sediment and mud. Elsewhere the surface is glazed with bubbles and flows, a varied reflective tableau painted by winter's hand. The true depth of the ice can best be judged where jagged fissures zigzag across the face, revealing a thickness of perhaps six inches or more. Air is trapped in bubbles of every size and configuration. Deep veins of sequestered oxygen run for dozens of feet. Here and there, bits of algae and the leaves of oak, elm, hackberry and ash are fixed in the ice where they fell.

I have come to skate, to exercise some little-used muscles, to experience the marvel of not only walking on water, but gliding across water phenomenally transformed by cold. And skate I do. But that has taken second place to what really holds me here, exploration of a marvelous montage that will not be repeated in a thousand years.

DECEMBER

December 4: Turkey Hunt

Just after Thanksgiving our local population of wild turkeys, the eastern race of *Meleagris gallopavo sylvestris*, apparently decided it was safe to come out of hiding. We hadn't seen a wild turkey on the place for days, so I was delighted to hear the comforting clucks of turkey hens on the eastern hill. Warm days have returned and the sun is bright. The marks and stains on our sun-facing solar windows are impossible to ignore, and my excuses for not washing them have evaporated with the sun. If I am to accomplish the task before winter sets in for good, today is the day. I fill a bucket with soapy water, gather sponge, squeegee, ladder and towel and head outside.

I have finished the hard part, the second floor windows that can be reached only by ladder, and am just beginning the first floor glass. In some part of my consciousness, the gargling peeps of turkey hens have grown stronger, and the constant chatter tells me that this is more than a handful of birds. But my concentration is on glass, methodically rubbing down streaks of insect offal, dust and grime, so I am ill prepared for the appearance of the first big hen to enter peripheral sight.

She stalks calmly around the corner of the house, thirty feet to my east, clucking and pecking, clucking and pecking, oblivious to the human who stands like an awkward tripod at the glass, legs spread to avoid trampling still live chrysanthemums in the flower bed, left hand propping his body against the glass, right arm scrubbing away. I freeze in this uncomfortable posture, knowing that dim though my visitor's senses might be, any movement will alert her to my presence and prompt a panicked rush for cover. Then a sister appears, and the chorus behind the pair grows stronger, telling me there will be more to come.

One by one, the meter-long birds round the corner and follow the leader across the front lawn. By the time the first hen reaches the bird feeder and discovers fallen sunflower seeds, half a dozen are in her wake. And still they come. How long can I hold my dead man pose? Already my arms are cramping and my twisted neck feels locked in place. I begin to count. When the twentieth turkey appears, the leaders have already rifled what other birds had kicked out of the feeder and are heading down the hill toward the garden. And still turkeys come, thirty, forty, fifty, will the procession never end? My body can stand no more strain, so very slowly I begin to move my limbs, feet inching together, back straightening, arms relaxing at my side. But still my neck is cramped far to the right, so I very slowly squirm my body half a revolution to the south.

Finally the last and perhaps most indolent or well-fed hen rounds the corner, and gradually the parade moves past me and away. Once the last eyes face the garden, I crouch low and make for the front door. I grab the camera, sneak out the back door and circle behind the house, into the trees and then the tall native grasses. I crouch and crawl to a vantage point above the pond just in time to see the leaders descend to the water, dip their beaks and drink. Each hen follows suit, pecks morsels at the water's edge, then proceeds over the hill into the next broad valley and up the long hill to our west. I pursue them for half an hour, discreetly snapping photos of the vast herd, as well as individual birds as they pass. If at any time a single turkey becomes aware of my presence, it is not apparent.

An hour after the first hen came into view, the last disappears on the western horizon. By now the sun is sinking low. My hour as peeping Tom is over, and I still have windows to wash. But the turkey hunt—theirs, not mine—goes on, though what they seek I can't say for sure. Is it only something to eat, the insect and seed remnants of summer still available on a warm December day? Is it new territory, a distant woods where they might winter near a farmyard with a predictable supply of food? Or perhaps just a leisurely stroll on a fine afternoon? Perhaps it is something else…or all of the above. But watching the turkeys hunt, as an uninvited and unacknowledged participant, has been a far greater reward than an unobstructed view of turkeys or anything else through unspattered glass.

December 7: A Bridge to Somewhere

For years I eyed the ridge of land between the two creeks that feed the big pond. The west slope is gentle, shaded by towering burr oaks and hackberries, the east a steep glacial ravine marked by seeps and outcroppings of chalk rock, the bedrock from which both streams spring. The peak between the two rises perhaps a hundred feet above the water. We had often crossed the frozen pond in winter and hiked this secluded spot, but in other seasons the peninsula could be reached in three ways: Hike north to the upland meadow above the gorges, wade the west creek, or hop across from stone to stone. Often I gazed across to the ridge, so near yet so far away, and thought of bridging the stream.

The western hill declines gently, so that fifty yards from the pond the banks stand just fifteen feet above water. This seemed the most likely place for a bridge, but even here I would need to span sixty feet. That posed two problems: Where would I find materials to build a bridge that long, and lacking a crane or other heavy equipment, how could I get a bridge into place? The answer to both questions came at once.

The water in the western neck is slow to freeze, fed by a perennial spring that flows fifteen gallons per minute, but two weeks of cold nights since I skated the area might make crossing with a load safe. And this week a crew employed by WAPA, the Western Area Power Administration, rolled in with big trucks and assorted power line servicing equipment to replace two fifty-year-old poles that support the high-voltage power line just north of our fence. These are no ordinary poles. They are massive western redcedars, sixty feet long and eighteen inches thick at the base. The foreman said WAPA had no use for the decommissioned poles; they were typically left behind.

I wrapped a log chain around the base of one and hooked it to my Ford, put the tractor in low gear, and inched the pole across field and prairie and down a ski trail I had carved through the woods to the edge of the stream, then returned for the second pole. When both were positioned beside the trail, I wrapped the chain around the smaller end of the first pole and attached my come-along, a hand operated winch that combines the principles of pulley and lever action, thus enabling an ordinary human to move many times his weight. The other end of the chain I wrapped around a tree at the edge, and began to crank. The first pole glided readily across frozen soil and down the bank, leaving hardly a mark. In an hour's time, both were positioned beside the stream.

Stringing together every piece of chain I owned, I crossed the ice and attached the come-along to a tree on the peninsula and again began to crank. The pole inched forward, literally. Every stroke of the lever advanced the timber an inch or two. Little effort was required in the early phase; gravity was on my side. Even when the pole hit the frozen stream it glided readily across the ice. But eventually it reached the other shore, and that is when the real work began. Now I was not merely dragging the pole, but lifting it eight feet to its resting place on the eastern bank. A cheater was required. I slid a piece of pipe over the handle, thus halving the force required to raise the pole inch by inch. After a long afternoon of strained muscles, both logs lay side-by-side and nearly level across the chasm. I drove steel stakes in the ground and lashed the poles to the posts to hold them in place. The hard work was done.

Friends Clarence and Sandy joined Norma and me on Sunday afternoon to nail lengths of two-by-six across the poles, spanning the creek and providing easy access to the peninsula year-around. Besides its primary function of bridging a forbidding ravine, the bridge is a place to sit, fish or contemplate, and a place where raccoons love to dine. But there is another unexpected benefit. The bridge is among the world's largest xylophones! The long trunks of the western red cedars taper from eighteen inches at one end to half that diameter at the other. As we cross the bridge, our feet play a rising or descending scale, depending on the direction of travel, thus expressing the timbre of the timbers.

December 9: Digging Out

We awoke this morning to howling wind and horizontal snow. Lots of snow. Already it is piled high on the patio, and the sidewalk is nowhere to be found. At this time of year, sunrise comes just after eight—if at all. Today we will see no sun. Snow swirls across the horizon and spins like dust devils across what once was lawn. In the dim light I watch the drifts rise and fall, shift and settle, then do it all again; with each stroke, the texture changes and the drifts rise a little higher than before.

At the feeders, the early birds—cardinals and blue jays—huddle on the leeward side, grab a sunflower seed and wheel away to the shelter of the juniper bush to dine. Hungry deer rise from shelter southeast of cedar trees, stretch, defecate and begin the trudge through knee-deep drifts to the garden, hopeful that I will emerge from the garage with a can of corn. I go to the garage for an armload of wood and build up the fire in the stove. While the coffee drips, I pull on boots and coat to take out corn. But first there's a wall of snow to move from the door. I shovel a narrow path away from the house and venture out to satisfy the deer. I slip and slide on a layer of ice beneath the snow. Apparently the overnight storm began with freezing rain.

Back in the recliner with a hot cup of coffee, I contemplate my favorite part of semi-retirement. No longer do we need to leave the house in the dark to be in an office when daylight comes. Luna the cat purrs in my lap, fire crackles in the stove and the sky turns a lighter shade of gray. We have no place to go, and even if we did, as long as the wind blows, the roads will be blocked. So there is no point in digging out, no urgency to do anything besides watch the shifting snow.

By noon, the wind howls less ferociously and snow seems

to be playing itself out. Sooner or later we will need to leave the bluff, perhaps tomorrow; so sometime before dark I should move some snow. After lunch I dig out my insulated coveralls and my warmest coat and head for the barn, where the tractor waits. Thanks to the new twelve-volt battery, the starter cranks, the spark plugs spark, and fire ignites inside the ancient zero-degree hunk of cast iron. The engine sputters, then roars. Congratulating myself on finally upgrading the old beast, I slip the shifter into first and crawl out of the barn.

We built this shed that we call a barn a quarter century ago to house the pair of Shetland ponies and a paint mare. The horses are long gone, so now it's a winter home for straw, mice, a riding mower and the Ford. But it wasn't built for the Ford. It's beside the creek in the bottom, well below our hillside house—a hillside now covered with half a foot of snow, drifts more than twice that deep, and under all a sheet of ice.

First I try the usual tractor trail to the top. I shift to third gear to pick up speed, but when I reach the slope, the driving wheels begin to spin. Fifty feet up, momentum halts and it's back to the bottom to try again. With each run I gain a few more feet, but then the hill steepens slightly and that's the end of the run. I long ago wired cast iron wheel weights on the rear blade to increase traction, two hunks of iron that together weigh at least 300 pounds, but they are not enough. I try another approach, through native prairie grass. The hill is gentler here, and normally the grass would provide good traction, but not today; it's coated with ice. Another failure. I try another approach and then another. The fourth takes me on a trajectory that will end by crossing the front lawn. I make it almost to the top this time before the Ford can go no more.

What to do now? I trudge to the garage for my trusty come-along, the hand winch with which I inched the power poles across the creek to build the bridge. It's gotten me out of more than one bind in the past, including the time I slid the pickup sideways into a tree on a trail in the woods. I connect one end to the tractor and the other to a log chain, wrap the other end of the chain around a tree, and inch the tractor over the crest and onto the lawn.

An hour after the tractor first came to life, I'm finally ready to move the snow. Already the day is dimming, so I will need to work fast. But at ten degrees, fast is good. By dark the sidewalk and driveway are cleared, and we are ready for an early morning escape tomorrow—assuming neither snow nor wind return. I leave the tractor on top just in case. I have guarded confidence that it will start on command, but now it appears I must contemplate the next innovation—a pair of wheel chains.

December 14: The First Skis of Winter

Monday night's blizzard brought eight inches of snow—dry fluffy stuff that roared and drifted across the prairies in horizontal mode. On Wednesday the wind finally blew itself out; I eyed the skis, knowing that trails through native prairie, and especially through the woods would be full of snow. But the snow I cleared from the driveway Tuesday afternoon had been replaced by new drifts. Slave that I sometimes am to an ingrained work ethic—the absurd notion that mature humans are supposed to work first, then play—I pulled out the coveralls again and headed out to clear new drifts, first scooping off sidewalk and patio, then firing up the tractor to clear the parking area and the 500-foot driveway to the outside world. Four hours later, I dragged myself in to sit by the fire, enthusiasm for further exertion in ten-degree weather gone.

Thursday dawned crisp and calm. Afternoon brought brilliant sun and temperatures in the teens—perfect weather for our favorite winter sport. Norma and I clipped on skis at the back door and headed out to survey the land. Exposed hillsides were swept nearly clean by the blizzard wind, but as I had expected, the five-foot-wide tractor-mowed trails through head-high native grass held plenty of snow. This was not a day for shady woods; it was a day to bask in the sun. So we took to the hills of the north forty, trudging to summits and gliding back to valleys until the sun was low and we found the first ski of the season telling on poorly-exercised triceps, calves and thighs.

Yesterday morning the thermometer was frozen at zero—the perfect time for splitting the last of the firewood logs. Again, by the time the last chunk was stacked I'd had my exercise for the day. Reading by the fire seemed the best activity for a cold afternoon. Today is Saturday, five days into the first good snow of the season, and still we haven't skied the woods. But today is the day. Clarence, who still suffers the indignity of working five days a week, shows up early and off we go, Clarence, Norma and I gliding toward the big woods.

I am especially eager to try the new run I opened this fall. I had cleared cedars and brush in a generally straight shot down the front of the bluff. The trail begins and ends in tallgrass prairie, but in between, runs through a dense forest of cedar, hackberry and ash. So here we go—nearly a quarter mile glide from the highest point on the meadow bluff to the edge of the river bottom, a steady drop of a hundred feet. The short steep plunge near the top produces more than enough speed and thrill for the rest of the run. Somehow all three of us reach the bottom not only alive, but without a tumble. A great new run has been inaugurated.

In my younger years I twice drove to the Rockies to downhill ski, once to Colorado and another time to New Mexico. My friends and I kicked out a day's wages for lift passes and rental, stood in long lines for a ride up, and felt the quick thrill of zooming back to ground zero to rejoin the waiting line. I don't regret those trips, and I understand the allure of downhill skiing, but I don't need to go back. I have thrill enough on the bluff, plus the great exercise of the climb. I'm still enjoying the same skis I've used for more than ten years, and even with last year's upgrade of new boots and poles, my total investment for a decade of exercise and fun is about $200. But best of all, we needn't start the car, and we ski on a whim. We step out the back door, clip on the skis, and enter our wonderland.

December 15: Birds Great and Small

Yes, we're skiing two days in a row. Norma, Clarence and I shuffle up the snow-packed trail through the big woods. We have left Boulder Creek behind and headed up the gentle valley that leads to the upland prairie. As usual, I have forgotten my binoculars, but Clarence has remembered his. We stop occasionally to admire at closer range the various birds we encounter along the way—blue jays, crows, a downy woodpecker, a flock of cedar waxwings. Then Clarence spots a small bird hopping up the trunk of a dying elm.

The profile resembles that of the white-breasted nuthatch, but the color is wrong and so is the hop. Nuthatches are famous for conducting their food searches from top to bottom, short skips down the trunks of trees, head down, tail to the sky. This bird hops up. "Might be a brown creeper," Clarence ventures. He pulls out the binoculars to confirm.

When I completed *Waiting for Coyote's Call* a decade ago, I had identified more than 100 species of birds on our bluff. I thought I'd perhaps noted all of our feathered residents and guests. But in the past decade I've been delighted several times by identifying yet another inhabitant or visitor. Probably my failure to identify a creeper illustrates the glaring gaps in seeing and knowing that remain for one whose eyes are usually open and who desires to know the fellow creatures with whom he shares his home—but who often forgets his binoculars.

What makes this late "discovery" surprising is the first word in one field guide's description of the brown creeper as a "common but inconspicuous woodland bird." Thus the creeper is one of a number of difficult to distinguish SBBs—small brown birds, a group that includes longspurs and sparrows of many kinds. And the brown creeper, *Certhia americana*, is "inconspicuous" indeed. It is small, just over four inches from beak to whisk broom tail, pointed feathers slightly fanned for camouflage and balance. Its streaked and mottled brown is perfect for hiding on the bark of a dying elm, the kind of place where the creeper is likely to find the insects in summer and larvae in winter that its long, curved bill can pluck. So only when it moves, or when it utters its double squeak, is it likely to attract the eye or ear. Even then, unless it is profiled against the tree, it is hard to detect with the naked eye.

So intent are Clarence and I on watching the creeper creep up the trunk in its unique spiral fashion that we completely miss the bald eagle sailing down the bluff, directly overhead and not more than a hundred feet above our heads, until Norma, who has skied ahead, spots the king of the skies and calls back to us. What a delight, a close visit by our most magnificent bird while contemplating one of our most inconspicuous. I'm glad we didn't miss the eagle. There are few greater thrills in our skies. But buoyed as I always am by their appearance, it is meeting the little brown creeper—and a great ski with friends—that makes this day.

December 16: Lighting a Christmas Tree

If the holiday economy depended upon us, the entire industry of raising conifers for Christmas trees would have folded long ago. We have purchased a spruce or pine only once in twenty years. Yes, the trees imported from Canada and those grown for the season on local farms are fuller, greener and more shapely than our Christmas trees, and such trees are a renewable crop not completely unlike corn or beans. The holiday tradition of decorating a tree is not the only time-honored bonding ritual for many families; choosing and cutting a holiday tree from a local farm is a great outing that boosts the local economy, and need not negatively impact the natural environment.

But in our household, for several reasons we have long opted for a homegrown redcedar instead. The ravines and prairies of the bluff grow hundreds of cedars, and more sprout each year. Cedars are one of our most dependable renewable natural resources. As I have noted elsewhere, cedars are actually a menace to other native species, and in the absence of fire that once controlled their spread, we must control them by more arduous means. A mature female cedar may produce many thousands of berries—seeds—each year, and each is a potential tree. Their proliferation, along with our restoration of native prairie and the general improvement in natural habitat, has brought an abundance of birds, including flocks of cedar waxwings and others who dine on cedar berries and subsequently deposit the seeds elsewhere, contributing to the spread. So cutting a holiday tree is a tiny part of the annual task of reducing the cedar population. But besides that, cedars make beautiful and aromatic traditional Christmas trees.

It is important to get a female, and not only to neuter its regenerative capacity. As with humans—my male perspective of course—the females of the species are most attractive. Their foliage tends to be greener and more abundant, and once the female cedar reaches "puberty" it is festooned with blue berries—already decorated before one brings it in and adds handmade ornaments. But there are two other related reasons to choose a female; the male produces pollen instead of seed, and once the tree begins to dry, pollen drifts down on foliage, ornaments, Christmas presents and across the floor. The male's pollen also produces an odd aroma—an odor some might call it—that to some nostrils resembles that of a cat's litter box.

A decade ago, in the early days of my cedarcide campaign—the continuing fight to eradicate cedars from meadows of native prairie or areas dedicated to prairie restoration—it was easy to find multiple cedars just the right size for the designated corner, seven or eight feet tall and half that wide. But after years of vigilance, most of the hundreds of remaining cedars are either in their infancy or are far too tall for our ceiling. So what to do? This fall I cleared all the mature females from a large grove of cedar and ash, partly to open the new ski trail down the bluff, partly to beat back cedars that border newly-restored native prairie. So at Christmas tree time, instead of cutting down another tree, we surveyed the fallen and chose a thirty-foot tree with a lovely, berry-festooned eight-foot top. We cut off the peak, and after soaking its trunk for a week in a bucket of water, it has regained its greenness and its look of life and health—a resurrected tree that perfectly symbolizes the Christmas season.

December 19: Joyfully Immature

One Webster definition of maturity is "being full-grown, ripe, fully developed, perfect and complete." Perhaps the definition relates principally to plants, but why not extend it to ourselves? A fully-developed person, one might think, has left foolishness, error and poor judgment behind, and henceforth will act in admirable ways. Perhaps the unwise and evil things we have done will be forgotten, overshadowed by the right choices we will now pursue and the perfection we will achieve.

But what happens to ripe fruit? It may be plucked from the tree and eaten, but if not, it soon falls to the ground to decay. A kernel of corn is mature when it has grown hard, when the plant that produced it has withered from green to brown, turns lifeless and brittle and rattles in the wind. Humans may imagine maturity as a desirable state, as a stage in our lives, whether at age twenty-one or sixty-five or some other arbitrary point, when we have grown complete. But nature tells us otherwise. The mature organism, at least amongst plants, is at the door of death.

Though I am a human and not a vegetable, I resist maturity. I hope to remain neoteric, to retain immature characteristics until my last days. I wish to be malleable as the greenest leaf, pliable like a tasty peach, not hardened like the stone at its center. Yes, the stone, the seed, is essential for the continuation of the peach's life, but the seed itself has ceased to grow and change. Applied to humans, the floral concept of maturity might suggest the end of growing, hardened arteries, head impervious to new ideas and experience, the notion that we've seen it all, or at least enough, that we have all the answers we need. No need for more questions, more encounters, more awe at the phenomena and ideas we have not yet witnessed or contemplated. For me, the proper time for maturity is the moment the heart stops, not one beat sooner.

In 2011, at age sixty-five, I was diagnosed with chronic lymphocytic leukemia. "If you're going to have cancer, this is one of the best kinds to have," my genial oncologist told me. "It is incurable, but it won't kill you right away, and we have weapons to beat it back and prolong your life." Nobody hopes to hear that they have cancer, but I must agree with my doctor. That the disease is chronic rather than acute means that the "victim" still has time—time to reflect on a lived life, time to plan for the future, including a future that he may not experience, time to do what needs to be done, time to grow in appreciation of the gifts of life, including family, friends and good fortune, time to develop a philosophy of death, and best of all, time to learn and grow. And in my case, the good fortune to receive a promising new drug.

But first, discard the concept of "victim." That is not me. I was born into privilege. Yes, when I was a boy my father worked for a dollar an hour and our family lived in a shabby house on a small sandy farm, but I was privileged to be raised by loving, hard-working parents, privileged to absorb attitudes and strategies for survival and growth. My parents taught me to clean up my messes, to keep tools sharp and clean and to wield them with all the skill I could muster, to assume responsibility for myself and for others. I was free to roam the hills, to climb the tallest trees, to learn the ways of fellow creatures even before I knew their names.

I was privileged to come of age in a time when a college education was affordable to children of the working class. I served two years in the Army, but escaped the horror of Vietnam. I married a beautiful, intelligent and caring woman, and we produced two children of whom we are rightfully proud. I have lived most of my life amidst uncluttered natural beauty. For sixty-five years, longer than most people have lived on Earth, I was the picture of health. I have been incredibly blessed, and if I died today, I should have no complaints. The real question is whether I will avoid maturity until my last breath.

In our woods stand mighty burr oaks, rooted in rich soil near the banks of an ever-flowing stream. A core sample demonstrated that the largest is two generations older than any human alive. And yet they live on, bigger each year than the year before, stronger, every year more fully-engaged in the processes of life, in their case the conversion and sequestration of light, water and minerals into the carbon at their core. Yes, some day they will die, but to that fact they seem oblivious. Every year they produce more acorns than the year before—more food for blue jays and squirrels and more potential oak trees, more promise for the future, more evidence that when individuals die, the ecosystem of which they are part can continue to thrive. I would be like the oaks, like all living plants. To them, maturity is not a goal. Perhaps if plants had anything like what we consider awareness or mindfulness, they too would consciously resist maturity to the end.

Humans might do well to follow their lead. In the animal kingdom, including *Homo sapiens*, we sometimes say that maturity has been achieved when we cease to grow bigger and instead are able to reproduce our kind. More difficult to pin down is the notion that maturity is tied to behavior, which we routinely describe as "mature," or not. But we are more than flesh and blood, more than bodies and reproductive organs, more than cells that fight off—and sometimes succumb to—debilitating or even fatal attacks. We are minds, intelligence, soul, will—call it what we may. When, and if, that abstract essence of a person ceases to evolve, what would be the point of keeping the body alive?

So, if life's goal is to keep the eyes open and ears attuned, to continue the quest for perception and understanding, how should that impact the ways we think and live? Perhaps it means that the brown thrasher that sings atop the cottonwood should retain his power to bring tears to our eyes. It means that anger should still rise in our throats at the report of human violence and injustice, or the desecration of our water, land and air. It means that even when we grow weary we continue to love, to think, to absorb knowledge, to create and to fight for sustainability and right. We may have produced some fruit, but when those sparks die out, we will be like a November corn stalk, brittle and slouching in the chilling wind.

Humans have always spoken of the "afterlife." To some that means walking streets paved with gold. To others it means that we live on as long as we, and what we have done as immature humans, are remembered by those still walking their own life's roads. Immortality is an enchanting idea, the notion that though the physical organism has "gone to seed" and like a fallen oak returned to the soil, an essence lives on. But immortality is not a proper goal of living. I am happy with mortality, for the essence of mortality is living, not in taking one intractable step after another toward the grave and the promise of something beyond, whether that something resides in heaven or on Earth.

All I know for certain is that in the midst of mundane struggles, violence and disregard, carelessness and mindlessness, heaven is in our midst—"under our feet as well as over our heads," as Thoreau put it. The day I forget this fact is the day I mature, and I know what that means. So this book is not about wisdom, but about wonder. It is about my daily walks through prairies and woods, about the hours passed watching hungry birds feed, about what I am learning from friends and books and fellow creatures that share our scrap of the Missouri River bluff. It is reflections from a mind that remains joyfully pre-mature.

Winter Again

December 21: Winter Solstice and Hope
Every year's successes and joys are mixed with disappointments and failures, the latter of which are opportunities to learn. Like all calendars we have known, this one turns, once again, to winter. But winter solstice, the longest and darkest night of the year, teaches us that every ending provides the opportunity and the obligation of renewal.

It is common for older people to observe that a year seems to speed by much faster than when they were young. For humans lucky enough to live out seven decades, each trip around the sun is an ever-smaller fraction of the life recalled. And yet this year has been rich and full. Life on our insulated bluff is remote from most of what passes for excitement in the larger world, but never a week has passed when "nothing happened." There is always a new wildflower in bloom, a blizzard to endure, a skunk perfuming our backdoor or the sighting of a bird I've never seen.

Among the pleasures of the year have been the mornings spent in my recliner, laptop glowing on my lap, my eyes flitting from the screen to the birdfeeders or the waving grasses, my ears tuned to the out of doors as much as to inner promptings, my mind freely following suit. As the year draws to a close, so I have noticed does the life of my computer's battery. It's down to a couple of hours at best. But that's OK. Sometimes I need help in maintaining a proper balance between physical and mental work, between work and play, between focused observation and freewheeling thought.

Two hours of writing is enough for one day. With a stronger battery, I might be tempted to work on, and might miss the most important encounter of the year outside.

It has been my honor to live close to nature for these many years, and to put down sometimes reasoned and sometimes random observations in this collection of stories and essays about life in our prairies and woods. Truth is, I've been carrying a pocket notebook for thirty-six years, recording daily observations, obligations, thoughts and encounters with serendipity. My environmental memoir *Waiting for Coyote's Call* grew, in large measure, from those notebooks, the observations and ideas that otherwise might have vanished; the narratives and observations in this book have evolved in a similar way. It is my hope that others might take interest in the musings of an amateur naturalist whose eyes and heart are open to the workings of the ecosystem, and more important, that some might be inspired to more fervently seek encounters in their own corners of the natural world. Thus, perhaps the end of another book is less a closing door than a door left ajar, a door that perhaps others will step through and a portal through which they will peer farther and further down the road.

Today is winter solstice, the shortest day of the year. But that means that even though winter officially returns tonight, tomorrow will be longer than today by a sliver of time, and with each ensuing day, my eyes will be open wider to the growing light…and there will be more to see. I close this account of the notes and thoughts of another year on Prairie Bluff with the still open question that followed the quarter century of *Waiting for Coyote's Call*:

Midnight, December twenty-first, the longest night of the year. Amongst plants and many fellow creatures, this is a time of sleep. In the morning, in the new year, in the spring, I tell myself, all will be revived. The annual cycle of rebirth will come. But in the post-modern world, not all women and men take note. Will we humans, like the rest of creation, open our eyes tomorrow to a new world, a world in which renewal is both possible and required? I remain waiting by the solstice fire for the coyote's call.

About the Author

Jerry Wilson lives with his poet wife, Norma, on Prairie Bluff in southeast South Dakota. For many years he taught literature and writing, then served as managing editor of *South Dakota Magazine*. He now devotes himself more fully to books that explore the natural world and to fiction that re-imagines history and contemporary life. More about his work is available at jerrywilson.us.

Also by Jerry Wilson:

American Artery: A Pan American Journey
Waiting for Coyote's Call: An Eco-memoir from the Missouri River Bluff
Blackjacks and Blue Devils
Across the Cimarron

CPSIA information can be obtained
at www.ICGtesting.com
Printed in the USA
FSHW022357010119
54771FS